ROUTLEDGE LIBRARY EDITIONS: URBAN STUDIES

Volume 9

SLUM CLEARANCE

SLUM CLEARANCE
The Social and Administrative Context in
England and Wales

JOHN ENGLISH, RUTH MADIGAN
AND PETER NORMAN

LONDON AND NEW YORK

First published in 1976 by Croom Helm Ltd

This edition first published in 2018
by Routledge
2 Park Square, Milton Park, Abingdon, Oxon OX14 4RN

and by Routledge
711 Third Avenue, New York, NY 10017

Routledge is an imprint of the Taylor & Francis Group, an informa business

© 1976 John English, Ruth Madigan and Peter Norman

All rights reserved. No part of this book may be reprinted or reproduced or utilised in any form or by any electronic, mechanical, or other means, now known or hereafter invented, including photocopying and recording, or in any information storage or retrieval system, without permission in writing from the publishers.

Trademark notice: Product or corporate names may be trademarks or registered trademarks, and are used only for identification and explanation without intent to infringe.

British Library Cataloguing in Publication Data
A catalogue record for this book is available from the British Library

ISBN: 978-1-138-89482-2 (Set)
ISBN: 978-1-315-09987-3 (Set) (ebk)
ISBN: 978-1-138-05719-7 (Volume 9) (hbk)
ISBN: 978-1-138-05750-0 (Volume 9) (pbk)
ISBN: 978-1-315-10532-1 (Volume 9) (ebk)

Publisher's Note
The publisher has gone to great lengths to ensure the quality of this reprint but points out that some imperfections in the original copies may be apparent.

Disclaimer
The publisher has made every effort to trace copyright holders and would welcome correspondence from those they have been unable to trace.

SLUM CLEARANCE

The Social and Administrative Context
in England and Wales

JOHN ENGLISH
RUTH MADIGAN
PETER NORMAN

CROOM HELM LONDON

First published 1976
© 1976 John English, Ruth Madigan and Peter Norman

Croom Helm Ltd, 2-10 St John's Road, London SW11

ISBN 0-85664-325-4

Printed and bound in Great Britain by
REDWOOD BURN LIMITED
Trowbridge and Esher

CONTENTS

Preface
1	Introduction	9
2	A Century of Slum Clearance	16
3	Slum Clearance in Principle and Practice	50
4	Housing Allocation in Centralised Systems – Newcastle, Manchester and Tower Hamlets	76
5	Housing Allocation in Decentralised Systems – Leeds and Liverpool	104
6	Residents' Knowledge of the Slum Clearance Process	124
7	Some Determinants of Attitudes Towards Moving	148
8	Housing Market Situation and Attitudes Towards Moving	170
9	Summary and Conclusions	189
Appendix A:	Supplementary Tables	198
Appendix B:	Definitions and Classifications	205
Appendix C:	Research Methods	207
Appendix D:	Form 26 (Housing Act 1957)	214

PREFACE

The research on which this book is based arose out of a two-fold interest, first, in the impact of local government redevelopment activities on existing physical and social structures and, second, in the administration of the growing stock of council housing. The field of interest was narrowed down to a specific concern with the administration of slum clearance; it was the main form of redevelopment affecting residential areas and a major source of new tenants of council housing. Yet many of the existing reports on slum clearance suggested that it was an alienating experience which failed to meet residents' housing aspirations. The intention was to explore whether this was really the case and, if so, how the situation might be improved. The research was financed by a grant from the Centre for Environmental Studies, awarded to Peter Norman, from October 1968 to September 1972.

The planning, field work and writing up of the study was undertaken jointly by the three researchers with a good deal of overlap and sharing of tasks. There was, however, some division of labour: John English was mainly responsible for work on the historical, legal and administrative background, Ruth Madigan for analysis of the residents' survey and Peter Norman for writing up the local authority allocation systems. Drafts of each section of the report were produced by the researcher principally concerned and were edited into their present form by Peter Norman.

Our thanks are due to the many people who made the project possible. First to the Centre for Environmental Studies and particularly to David Donnison who always showed a close interest in our work. Without the willing help of many officials in local authority departments neither the survey nor the analysis of administrative systems would have been possible; we are indebted to the staff of Newcastle-upon-Tyne C.B., Leeds C.B., Manchester C.B., Liverpool C.B., Tower Hamlets L.B., Bingley U.D., Doncaster C.B., Gravesend M.B., Haringey L.B., Norwich C.B., Portsmouth C.B., South Shields C.B., Stoke-on-Trent C.B., Warley C.B. and Wolverhampton C.B. Staff in other local authorities which we visited in the earlier stages of the project also gave freely of information and advice. We were dependent on the co-operation of the Ministry of Housing and Local Government (as it was then) in drawing the sample of clearance areas and we are particularly grateful to the Procedures Section of that department for their assistance.

The study would not have been possible without the forebearance and generosity of the clearance area residents whom we interviewed, particularly in Byker, Hunslet, West Gorton, Everton and Spitalfields. For their hospitality in providing us with temporary accommodation in survey areas we thank Vernon Gracie who gave us the use of his now famous Byker office; the Church Army for their hall in West Gorton; Rev. Neville Black for the use of his hall in Stanfield Road, Everton; and Toynbee Hall for their office in Spitalfields.

Interviewing in areas of poor housing can be a rewarding but also a draining experience. For their tenacity and willingness, our thanks to Diana Barnes, Tim Cantell, Jacqui Curwen, Elspeth Farmer, Phil Gaunt, Chris Madigan, Chris Paris, Isabel Senior and David Whitham. Maureen Robb, Anne Carey, Mary Smith and Sue Lindsay patiently prepared the survey data whilst Shona Hazelton and Moira Dougan bore the unenviable burden of typing successive drafts. To all these and to our colleagues in the Department of Social and Economic Research, University of Glasgow, who have given us support and encouragement we are very grateful.

1 INTRODUCTION

In 1970-71 when this study was undertaken, the post-war slum clearance drive was at its peak and some 70,000 houses were being dealt with each year. Since then the number of slum houses demolished or closed has declined drastically to 41,700 in 1974 and 49,000 in 1975.

This decline was accompanied by a sharp increase in the rate of house improvement; between 1970 and 1973 the number of improvement grants approved more than doubled. It looked for a time as though improvement was steadily replacing clearance as the main means of dealing with the problem of low quality housing but the number of improvement grants has also recently fallen. With houses becoming unfit at an estimated rate of 100,000 each year,[1] current rates of improvement and demolition will make very little impression on the total number of slum houses by the end of the century.[2]

It remains to be seen whether the impetus of the improvement programme can be recovered and whether the housing action areas and other procedures introduced by the Housing Act, 1974 will prove effective. If the amount of improvement work cannot be increased and sustained at a high level, reversion to a larger slum clearance programme seems inevitable. Even if improvement does recover it is inconceivable that investment in house improvement could ever reach a level at which obsolescence is eradicated. As a Shelter report on slum clearance pointed out:

> It is almost as if clearance had been dismissed as an outmoded method of treatment of unfit housing and yet there is a large number of houses which are in too bad a state of repair and structural unsoundness for improvement to be feasible . . . Houses do not have an indefinite life and while good maintenance and attention to repairs can extend the life of a house, all however, decay sooner or later and must eventually be pulled down. Clearance and redevelopment, then, will continue to be realities for a great number of people.[3]

Slum clearance is bound to remain numerically important but the significance of a study of clearance does not depend on numbers alone. Slum clearance puts the ordinary citizen in a situation of extreme dependence relative to his local authority. In carrying out a clearance scheme a council decides not only that people are to leave their homes but where and in what conditions they are to be rehoused. For most residents of a clearance area the local authority is the only source of alternative housing when their existing homes are demolished. The local authority not only destroys the existing physical and social fabric but also provides and manages its replacement. The context of slum clearance highlights both the control over the life chances of individual citizens which local government can exercise and its potential for physically and socially restructuring the city.

All three fields of study in which this book has its origin have acknowledged, implicitly or explicitly, the powerful position of local officials and the weak position of residents in the slum clearance situation.

First are the community studies such as Young and Willmott's widely read book on Bethnal Green.[4] The basic approach of early studies of this type was a before and after comparison of life in inner urban areas and new housing estates. The power of local government to nurture or to destroy existing ties of kinship and local mechanisms of mutual support was explicitly recognised but the relationship of citizens to officials during the slum clearance process was not a matter of direct concern. However, Jennings's later study of Barton Hill in Bristol paid a good deal of attention to the stages of slum clearance and their reception by local residents,[5] foreshadowing the central concern with the process as such in the locality based work of Dennis and his colleagues in the North east.[6]

Dennis's first book on Sunderland explores the broad framework of housing decisions within which particular slum clearance areas are defined and the supposed 'scientific' basis on which 'lifing' and demolition decisions are made. The work juxtaposes the fragility of official plans and the solidarity of opposition amongst many householders against the loss of their homes. In his second book, the Millfield area of Sunderland is taken as 'the concrete example in an analysis of the power relations between a group of citizens and their city bureaucracy'.[7] The issue of participation and the protection of individual rights becomes central to the community study.[8]

The second group of studies have taken a social administrative approach and are specifically concerned with the process of clearance itself as the object of study. Problems of information and communication between the local authority and residents, particularly over matters affecting individuals' rights, have been their main focus. But the legitimacy of the slum clearance objective and of the existing administrative machinery is not questioned; indeed, two such studies, by Norris and by Bull, originated in requests for assistance from local housing managers.[9] Norris began with a broad inquiry into the levels of satisfaction expressed by previous residents of clearance areas after their move to a new house. Her perspective on the administrative process was to seek ways in which tenant satisfaction could be increased and the gulf between 'they' and 'we' reduced. This gulf 'can only disappear as the citizens come to identify themselves with the administration, as they understand its problems and the limits within which it works'.[10] Bull's initial brief was narrowly focused on the clearance process and the need for welfare workers in affected areas. But his later work developed into a wider consideration of information needs and the possibility of resident participation within slum clearance thereby implicitly questioning the existing structure of power relationships.[11]

The present study begins with a similar orientation. Recognising the potential impotence of citizens caught up in a complex bureaucratic process it investigates the scope for individuals to exercise even the rights and choices which are ostensibly safeguarded by the existing structure. To what extent are the residents of clearance areas aware of the significance of the stages of clearance and rehousing? Are their decisions based on adequate information? How does the ideal embodied in the structure of Acts of Parliament and regulations match the reality of the system in operation? Answering these questions involves not only the study of residents' knowledge and experience of the process but direct investigation of the officials at work; a central objective of the study is demystification of the administrative process by which slum clearance and rehousing schemes are executed.

Subsequent development of this theme has placed even greater emphasis on the power relations of the slum clearance situation and has attacked directly the legitimacy of the *status quo.* Following the formal introduction of public participation into the planning process in 1968[12] and the Skeffington report[13] the discussion of the concept has extended into other areas of administration. Where, in the past, criticism and resentment were directed only at the planners, whose claim to 'comprehensive' control made them the obvious target, public dissatisfaction is now increasingly directed towards the housing, environmental health and legal departments which directly control the day to day administration of slum clearance and rehousing.[14] In many instances, clearance areas have been the battle ground on which community action has waged the struggle between residents and bureaucracy. Procedural aspects of clearance and rehousing have been redefined as the weapons of officialdom in the people's fight against the town hall.[15]

The third line of work to which this study relates is the school of urban sociology which has developed under the influence of Pahl's writings of the late sixties.[16] Although it is only in Chapter 8 that the material of the present book relates explicitly to a central theoretical problem of urban sociology — the theory of housing classes developed by John Rex — the broad approach of the study is to explore the general problems of access to scarce resources and the controlling operations of local officials which are central to Pahl's original formulation. The key argument propounded by Pahl was that 'there are fundamental social constraints on access to scarce urban facilities. These reflect the distribution of power in society and are illustrated by bureaucratic rules and procedures and social gatekeepers who help to distribute and control urban resources'.[18] Though Pahl's later writings have abandoned this 'managerialist' thesis arguing that it grossly inflates the power of the local government official in the dynamics of the urban system[19], the thesis is particularly applicable to a study of slum clearance administration.[20] First, the constellation of power is quite unambiguous with the local authority directly intervening in the expropriation and demolition of property and the allocation of alternative homes. Control of citizens' life chances through control of access to housing is meaningfully exercised at the local level. Second, the rules of access to compensation or to alternative housing are easily available for analysis since they are mostly laid down either in national legislation or in local rules and regulations governing eligibility or desert. The research problem is not so much to discover the rules but to explicate their realisation in practice through the study of procedure and detailed decision making.

The research for this study involved systematic interviewing of local housing officials and analysis of the performance of administrative systems. The Pahl thesis was highly relevant in directing the overall approach of this part of the study. But unfortunately, apart from the precept 'study the gatekeepers', the empirical researcher finds little to guide him in applying the managerialist thesis to a particular situation and few precedents of empirical work.[21] The conceptual framework which this book develops for a comparative analysis of allocation systems based on the interplay of organisational structure, rules of procedure and the work ideologies of housing managers is an attempt to operationalise some of the key factors identified in the Pahl thesis.

Apart from interviews with officials the main part of the present study was a survey of residents of slum clearance areas in fifteen towns and cities scattered across England. The study was designed to avoid the limitation of many previous surveys which drew their material from only one or two areas within a narrow geographical compass. The areas surveyed were selected by a random process to give as representative a sample as possible of the clearance area population at one point in time. Full details of the survey and other research procedures are given in Appendix C on research methods. As one objective of the study was to relate survey material to the analysis of administrative systems the main constraint on the survey design was the need to locate sufficient interviews in at least some areas to permit separate analysis of the data. The solution was to divide the sample of clearance areas into two and to select five large and ten small areas; interviews were then concentrated disproportionately in the large areas. The administrative process was analysed in the local authorities within which the five large clearance areas were located so that selection of these authorities was also based on a random procedure.

The five local authorities selected by this method were the old County Boroughs of Newcastle-upon-Tyne, Leeds, Manchester and Liverpool and Tower Hamlets London Borough.[22] They are referred to throughout the text as the 'main' areas and the samples which were located within each of these local authority areas are referred to as 'main' area samples. Survey results are not separately presented for the remaining ten areas, but are pooled for presentation; these areas are therefore referred to as 'pool' areas and the samples as 'pool' area samples. It was a matter of chance that none of the areas sampled happed to be located in Wales.

The main part of this book begins with an outline of the origins of the slum clearance procedures that exist today and of government policies and programmes regarding unfit housing.

The procedures which are most commonly used for slum clearance are considered in some detail in Chapter 3, as are their implications both for the local officials who must implement them and the residents who benefit, or suffer, from them. This chapter spells out the rules of access both to tangible resources such as compensation or a council house and to the intangible resource of information.

Chapters 4 and 5 provide a comparative analysis of the housing allocation systems in the five main area authorities, and of their strengths and weaknesses from the point of view of clearance area residents. Chapter 4 is confined to analysis of the three centralised allocation systems in Newcastle, Manchester and Tower Hamlets.

Chapter 5 continues with material on the two decentralised systems in Leeds and Liverpool and concludes with a summary and comparison of the 'operational styles' of all five housing departments.

In Chapter 6 the appraisal of clearance area and allocation procedures continues with an investigation of residents' comprehension based on the findings of the survey. The problem for clearance area residents is not only to understand information which is given them directly, but to grasp the significance of events which they experience such as official visits from local government staff. The survey therefore studied both residents' grasp of facts about slum clearance procedure and their interpretation of the jobs of the officials involved.

Since the acceptability of slum clearance policy is to some extent dependent on the public response, Chapters 7 and 8 present survey data on residents' views about having to leave their homes. In Chapter 7 support of or opposition to moving is related to broad background features, particularly of housing conditions, life cycle stage and tenure. But these characteristics of households are only crude indicators of the range of factors which are taken into account when considering the gains or losses likely to result from redevelopment. In Chapter 8 the market situation of some distinctive categories within the general population is considered in detail. This chapter relates the needs and aspirations of each group to the likelihood of their securing access to the housing which will best suit their needs.

Finally, Chapter 9 draws together the main findings of the book and their implications for the future administration of slum clearance and for the professionals involved.

NOTES

1. Department of the Environment, *House Condition Survey, 1971, England and Wales,* Housing Survey Reports, No. 9, Department of the Environment, 1973, p. 4.
2. Some commentators have argued that an objective of housing policy should be to reduce the average 'normal' life of dwellings by higher rates of replacement. Such an objective requires a far higher rate of clearance and rebuilding than anything yet achieved. See Simon Pepper, *Housing Improvement: Goals and Strategy,* Architectural Association, Paper No. 8, Lund Humphries for the Architectural Association, 1971, Chapter 1; see also the continuation of Pepper's reasoning in Fred Berry, *Housing: the Great British Failure.* Charles Knight, 1974, p. 6.
3. Shelter, *Slum Clearance,* Shelter, 1974, p. 1.
4. Michael Young and Peter Willmott, *Family and Kinship in East London,* Routledge and Kegan Paul, 1957; reprinted by Penguin 1962. Also

J.M. Mogey, *Family and Neighbourhood*, Oxford University Press, 1956; T. Brennan, *Reshaping a City*, House of Grant, 1959.
5. Hilda Jennings, *Societies in the Making: A Study of Development and Redevelopment within a County Borough*, Routledge and Kegan Paul, 1962.
6. Norman Dennis, *People and Planning: The Sociology of Housing in Sunderland*, Faber, 1970; Norman Dennis, *Public Participation and Planners' Blight*, Faber, 1971; Jon Gower Davies, *The Evangelistic Bureaucrat: A study of a Planning Exercise in Newcastle-upon-Tyne*, Tavistock, 1972.
7. Norman Dennis, *op. cit.* (1972), p. 13.
8. Norman Dennis, 'Half-beating City Hall – The Duke Street Story', *New Society*, Vol. 26, p. 6, 4th October 1973.
9. June Norris, *Human Aspects of Redevelopment*, Midland New Towns Society, Studies in Housing and Industrial Location No. 2, 1960; D.G. Bull, *The Welfare of People in Clearance Areas: A Housing Management Problem*, Department of Social Administration, Manchester University, mimeo, 1967.
10. June Norris, *op. cit.*, p. 75.
11. D.G. Bull, 'Public Relations in Clearance Areas: Whose responsibility?' *Housing Review*, Vol. 18, No. 2, March-April 1969; D.G. Bull, 'Rehousing from Clearance Areas: People's Rights and Local Authority Obligations', *Housing Review*, Vol. 19, No. 1, January-February, 1970.
12. Town and Country Planning Act 1968.
13. Ministry of Housing and Local Government, *People and Planning: Report of the Committee on Public Participation in Planning.*, HMSO, 1969.
14. A discussion of the relative power of these officials compared with that of the planners is contained in P. Norman, 'Corporation Town', *Official Architecture and Planning*, Vol. 34, No. 5, May 1971.
15. Sidney Jacobs, *The Right to a Decent House*, Routledge and Kegan Paul, 1976.
16. Especially, R.E. Pahl, *Spatial Structure and Social Structure*, Centre for Environmental Studies, Working Paper No. 10, 1968; reprinted with other essays in *Whose City?*, Longman, 1970.
17. See John Rex and Robert Moore, *Race, Community and Conflict*, Oxford University Press for the Institute of Race Relations, 1967; also John Rex, 'The Sociology of a Zone of Transition', in R.E. Pahl (ed.), *Readings in Urban Sociology*, Pergamon, 1968.
18. R.E. Pahl, *op. cit.* (1970), p. 215.
19. R.E. Pahl, 'Urban Managerialism Reconsidered',*Whose City?*, 2nd Edition, Penguin, 1975, Chap. 13.
20. For a general discussion of the applicability of the Pahl thesis see P. Norman, 'Managerialism – a Review of Recent Work', *Proceedings of the Conference on Urban Change and Conflict*, Centre for Environmental Studies Conference Papers No. 14, 1975.
21. At the time the research was undertaken the available published work was J.R. Lambert, 'The Management of Minorities', *The New Atlantis*, Vol. 2, No. 1, 1970; R.E. Pahl and Edward Craven, 'Residential Expansion: The Role of the Private Developer in the South-East', *Journal of the Town Planning Institute*, April 1967, reprinted in *Whose City?*, Chap. 9.
22. The study is based on these local authorities as they were constituted before local government reorganisation in 1974.

2 A CENTURY OF SLUM CLEARANCE

The Origins of Slum Clearance 1868-1930

A major objective of the public health movement in Britain from the 1840s onwards was the improvement of housing conditions. As early as the forties and fifties various Nuisances Removal Acts empowered local medical officers of health, as a last resort, to prohibit the use for human habitation of premises which were injurious to health. Early legislation thereby established an intimate connection between unhealthiness and unfitness which was weakened only slowly over the years.

The first measure specifically concerned with slum clearance was the Artizans' and Labourers' Dwellings Act 1868, which was generally known as the Torrens Act after the backbencher who introduced it.[1] Under the Act the medical officer of health was required to report on the condition of individual premises which were 'in a condition or state dangerous to health so as to be unfit for human habitation'. Unfit houses could be closed and if owners failed to undertake repairs they could be required to demolish the offending houses. The Torrens Act was amended on a number of occasions and it is the origin of the procedures for dealing with individual unfit houses in Part II of the Housing Act 1957.

Under the Torrens Acts neither rehousing nor demolition were the legal responsibility of local government. Until the Land Compensation Act 1973 laid down a general duty[2] there was no obligation on local authorities to rehouse displaced occupiers of individual unfit houses. Since the widespread development of council housing in the 1920s local authorities have accepted a rehousing obligation in practice but before that time displaced occupiers had to fend for themselves. The costs of demolition fell on the owner of an unfit house and the local authority was not required to purchase the cleared land. For these reasons under the Torrens Acts action was relatively cheap. Nevertheless very little action was taken at least until the twentieth century.

The second strand of slum clearance legislation, dealing with areas of unfit housing, was initiated by the Artizans' and Labourers' Dwellings Improvement Act 1875, which was introduced by the Home Secretary in Disraeli's government and has been known as the Cross Act. It applied initially to London and urban sanitary districts with a population of 25,000; though it was subsequently extended to all urban districts it never applied to rural districts. The Act was amended many times but the basic procedure survived until the fundamental remodelling of 1930. The Cross Acts provided for improvement schemes which encompassed both the clearance of an area and its subsequent rebuilding. There were two alternative criteria for declaring an improvement scheme: first, unfitness for human habitation of houses or, second, unhealthiness resulting from generally bad conditions in an area.

Procedure for undertaking an improvement scheme was complicated by the need to provide for both the demolition of existing buildings and the future use of the cleared land. The confirmation of an improvement scheme involved a lengthy and expensive process. Under the 1875 Act an improvement scheme had first to be submitted to the Local Government Board; if they approved it a provisional order was issued which then had to be confirmed by Act of Parliament. Eventually, however, the Housing, Town Planning, Etc. Act 1909 abolished the requirement for parliamentary approval and in effect introduced the compulsory purchase order.

The rehousing requirements of the original Cross Act of 1875 were extremely stringent: an improvement scheme was required to '... provide for the accommodation of at least as many members of the working class as may be displaced ... in suitable dwellings, which, unless there are any special reasons to the contrary, shall be situate within the limits of the same area, or in the vicinity thereof ...'[3] Alternative accommodation had to provide an equivalent number of replacement dwellings but there was no reference to rehousing displaced occupiers until 1930. In fact, it was notorious that delay in rebuilding and higher rents prevented most slum inhabitants from occupying the new houses that were provided.

Nevertheless these rehousing requirements proved to be a major disincentive to local authorities because of the cost. Land included in improvement schemes had to be bought at its market price which, especially in London and other big cities, often reflected its value for commercial use. Its value for working class housing, even at rents higher than the former inhabitants could afford, was only a fraction of its cost; if the land was sold for rehousing (at first local authorities were not normally allowed to build themselves) a heavy loss had to be borne by the rates. Consequently, the rehousing provisions were successively weakened over the years. As early as 1879 an amending Act permitted the Local Government Board to approve rehousing away from the area. Finally, in 1882 rehousing was made discretionary unless it was required by the Board.[4] By successive amendments of the rehousing provisions an estimable feature of the original measure was progressively weakened in a vain attempt to encourage local authorities to use the legislation. The rehousing obligation was strongly supported by the 1885 Royal Commission on the Housing of the Working Classes and an important body of opinion believed that, without adequate provision for rehousing, slum clearance schemes were positively harmful as they increased overcrowding in surrounding areas.

Procedural complexity and the rehousing obligation were two major disadvantages of improvement legislation from the point of view of local authorities. The third was the high cost of land purchase. The Land Clauses Consolidation Act 1845 failed to lay down the basis on which compensation should be assessed and it seems to have been assumed that valuers and, in the case of disputes, the courts could work without legislative guidance. The result was that valuations were commonly greater than the ordinary market price of land and a practice grew up of adding an allowance of 10 per cent to soften the blow of compulsory purchase. This, of course, compounded the financial problems of using the land for working class housing. The compensation problem was not effectively tackled until the Acquisition of Land (Assessment of Compensation) Act 1919 laid down the basis of the modern code. But the introduction of exchequer subsidies at this time meant that financial obstacles became less important in any case.

Actual progress on improvement works was very slow. In the first five years after the first Cross Act of 1875 some ten provincial local authorities initiated improvement schemes, not all of which were completed. Progress then fell away until after the consolidating Act of 1890 when there was some recovery. The position in London was rather different; the Metropolitan Board of Works had initiated twenty-two improvement schemes by 1888 and the work was carried on by the London County Council. Nevertheless, just before the First World War only two or three improvement schemes were being confirmed each year in the whole country and only thirty-two schemes were completed between 1890 and 1914.[5] There is little doubt that the principal reason for this poor performance was the high cost of improvement schemes. After some initial enthusiasm local authorities realised the implications of improvement for the rates; there were a number of instances of refusals to act on official representations by medical officers of health. Those few local authorities which had taken action found themselves faced with greater expense than had been anticipated and improvement schemes were usually not completed for years. With earlier schemes uncompleted and requiring large subsidies from the rates most councils were unwilling to take on further commitments. An indication of the delays is that the Ministry of Health was still issuing orders in the 1920s modifying uncompleted schemes from the previous century.

Following the five-year hiatus in house building and slum clearance occasioned by the First World War, the government became much more directly concerned with housing problems, but initially attention was focused on dealing with the overall shortage of houses. The Housing, Town Planning, Etc. Act 1919 provided an exchequer subsidy for local authority house building covering costs in excess of the product of a penny rate, thereby inaugurating large-scale council house building. This subsidy was also available for slum clearance schemes and, combined with the new compensation arrangements, eased financial constraints. Nevertheless, slum clearance did not restart on a large scale. In 1921 the Annual Report of the Ministry of Health stated that '... until much more has been done to overcome the existing shortage of housing accommodation, it would obviously be unwise to attempt to put into operation drastic measures for clearing unhealthy areas'. Only eight improvement schemes had been submitted during the year and most had not been approved as it was felt that it would be 'inexpedient to proceed with them at the moment'.[6]

The subsidy under the 1919 Act was terminated in the public expenditure cuts of 1921. The Housing Act 1923 provided a less generous subsidy of half the loss on slum clearance schemes; this arrangement remained until 1930. The volume of slum clearance did increase in the twenties though mainly through action on individual unfit houses. Each year between two thousand and five thousand houses were subject to closing and demolition orders. As far as unhealthy areas were concerned, between 1919 and 1928 121 improvement schemes were confirmed involving the demolition of about 15,000 buildings and the rehousing of approximately 74,000 persons. But only about 11,000 houses included in these schemes had actually been demolished by 1930.

In 1928, however, the archaic procedure for initiating improvement schemes, basically unchanged since the nineteenth century, finally broke down. An objector succeeded in having an improvement scheme set aside by the courts on the ground that it had failed adequately to specify the future use of the land. But it was impracticable to provide the amount of information required so that no more improvement schemes could be confirmed by the Ministry.

These problems were, however, only one factor leading to a fundamental reappraisal of the legislative framework for slum clearance. In the late twenties slum clearance had become a political issue. The general housing situation had improved but there was growing concern at the failure to do anything directly for the worst housed. In 1928 the National Housing and Town Planning Council set up a committee to examine slum clearance and there was a spate of books and pamphlets on the need for action. One of the most influential was by E.D. Simon[7] who had had considerable experience of housing in Manchester. The policy in the twenties of building council houses for artisans was failing to meet the needs of the poorest and worst housed; a large slum clearance programme was essential. The outcome was the Housing Act 1930 which marked a turning point in the history of slum clearance. The old legislation, with its origins in 1868 and 1875 had clearly failed and was almost entirely swept away. The 1930 Act introduced the procedures which basically still exist and inaugurated a national slum clearance campaign.

The Inter-War Slum Clearance Drive, 1930-39

The redirection of housing policy and the new emphasis on slum clearance was described in the Annual Report of the Ministry of Health in 1931:

> The Housing Act, 1930 marked a turning point in post-war housing policy. The policy previously followed by all Governments had been to concentrate almost exclusively on the provision of new houses in order to increase the total pool of accommodation available for the working classes; and, while a limited amount of slum clearance was undertaken under the Housing Acts from 1890 to 1925, it was considered that any direct and comprehensive plan to clear the slums and to meet the needs of the poorest workers must meanwhile be deferred. It was, however, hoped and expected that their conditions would be indirectly improved by a general process which has been described as 'filtering up'.[8]

During the twenties over one and a quarter million new houses had been built in England and Wales, nearly half a million of them by local authorities; nevertheless little had been achieved to improve conditions for the worst housed section of the population.[9] There were at least two reasons for this. First, the increase in the total number of available houses had been insufficient to satisfy demand amongst better off members of the working class; consequently, few houses had become available for people from the slums and the process of 'filtering up' had not worked. Second, the poorest households could not afford the rents of council houses and, in any case, local authorities tended to select tenants according to criteria of respectability, cleanliness and rent paying capacity which worked against the worst off.

In moving the second reading of the bill which became the Housing Act 1930 the Minister of Health, Arthur Greenwood, identified three reasons for the slow progress of slum clearance during the twenties; first, there was the complicated procedure, which has already been discussed; second, the inadequacy of a subsidy of 50 per cent of losses incurred and, third, the concern of local authorities with 'normal housing requirements'.[10]

As far as procedure was concerned the keynote of the Act was simplicity compared with previous legislation. In particular the clearance of an area was completely separated from procedures for redeveloping the site. After 1930 a clearance scheme did not have to make provision for using the land and procedure for compulsory purchase was also simplified. The machinery of clearance areas and compulsory purchase orders remains basically unchanged today. For the first time unfitness for human habitation was defined[11] and the emphasis moved away from unhealthiness to bad housing conditions as such. This definition, relying to a large extent on local standards, remained in use until 1954.

The second main obstacle identified by Greenwood was finance and the 1930 Act introduced substantially larger subsidies paid on a new basis. Exchequer subsidies were no longer based on the loss incurred by a local authority but on the number of persons displaced and rehoused. The basic subsidy was £2. 5s for 40 years per person rehoused (slightly more in agricultural parishes) with an additional subsidy for expensive sites in urban areas. This form of subsidy had two advantages; as the amount increased with the number of persons rehoused it was particularly useful in meeting the needs of large and poor families and it provided an incentive for local authorities to carry out fully their obligation to rehouse people displaced by clearance.

The legislation included a measure of central government pressure on local authorities which was entirely new. Every urban authority with a population exceeding 20,000 was required, every five years, to submit a statement to the Ministry of Health giving proposals for dealing with housing conditions in their area, including slum clearance. Programmes submitted at the end of 1930 provided for demolition of some 96,000 houses during the subsequent five years.

The slum clearance drive initiated by the 1930 Act had an abortive start when the financial crisis in 1931 was followed by a general retrenchment in public expenditure. Then the government decided that exchequer subsidies should be concentrated on building for rehousing, although it had been intended that subsidised building for general needs should continue alongside. With interest rates and building costs falling the official view was that private enterprise and, if necessary, unsubsidised building by local authorities could adequately supply the need for ordinary working class housing. Following this line of argument the general needs subsidy was abolished by the Housing (Financial Provisions) Act 1933, leaving only the slum clearance subsidy under the 1930 Act. It is impossible to say whether local authorities would have extended their concern from 'general housing requirements' to include slum clearance without this change but they now had no alternative.

The new policy was outlined in 1933 in the Annual Report of the Ministry of Health.

> During the year under review special attention was devoted by the Government to the problem of clearing the slums and improving the bad housing conditions which they regard as a matter of urgent importance deeply affecting social welfare and the health of the people. They have formed the view that the present rate of progress is definitely too slow and that the time is opportune for an intensive and concerted effort to put an end to this national evil . . . A circular letter has accordingly been sent to all Housing Authorities . . . In their programmes Local Authorities are required to show the areas which should be dealt with as clearance areas . . . and the timetables for the clearance . . . and for the provision of the necessary rehousing accommodation. The programmes are to be drawn, as far as possible, on the basis that all areas that require clearance will be cleared not later than 1938, and Local Authorities are urged to make an immediate start in dealing with clearance . . . areas that can be dealt with at once.[12]

Thus the first slum clearance drive was inaugurated.

Initial returns from local authorities in 1933 envisaged the demolition of about 266,000 houses with well over a million inhabitants and erection of a rather larger number of replacement dwellings.[13] This programme was over two and a half times larger than the 1930 programme. In its own terms the campaign to abolish the slums in five years was less than successful; even by the outbreak of war not all the houses in the original programme had been demolished. On the other hand, far more slums were dealt with than ever before and by 1939 houses were being demolished at the rate of about 90,000 a year. This rate of progress has never since been equalled. Altogether about 273,000 houses were demolished or closed during the thirties but local authority clearance programmes were continuously revised so that by 1939 they contained 472,000 houses. In 1939 almost exactly the same number of scheduled slums remained to be dealt with (about 266,000) as had been contained in the original programme.

The main concern of the Housing Act 1935 was overcrowding which was precisely defined and made a statutory offence. The duty of local authorities to deal with overcrowding gave an added impetus to slum clearance since the two problems were were often concentrated in the same houses; subsidies for dealing with overcrowding were smaller than for clearance so there was a strong incentive to adopt the latter procedure wherever possible. The 1935 Act made a number of procedural changes affecting slum clearance and, in the sphere of compensation, introduced well-maintained payments. Housing legislation was consolidated by the Housing Act 1936 which remained the principal act until 1957.

Although there were signs by 1939 that the rate of slum clearance might slow down as local authorities completed their five-year programmes a great deal had been achieved. Rising standards and a growing recognition of the real magnitude of the problem were mainly responsible for the apparent paradox that the number of houses still to be cleared was as great in 1939 as in 1933. On anything but the narrowest view the slum clearance drive of the thirties must be counted a success. Slum clearance came to an abrupt halt when war broke out in September 1939. There was virtually no clearance for the next fifteen years and little new building or repair and maintenance. If the rate of clearance had remained as high as in 1939 a million more unfit houses would have been cleared during that time.

Slum Clearance Resumed, 1945-56

Resumption of slum clearance was out of the question in the immediate post-war period; there was a desperate shortage of accommodation and even a slum house was better than being homeless. The Housing Act 1949 did not deal with clearance and there was little discussion of the slum problem in Parliament. The chief significance of the 1949 Act for slum clearance was its removal of any reference to 'the working classes' in the Housing Acts; thereby the operation of the Acts, including the obligation to rehouse, was extended to the whole population. Aneurin Bevan, the Minister of Health, argued that clearance could be resumed only after the needs of homeless families had been met and resisted pressure to withdraw the circular which had suspended clearance.[14] This remained the situation until a change of policy by the Conservatives in 1953.

The Conservatives fought the 1951 election partly on a promise to build 300,000 houses a year, a target which was achieved in 1953.[15] Their success provided an opportunity to reappraise the direction of housing policy and to accommodate the growing pressure for action on rents, repairs and maintenance and the replacement of slum houses.[16] The National Housing and Town Planning Council were particularly vociferous in support of a new clearance programme. In May 1953 they stated that 'never before has the public conscience been so alive to the need for good healthy housing conditions'. It was, therefore, 'precisely the right moment' to eliminate low standards and local authorities should introduce new slum clearance schemes as soon as possible.[17]

The Queen's speech in November 1953 heralded 'a vigorous resumption of slum-clearance' and in the Debate on the Address Harold Macmillan, then Minister of Housing, made a major speech outlining his proposals.[18] Although there was still 'a great problem of overcrowding' and 'of families with no home of their own' we could no longer 'leave people living in cramped, dark, rotten houses'. Whilst reliable figures were not available there were certainly 'many hundreds of thousands' of slums. 'In some great cities it will take perhaps 10, 15 or 20 years for us to clear away the whole thing' although, by implication, most authorities were expected to finish the job of clearance within five years.

The White Paper *Houses – the Next Step*[19] explained the Better Housing Campaign in detail. In the private sector the policy for sound houses was an increase in rents and encouragement to landlords to make repairs. Substantial repairs to 'dilapidated' houses were to be enforced by the local authorities and improvements encouraged by easing conditions for the improvement grants which had first been made available under the 1949 Act. For slum houses 'it is an essential part of the Government's plan that local authorities should take up again the great campaign of slum clearance which the war interrupted'. Pre-war clearance programmes had included 472,000 houses; about 140,000 houses from these schemes were still outstanding and there were hundreds of thousands more which would qualify as slums. Following the precedent of the thirties the Minister would require submission of programmes from local authorities and, where they could not clear all slums within five years, new powers of deferred demolition would be available for acquisition and 'patching' of properties.

The clearance element in the plan was justified, first, by 'the need for slum clearance from the human point of view' and, second, by encouragement to central area redevelopment. By enabling the transfer of some council building from virgin sites it was hoped to minimise decay of the inner cities and the loss of good farmland to housing. Additionally, it was felt that rehousing on cleared sites was inherently preferable 'to avoid uprooting people' who wished to remain near their old homes and places of work.

Slum clearance was only one element in the Better Housing Campaign and, politically, not a contentious issue. In debate on the Housing (Repairs and Rents) Bill there were two lines of attack from the opposition apart from rejection of rent increases. The first was the impossibility of ensuring that repairs would be undertaken. Indeed, Bevan seriously doubted whether the building industry had the capacity to manage repairs and improvements in addition to the load imposed by an unprecedented production of new buildings.[20] Other major speakers attacked the deferred demolition proposals. But these were minor points; everybody agreed that poor housing was unacceptable and that a clearance programme was now due.

The Housing (Repairs and Rents) Act 1954 made only minor changes in slum clearance law. Apart from the deferred demolition procedure the main innovation was to implement a new definition of unfitness for human habitation which had been recommended by the Central Housing Advisory Committee in 1946[21] Unlike the 1930 definition the new definition was not framed in relation to locally variable standards but attempted a universally applicable measure of unfitness. This definition of unfitness with slight amendment is still in force today under the Housing Act 1957.[22]

Local authorities were encouraged by the Minister to take up slum clearance again without waiting for the new Act. In March 1954 the advice contained in previous circulars was withdrawn and authorities were informed that they should 'forthwith resume the full exercise of their powers under Part II and Part III of the Housing Act, 1936 and continue to do so until the proposals they will submit under the Bill . . . have been approved'.[23] These proposals were requested in August 1954.[24] Submissions were to be in within twelve months and programmes of action for the first five years would require Ministry approval. But many authorities responded to government stimulus and began clearance again without waiting for ministerial approval of their plans.

At the general election in May 1955 the Conservatives capitalised on the apparently successful resumption of slum clearance, promising to rehouse at least 200,000 people a year and to provide 60,000 new dwellings each year for this purpose. This target was to be reiterated by Duncan Sandys, the new Minister of Housing,[25] and its eventual achievement in 1958 was marked by a planted parliamentary question to his successor, Henry Brooke, in April 1959.[26] But the returns submitted by local authorities during the summer of 1955 showed that, at the proposed rate of clearance, it would take much longer than five years to complete the job. The published figures for England and Wales gave 847,000 unfit houses out of a total of 12,935,000.[27] Action in the first five years was expected to clear only 375,000, well under half the 'official' number of slums. It was also quite clear from the detailed returns that there was tremendous variation in the basis of the figures from one local authority to another, a blatant deficiency which has been extensively criticised elsewhere.[28] The problems of some authorities seemed beyond solution even within the twenty years suggested by Macmillan; Liverpool returned 88,233 unfit houses — 43 per cent of the city's housing — but proposed demolition of only 7,025 in the first five years. Manchester returned 68,000 and proposed action for only 7,500. Oldham's return implied a similar fifty-year programme of 11,169 unfit houses with only 1,150 demolitions in the first five years. But despite the glaring anomalies in the returns they were to remain the basis of government planning until the early 1960s.

The abolition of the general needs subsidy by the Housing Subsidies Act 1956 was presented by the government in part as a further boost to the slum clearance programme. Introducing the Bill, Duncan Sandys argued that it was time that slum families secured a share of the new houses provided by local authorities. Since the government could not direct housing authorities in this way they were obliged to use incentives, in this case the retention of subsidy for houses built for slum clearance while general needs subsidies were abolished.[29] In fact, the inequity of subsidising council tenants who allegedly did not need it was a far more important theme of the government's case and the opposition rightly argued that it was deceitful to give the impression that maintaining an existing subsidy was an advance.

The slum clearance drive which was built up in the years 1954 to 1956 was not innovative in the sense that it followed closely the lines of the pre-war campaign and was seen as such by politicians and administrators. The main improvements were a tighter specification of unfitness and slightly more generous compensation arrangements. But against these strengths must be set the fundamental weakness of a programme based on totally inadequate information which nevertheless indicated clearly that the projected rate of action was pitifully slow. Housing conditions had worsened substantially since 1939 while standards of what was an acceptable house had risen. Nevertheless the government were prepared to go ahead with the programme without attempting a thorough appraisal of what was realistically required. But local authorities were soon to find that there were real difficulties in the way of achieving even their own modest targets. A combination of rising interest rates and the restriction of subsidies forced a cut-back in their building programmes. The strain on technical staff limited the scale of clearance activity that could be attempted but there was no provision for improving support facilities for local authorities. Decontrol of rents under the Rent Act 1957 combined with the economic and demographic trends of the late fifties were soon to place an increasing burden on housing authorities which diverted their energies from slum clearance.

The Campaign in Progress, 1956-64

Once the slum clearance programme had been established policy changed very little for some years until, in the sixties, a crescendo of criticism from inside and outside Parliament forced the government into more dynamic action. In the build-up to the 1959 election the government congratulated themselves on achieving their aim of 200,000 people a year rehoused from the slums and the Conservative election manifesto promised to rehouse another million by 1965. But constant probing by the opposition and the accumulation of independent evidence outside Parliament began to reveal the inadequacy of the programme. Whilst the government celebrated the achievement of their target the opposition pointed out that at the prevailing rate of progress the 847,000 unfit dwellings identified in 1954 would take 29 years to clear.[30]

The first serious academic critique of housing targets was published in 1960. Cullingworth's *Housing Needs and Planning Policy* asserted not only that the local authority statements of unfit houses were 'a gross under-estimate' but that the process of obsolescence would itself produce the need for an annual replacement of 141,000 houses given a life of 100 years. 'Even if two million slum houses were replaced immediately there would still remain the problem of gradually replacing the remaining 86 per cent. At a 1 per cent annual replacement rate this would involve the building of 121,000 houses a year.'[31] The rate of

80,000 demolitions a year implied by local authority targets probably meant that the country was falling behind. Cullingworth concluded that 200,000 a year was the desirable rate of demolition. Since this could not be managed a substantial programme of subsidised improvement was necessary.

The government's reply to critics was set out in a White Paper in February 1961.[32] The new policy on slum clearance was to concentrate on the hardcore problem of some fifty authorities whose programmes and progress showed that they had a long period of clearance ahead of them. Over the rest of the country 'unfit houses should have practically disappeared within the next 10 years'. The White Paper hinted at greater financial assistance for the hardcore areas and the Minister saw them benefiting, at least in the staffing of their overworked technical departments, by the cessation of clearance programmes elsewhere. But the programme continued much as before. By the end of March 1961 Birmingham had demolished or closed only 7,600 of the 50,000 houses defined as unfit in 1954. Liverpool had cleared only 5,900 of its 88,000 slums.[33] In the five years from January 1955 to the end of 1960 the Welsh authorities had demolished only half the houses in their 1955 five-year programmes and the English authorities lagged by 90,000.[34]

During Dr Hill's short spell as Minister of Housing (from November 1961 until July 1962) the critique of the government's clearance programme was substantially strengthened by a number of independent studies. Needleman's article in the *National Economic Review* of November 1961[35] reached conclusions similar to Cullingworth's: again assuming that the life of a property was 100 years the rate of demolition required up to 1980 would be 200,000 houses a year and from then on about 100,000 a year.

A more polemical piece in the *New Left Review* of January 1962[36] extended Cullingworth's exposure of the 1954 returns to demonstrate the absurdity of figures which put Darlington and East Grinstead or Derby and Aylesbury in the same situation. Even more damaging, the extrapolation of progress since 1955 showed that Liverpool would take 94 years to clear its slums, Manchester 46 years and Pembroke 480 years.

The following March, Burnett and Scott, two members of the Ministry's staff, published an appraisal of housing conditions based mainly on census figures and rating information.[37] Their analysis identified ten areas mainly in the conurbations of the North, the North East, the Midlands and South Wales, where the problem of housing obsolescence was greatest. These were then examined in more detail. In

A Century of Slum Clearance

Tyneside the authors found that although only 21,800 houses had been returned as unfit in 1955 'the total stock which does not measure up to modern standards may be between 50,000 and 100,000 dwellings'.[38] In East Lancashire 'all the clearance and improvement which has been done so far is a sporadic effort compared with the total of about 120,000 unfit houses that remain and the possible maximum of about 300,000 substandard dwellings'.[39] In fact, within these ten areas the rate of progress was even slower than elsewhere. The summary conclusion of this paper, reporting internal research conducted by the Ministry, put a final nail in the coffin of the 'official' clearance programme:

> The evidence that is available indicated that the problem of obsolescent housing extends well beyond the 850,000 dwellings recorded as unfit. In England and Wales there were in 1951 about 1,984,000 dwellings of three rooms or less; 4,850,000, one in three of all households, without a fixed bath; 2,800,000 without exclusive use of a W.C. and nearly 2,250,000 dwellings rated in 1958 in the lowest category of £10 or less. Some 3,250,000 houses were estimated to be over seventy-five years old and a further 1,400,000 between sixty and seventy-five years of age in 1951.[40]

Despite the indirect data[41] used this was a powerfully argued case.

Gray and Russell's *The Housing Situation in 1960* which had been commissioned by the Ministry in April 1960 and was published in May 1962[42] provided confirmation from another official inquiry. The survey gave for the first time an estimate of the number of accommodation units likely to be pulled down in successive five-year periods and hence a realistic estimate of replacement needs. Taking unfit accommodation, which should be eradicated immediately, together with property having a life of less than five years there were 832,000 units which should be demolished by 1965. But only 486,000 of these were likely actually to be removed by planned action. To clear the 1,954,000 units with lives of less than 15 years within a 15-year period would mean a clearance rate of 130,000 per annum. On the other hand, 735,000 units were thought to be capable of repair at reasonable cost thereby reducing the total replacement to 1,219,000 and the annual rate for 15 years to 81,000. But even this rate was a good deal higher than the 60,000 houses demolished or closed in 1959.[43]

Some of this evidence began to permeate political discussion in successive debates on housing. The concentration on areas of greatest need became more precise. Dr Hill promised a 'special drive' in the worst-off towns and reported that forty authorities with the worst problem had been approached for a statement of their difficulties. Ministry staff were to be sent to visit them to see what special help could be given.[44] But the financial priority promised in the 1961 White Paper was not introduced.

When Sir Keith Joseph took over from Dr Hill in July 1962 he immediately implemented plans for a regional office in Manchester to help local authorities with their clearance effort. Areas with the worst slum problems were to double and treble their rates of clearance and industrialised building methods would boost council house building in these areas. By May 1963 thirty-eight local authorities had been scheduled for special treatment. They were expected to increase their clearance rate by at least 100 per cent over the average of the previous three years.[45]

Programmes for council building were agreed for a five or six year period with the thirty-eight authorities doubling their rate of building compared with the previous three years.[46] A White Paper[47] stated overall policy as the eradication of most of the remaining 600,000 slum houses in the next ten years together with an increased rate of house improvement. But the scandals of homelessness and Rachmanism, pursued with vigour by the press and politicians, overwhelmed all other issues. In July 1963 Sir Keith Joseph announced that Sir Milner Holland had agreed to chair a Committee of Inquiry into London's housing.[48] These immediate problems dominated debate in the last months of the Conservative government during 1963 and 1964. According to the Minister progress in slum clearance amongst the thirty-eight authorities gave promise that all but twelve would clear all their slums by 1973.[49] But the Conservatives were not given the opportunity to pursue their plans as they were defeated in the general election of October 1964.

Labour's Reappraisal, 1964-70

Early in 1965 Richard Crossman, Minister of Housing in the new Labour Government, took the first steps in a review of policy on older houses. A Ministry circular in February announced that a subcommittee of the Central Housing Advisory Committee had been set up to consider standards of housing fitness.[50] The circular also required local authorities to submit returns of all remaining unfit houses in their areas regardless of the time it would take to clear them. The replies to this circular greatly increased the number of 'official' slums remaining in England and Wales. While there were approximately 250,000 unfit

A Century of Slum Clearance

houses still standing according to the 1955 estimates the new returns gave a total of 771,400 in the first quarter of 1965.[51]

In fact it had become quite apparent that the local authorities' own estimates of slum housing were seriously misleading as a basis for national policy and that government intelligence on housing was generally inadequate. The 'pathetic record' of government sponsored research on housing in Britain had been castigated by Donnison in an article in *The Times* (19 November 1962).[52] At a time of rapid social and economic change, he argued, the government required an independent research programme and regular surveys if a satisfactory balance and mix of housing was to be supplied for the country as a whole. The miscalculation of the number of houses which were expected to be decontrolled by the 1957 Rent Act was cited as one example of the costs of poor intelligence in the housing field.

The first steps to improve government intelligence had been made by Sir Keith Joseph, early in 1964, when a Chief Statistician was appointed at the Ministry and the Statistics Section expanded into a Statistics Branch.[53] In May 1964 the Ministry commissioned the Government Social Survey to undertake a second general study of the housing situation along the lines of Gray and Russell's earlier work.[54] However, the main contribution initiated under the Conservatives was the exhaustive inquiry undertaken by the Milner-Holland Committee. The thoroughness of this inquiry was not a matter of direct government responsibility and may well have exceeded their expectations.[55] In a debate on the Milner-Holland Report, Crossman scorned the Conservative's record on research and announced a reorganisation of information services. For a start the tabulation of 1961 census results was to be speeded up and the statistical staff of the Ministry increased.[56]

The improvement of intelligence was to be an important theme of development during the Labour period 1964-70. In 1965 regional offices were established in Birmingham, Leeds, Bristol and Nottingham and at the centre the research section was strengthened. The White Paper *The Housing Programme 1965 to 1970*,[57] published in November 1965, contained an Appendix describing the improvements to be made in information sources. These included confirmation of the decision to hold a census in 1966 and a series of studies of housing conditions in the conurbations. Further national investigation of housing conditions was to await the report of the Denington Committee.

The substantive proposals of Labour's five-year programme outlined in the White Paper were centred on the target of half a million new houses a year by 1970. Replacement of 'about one million unfit houses already identified as slums' and up to two million more 'old houses not yet slums but not worth improving' provided the main justification for this increase in the house building programme. The decline of private landlordism meant that public sector building must be increased if low income families were to find somewhere to rent. At the end of 1965 the prospects for house building seemed good. Total houses built during the year were 347,000 in England and Wales, a post-war record. But the upward trend continued only until 1968, when 372,000 houses were completed, and in the same year the half million target was officially abandoned.

Apart from greater central government assistance through the local offices of the Ministry and of the new National Building Agency, the main inducement to slum clearance was the more generous subsidy arrangements for priority areas under the Housing Subsidies Act 1967. Robert Mellish, Joint Parliamentary Secretary to the Ministry of Housing, talked of 'one hundred and thirty priority local authorities with major slum and over-crowding problems',[58] which were to be given 'maximum targets' for new building and a four-year rolling programme of construction. Another 177 authorities would have the advantage of a three-year rolling programme making 300 authorities in all. But the actual implementation of the proposal was not so widespread. The criteria applied to local authorities for backdating subsidies were that they should have:

i) more than 12½ per cent slums according to the returns submitted to circular 11/65; *or*
ii) 10 per cent or more excess of households over dwellings according to the 1961 census; *and*
iii) 100 or more houses or flats approved but not started, or under construction, at the end of November, 1965.

By these criteria some sixty-five authorities qualified.[59] Nevertheless, compared with the selective assistance provided in the later years of the Conservative Government inducements were more widespread and involved hard cash. On the other hand, the criteria depended on outdated census information and the doubtfully accurate 11/65 returns. Geographically the policy involved a new concentration on Welsh authorities and on authorities within the GLC area compared with the list of thirty-eight authorities singled out by Conservative measures.[60]

The report of the Denington Committee in 1966[61] provided the initial impetus for a substantial reappraisal of the slum problem. As part of their work the Committee took practical steps to encourage surveys of housing conditions; six small surveys were undertaken to assess the difficulty of such work and the Committee also assessed the burden on local government staff of more fact finding enquiries. Their recommendation was that both forms of enquiry should be more widely used. At the national level they suggested that 'for the purpose of making a first quick assessment of the total problem, the Minister might well have a national sample survey made'. This recommendation was quickly accepted. Fieldwork was carried out in February and March 1967 and data were available by June. The speed with which the survey was mounted and the information produced owed much to previous work which the Ministry had carried out as part of their study of improvement possibilities in Deeplish, Rochdale.[62]

Compared with previous estimates the 1967 survey showed that the problem of poor condition housing was both much larger and more widespread than had been thought.[63] Unfit dwellings numbered 1.8 million compared with only 820,000 identified in 1965. Compared with the 1965 returns the conurbations of the north accounted for a smaller proportion of unfit houses and the smaller urban areas and rural areas a larger proportion; not only was the scale of the national clearance programme inadequate but the policy of concentration on the remaining hardcore areas was shown to be ill-founded. In addition to the 1.8 million unfit dwellings some 4.5 million required either £125 or more spent on repairs or lacked at least one basic amenity. The Denington Committee had not recommended a change in the standard of unfitness, partly because so many unfit houses still existed by the old standard. However, they had argued that 'we would expect those authorities which cannot deal with all their present unfit houses within seven years to justify their programmes to the Minister, and, for those houses which must stand between seven and fifteen years, to undertake programmes of acquisition and patching.'[64] The extent of poor conditions revealed by the survey ruled out even this possibility.

For the government these figures were a challenge to existing policies that could not be ignored. Frank Allaun, an MP for Salford, had for some time urged action on the Deeplish and Denington reports.[65] In October 1967 Anthony Greenwood, then Minister of Housing, announced a review of legislation.[66] In April 1968 the White Paper *Old Houses into New Homes*[67] announced a switch of public investment from new house building to the improvement of older houses. Although the opening paragraphs presented this as a response to a changing 'balance of need between new house-building and improvements' the vast pool of poor housing revealed by the Ministry's survey was the most pressing consideration. The White Paper claimed that a switch of resources to improvement would not affect the rate of clearance which would have to remain high if the state of affairs revealed by the survey was to be tackled effectively. But the main effect of the switch was to make large-scale improvement a real possibility. The subsequent Housing Bill introduced new procedures for area improvement, in particular general improvement areas, but made only minor adjustments to slum clearance by increasing compensation in some cases and slightly altering the criteria of unfitness.

Although Frank Allaun had long been one of the chief supporters of a more vigorous improvement campaign he was the main critic of the Bill. Local authorities he said would find it difficult to bear the increased costs of compensation; decontrol of rents of houses provided with standard amenities would cause hardship and without the addition of compulsory powers for area improvement the Act would have no teeth.[68] The Bill received the Royal Assent in July 1969 and its effects had hardly begun to emerge before the Conservatives returned to office in June 1970.[69]

The Swing Away from Slum Clearance, 1970-75

Shortly after the Conservatives took office, in November 1970, ministerial responsibilities were reorganised and the Ministry of Housing and Local Government was absorbed into a new Department of the Environment. The first concern of Peter Walker, Secretary of State for the Environment, was the reform of housing finance. Preliminary information was given in a statement in November but full details of the sweeping changes in rents and subsidies were not ready until the publication of a White Paper the following July.[70] As a minor item in the package of reforms slum clearance was to be put on a new financial basis. Under the existing system subsidy was not directly available on slum clearance operations but only on the council housing which was built to rehouse displaced residents. According to the White Paper local authorities were finding, in many instances, that they did not need the cleared land for council housing but might prefer to use it for other purposes 'including redevelopment for owner occupation, commercial purposes or as public open space'.[71] To assist local authorities in these circumstances there was to be a new Slum Clearance Subsidy to meet 75 per cent of the loss to the general rate fund incurred through acquisition and clearance of slum property.

In the acrimonious debates on the Housing Finance Bill government speakers made much of the stimulus to slum clearance which the new subsidy was expected to provide. Julien Amery, Minister for Housing and Construction, joined the long line of Ministers who have committed themselves to a ten-year deadline for clearing the remaining slums. The Secretary of State for the Environment was more circumspect claiming only that 'the provision means that there are no financial reasons why the slums should not be cleared in the coming ten years'.[72] By implication this involved a substantial increase in the level of activity since Peter Walker also castigated the record of the Labour Government under whom, he said, the rate of clearance would have involved another twenty-five years' work to clear the backlog.[73]

By the time of the third reading of the Bill, in May 1972, Amery was in possession of the first results of the House Condition Survey which had been undertaken in September 1971. The findings showed an apparent drop in the numbers of slums in potential clearance areas from 1.1 million in 1967 to 700,000 in 1971 — a decline of 100,000 a year. The number of substandard houses lacking amenities had fallen from nearly four millions to less than three millions.[74] Amery reiterated his target of eradicating slums and substandard housing within the decade and issued a circular to all local authorities urging them to join a final drive to achieve this objective in a concerted programme. Significantly the circular pointed out that the new subsidy enabled local authorities to encourage private rather than public redevelopment of cleared sites.[75]

Euphoria about future prospects was based more on the increase in improvement activity than on the rate of clearance. Grants approved in March 1972 were the highest ever and Amery predicted at least a quarter million for the year.[76] But slum clearance was up by only a few thousand on 1970. The Housing Act 1971 had boosted the improvement effort by temporarily increasing grants in development areas and intermediate areas to 75 per cent and the time limit for higher grants was to be extended for another year to June 1974.

In October 1972 when the fight over the Housing Finance Bill was finished Geoffrey Rippon took over as Secretary of State for the Environment and Paul Channon as Minister for Housing and Construction. Official policy moved steadily against slum clearance and in favour of improvement. Although Reginald Freeson raised serious doubts about the real impact of the improvement programme and the statistical accuracy of the 1971 House Condition Survey[77] improvement grant approvals were rising steadily. Amery's forecast of 250,000 approvals for 1972 was exceeded by 69,000 and in 1973 grant approvals reached 361,000. On the other hand slum clearance languished and the ten-year target receded into the background.

The general climate of thought and opinion in the country favoured the shift in official policy. Academic and journalistic commentary during 1971 and 1972 provided a variety of arguments against slum clearance continuing at its existing rate. Ungerson's report on Southwark and Brent portrayed the difficulties of life in areas of protracted redevelopment[78] and Dennis's second report on Sunderland exposed the depth of opposition between town hall and residents opposed to clearance plans.[79] Shelter, realising that slum clearance for many poor households meant only a transfer to a poor council estate, argued for a *Reprieve for the Slums*.[80] Around this time local and national community action magazines were established to assert the rights of the citizen under redevelopment.[81] From the opposite political perspective McKie's *Housing and the Whitehall Bulldozer* proposed a policy of 'cellular renewal' better suited to the realities of the housing market, particularly in provincial towns[82] and Pepper's careful review of the problems of improvement legislation provided many elements of a blueprint for such an approach.[83] But it was an article in *Official Architecture and Planning* which spelled out the plain message 'Stop Slum Clearance – Now'.[84] Alan Stone's polemic on Liverpool argued that the city's clearance programme had outstripped its capacity to rebuild. Acres of derelict land in the city centre and problem estates on the outskirts, destruction of existing communities and growing vandalism all pointed to the need to stop the big clearance schemes and adopt improvement and small-scale redevelopment instead.

During 1973 the only legislative change affecting slum clearance was the new compensation arrangements introduced by the Land Compensation Act, with the support of both major parties. Introduction of Home Loss Payments and Disturbance Payments for both tenants and owner occupiers substantially increased the amount of cash that residents affected by redevelopment could expect to receive. But the new arrangements were not particularly concerned with smoothing the progress of slum clearance; they arose from a general review of compensation and a report on the impact of road proposals.[85]

Meanwhile the alternative to large-scale slum clearance and redevelopment was worked out. The first of two White Papers developing a new philosophy and new machinery was issued in April.[86] It placed slum clearance in the context of widening the choice of housing available. Home ownership was to be increased by ensuring adequate land and mortgage funds. To check the decline of the private rented sector the voluntary housing movement would get more help from the Housing Corporation and the National Building Agency. Slum clearance, which for years had provided the principal means of municipalisation, was no longer to take place on the same scale: 'wholesale demolition of residential areas displaces and uproots settled communities. The alternative is systematic and thorough improvement of older housing, and the rehabilitation of whole sections of a town through the medium of general improvement areas'.[87]

New measures for dealing with the problems of older housing followed in a White Paper in June.[88] Again the argument stressed the social considerations that justified a move away from large-scale clearance:

> The Government believes that in the majority of cases, it is no longer preferable to attempt to solve the problems arising from bad housing by schemes of widespread, comprehensive redevelopment. Such an approach often involves massive and unacceptable disruption of communities and leaves vast areas of our cities derelict and devastated for far too long. Regardless of the financial compensation they receive, many people suffer distress when their homes are compulsorily acquired. Increasing local opposition to redevelopment proposals is largely attributable to people's understandable preference for the familiar and in many ways more convenient environment in which they have lived for years'.[89]

To avoid these problems local authorities should instead introduce a programme of 'gradual renewal' in which slum clearance and house improvement procedures would operate side by side in programmes of 'continuous, flexible and gradual redevelopment on a relatively small scale'.[90] Housing action areas in localities of particular housing stress would provide a new method of achieving this objective.

By the time the Housing and Planning Bill was prepared early in 1974 the steady decline in public sector house building had substantially altered the balance between demolition and replacement. *New Society* pointed out in April that 'slum clearance which removed a house for every two built by councils in 1968 removed more than two for every three built in 1973'.[91] Figures for the conurbations in 1972 showed that in most cases the big cities were clearing slums faster than they were rebuilding. 'The answer is not to stop slum clearance — but it could well be slowed down until councils are coping again'.

In fact many authorities had already begun a reappraisal of their programmes for older housing. In 1973 Leeds Metropolitan District established a Housing Working Party to review policy in the new authority and particularly the Housing Renewal Programme of the previous Leeds County Borough. Their final report transferred 2,600 dwellings from the clearance programme to improvement instead, among other reasons, because of increasing public opposition.[92] Newcastle began a review of policy which identified a minimum clearance programme of some 5,000 houses but reconsidered the future of 4,000 which might now be saved.[93] Manchester's House Conditions Survey in 1972 led to adoption of the preferred alternative of gradual renewal and phasing out of the clearance programme at the end of 1976[94] and Birmingham adopted a massive programme of general improvement areas and 'renewal areas'.[95] The effect of such changes of direction by local authorities showed clearly in the clearance statistics for 1974. During the year only 42,000 houses were demolished or closed, the lowest total since 1956.

The Conservative's Housing and Planning Bill lapsed when the government were defeated in the general election in February 1974 but the measure was revived in almost identical form by the Labour Government and enacted as the Housing Act 1974. Apart from introducing housing action areas the Act abolished the procedure for clearance orders. Circulars issued since the introduction of the new Act make it quite clear that slum clearance is now definitely a second best.[96] Circular 13/75 in particular reminds local authorities that they have to be satisfied, before declaring a clearance area under the Housing Act 1957, that demolition of all the buildings in the area is the most satisfactory way of dealing with that area. 'In declaring a clearance area, therefore, a local authority will have to establish, for example, that a housing action area declaration is not more appropriate'.[97]

An Overview of the Slum Clearance Campaign

Taking a broad view of slum clearance since the introduction of modern procedures in 1930 there has been a remarkable continuity of effort and direction until the recent move towards gradual renewal. The post-war drive which began in 1955 took up the same basic objectives and machinery as the pre-war effort of the thirties. The main problem for successive governments of either party was to raise the rate of clearance to higher levels in the face of constant upward revision of the numbers of unfit houses. But the post-war rate of clearance never reached pre-war war levels.

The build up of the post-war slum clearance drive and the relative achievements of Labour and Conservative Governments can be seen from Table 1. By 1951 annual closures and demolitions totalled 11,000

Period	Houses demolished in clearance areas			Houses not in clearance areas			Total* demolished or closed	Persons Moved
	Unfit	Others	Total	Demolished*	Closed	Total*		
1930 – 31. 3.45	221,987	6,765	228,752	92,692	15,517	112,209	340,961	1,340,293
1. 4.45 – 31.12.54	31,772	1,683	33,455	37,479	18,924	56,403	89,858	308,737
1955	8,066	495	8,561	8,731	7,081	15,812	24,373	79,965
1956	13,777	593	14,370	10,620	9,346	19,966	34,336	115,093
1957	21,099	933	22,032	13,053	9,430	22,483	44,515	159,223
1958	28,376	1,521	29,897	13,752	9,074	22,726	52,623	159,923
1959	32,685	2,224	34,909	13,506	9,140	22,646	57,555	154,853
1960	31,334	2,286	33,620	13,789	9,152	22,941	56,561	167,679
1961	34,668	5,273	37,941	15,205	8,823	24,028	61,969	168,032
1962	35,328	3,379	38,707	15,474	8,250	23,724	62,431	173,014
1963	37,216	3,313	40,529	13,383	7,533	20,916	61,445	163,160
1964	37,629	3,524	41,153	12,601	7,461	20,062	61,215	161,861
1965	38,964	3,624	42,588	10,447	7,601	18,078	60,666	171,595
1966	42,847	5,229	48,076	10,930	7,776	18,706	66,782	177,283
1967	46,913	4,604	51,517	11,774	7,861	19,635	71,152	185,132
1968	47,637	6,238	53,875	10,083	7,628	17,711	71,586	188,895
1969	46,746	6,653	53,399	8,499	7,335	15,834	69,233	173,447
1970	47,259	5,279	52,538	8,591	6,675	15,266	67,804	169,598
1971	49,676	6,510	56,186	8,188	5,683	13,871	70,057	157,125
1972	47,964	5,478	53,442	7,140	5,516	12,656	66,098	148,338
1973	46,841	5,898	52,739	6,141	4,677	10,818	63,557	132,703
1974	33,319	3,554	36,873	2,592	2,233	4,825	41,698	96,193
1975	36,586	4,458	41,044	4,659	4,380	8,039	49,083	117,183

* in columns marked with an asterisk the figures from 1945 onwards of demolished houses not in clearance areas exclude demolitions of houses previously returned as closed

Sources: Pre-war figures from: M.H.L.G. *Housing Return for England and Wales*, 31/3/56 Cmd. 9749 HMSO
Post-war figures from M.H.L.G. *Housing Statistics Great Britain*, quarterly, and since 1972, Department of the Environment *Housing and Construction Statistics*, quarterly.

houses and had increased to 18,000 per annum by 1954. Almost two thirds of the houses affected were individual houses not located in clearance areas. When the drive began in 1955 the rate of clearance grew rapidly for the first three years increasing by some 10,000 dwellings a year. Thereafter the total rose only gradually to reach a plateau around 60,000 per annum by 1961. Initially the demolition of individual houses outweighed clearance area action, building up rapidly to around 22,000 per annum by 1957. This level of individual action was maintained until 1963 when it began a steady decline, which was reversed only in 1975. Clearance area action, on the other hand, built up only gradually but steadily increased in scale through the entire period 1955 to 1971 and fell away substantially only in 1974.

The gradual and stable trends of demolition rates indicate a situation which was relatively impervious to changes in emphasis within the overall policy. Shifts from year to year were usually slight and the overall direction of the trends remarkably stable. The only exception was the sudden steep rise in clearance area action during Labour's administration in 1964 to 1970. During the last three full years of the Conservative Government, 1961 to 1963, an average of 61,950 houses were cleared annually of which 63 per cent were in clearance areas. When the increase under Labour levelled off in the three years 1967 to 1969, the government's last three full years, demolitions averaged 70,660 per annum of which 75 per cent were in clearance areas.

Under successive governments the rate of new building in the public sector was regarded as a key determinant of slum clearance progress. The clearance drive did not start until a high rate of new house building had been achieved and the building programme and demolition programme were explicitly linked in successive policy statements and in academic and political debate.

Development of industrialised building methods and government approval of advance construction programmes were both pursued as inducements to clearance activity. But it is doubtful whether the link between provision of new houses and demolition of old was ever quite so direct as implied. During the build-up of slum clearance from 1955 to 1959 public sector building declined steadily. A fairly constant level of clearance at around 60,000 was maintained until 1965 while public sector building increased by over 40,000 houses per annum between 1963 and 1965. The move to a new 'plateau' around 70,000 demolitions per annum under Labour contrasts with a peak of public house building in 1967 and subsequent steady decline. It was only during the dramatic slump in house building in 1974 that slum clearance appears

A Century of Slum Clearance

to have followed closely the trend of construction figures but there are many other reasons for the dramatic fall at this point.

Two factors served to insulate clearance programmes to some extent from the vicissitudes of building performance. On the one hand, local authorities could cut back heavily on allocation of waiting list cases giving priority instead to applicants displaced by slum clearance. In some central London boroughs housing of waiting list cases was stopped altogether.[98] Many other cities gave slum clearance families first priority; in Manchester, for example, 72 per cent of lettings in 1969, excluding lettings to transfer cases, went to families occupying unfit houses.[99]

On the other hand, the growing pool of council housing provided increasing numbers of annual relets available for slum clearance applicants. By 1969, Liverpool C.B. produced about 3,000 relets a year which almost exactly balanced the average number of demolitions at the time.[100] In the same year Manchester C.B. let 4,536 houses to households occupying unfit property. Almost half of these were relets and, in total, 3,507 relets came available during the year.[101]

However much central government might exhort, the implementation of national slum clearance targets is dependent on the performance of local authorities. Direct administrative assistance through the decentralised offices of the Department and through the National Building Agency never overcame completely the chronic problem of staffing difficulties in heavily burdened public health, surveyors' and town clerks' departments. But there is some evidence that this assistance had a direct pay-off in terms of improved local authority performance. The thirty-eight authorities singled out for special attention in 1963 together cleared an average of 11,000 houses per annum in the years 1955 to 1961. The total increased substantially in subsequent years to a peak of 29,000 in 1967.[102] Individual authorities varied widely in their response. Some of the thirty-eight appear not to have responded at all. Sheffield maintained a steady rate of 1,000 to 1,600 demolitions for most of the period; the rate in Leeds remained around 2,000 per annum. On the other hand, the response could be quite dramatic. In 1961 and 1962 Manchester cleared about 1,350 slum houses; from 1963 onwards this was increased to about 4,000 houses per annum. Oldham almost tripled its performance between 1963 and 1965. In 1965 Birmingham reappraised progress and raised the level of clearance from around 2,000 per annum to over 4,000 while Liverpool moved from around 1,700 per annum to over 3,000 per annum as a result of a National Building Agency Report in 1965.[103]

Despite these local successes the slum clearance drive was never big enough to provide a solution to the problem of bad housing. Even before the 1967 survey it was clear that the programme was inadequate. In Table 2 the totals of unfit dwellings in official estimates are compared with average rates of clearance during subsequent years of the programme.

Table 2: Estimated unfit dwellings and slum clearance progress since 1955

England and Wales

	1955 local authority returns	1965 local authority returns	1967 Independent Survey	1971 Independent Survey
Total dwellings	12,935,000	15,040,000	15,700,000	17,100,000
Unfit dwellings	847,000	823,000	1,836,000	1,244,000
% Unfit	6.5	5.5	11.7	7.3
Average rate of clearance	51,700 (1955-64)	67,900 (1965-69)	70,600 (1967-69)	66,600 (1971-73)
Approximate years to clear all unfit dwellings	16	12	26	19

None of these estimates made any allowance for the process of obsolescence which transfers many thousands of houses each year into the unfit category. Nor was there any allowance for houses requiring action because of rising standards such as a move to the 12 point standard which was considered by the Denington Committee.[104] But even taking static estimates of unfitness the levels of clearance achieved implied a very long-term programme which made nonsense of ministers' claims that slums would be cleared within the decade.

Realisation of the inadequacy of demolition progress was an important impetus behind improvement policies. But improvement of older houses emerged only slowly as an important area of government intervention.

Discretionary grants introduced by the 1949 Act were not widely used and by 1958 only 160,000 such grants had been approved (see Table 3). The House Purchase and Housing Act 1959 introduced a standard grant for providing basic amenities which rapidly outstripped discretionary grants as the main source of government support. Total grants approved annually jumped from a few thousand in 1958 to 130,000 in 1960. But they then declined from that high point. The solution was to be a more systematic area approach initiated by the Housing Act 1964. Under the 1964 Act local authorities could declare 'improvement' areas within which 50 per cent of dwellings lacked one or more of the basic amenities. Private landlords could be compelled to improve their houses with basic amenities even outside improvement areas as long as tenants were willing to accept the consequent increase in rent; owner occupiers could not be obliged to co-operate. Unfortunately, this area improvement policy did not produce significant results; by 1968 only 400 improvement areas had been declared and only some 4,000 dwellings within them improved.[105] The total of discretionary and standard grants approved dropped to 114,000 in 1968 and 109,000 in 1969.

Table 3: 'Improvement' grants approved annually, England and Wales, 1949 to 1975

Year	Grants approved		Total
	Discretionary	Standard	
1949-1958	159,869	–	159,869
1959	45,935	33,061	78,996
1960	48,013	82,819	130,832
1961	47,945	79,831	127,776
1962	41,768	68,738	110,506
1963	42,701	77,278	119,979
1964	45,050	76,635	121,685
1965	40,100	82,893	122,993
1966	39,960	67,760	107,720
1967	46,606	66,536	113,142
1968	46,178	68,038	114,216
1969	49,376	59,562	108,938
1970	87,398	69,159	156,557
1971	137,608	59,873	197,481
1972	260,007	59,162	319,169
1973	316,438	44,516	360,954
1974	207,561	24,357	231,918
1975	115,718	11,170	126,888

Source: M.H.L.G., *Housing Statistics Great Britain*, quarterly and since 1972, Department of the Environment, *Housing and Construction Statistics*, quarterly.

The Denington Report had recommended that powers of compulsion should be introduced covering all types of property but a note of reservation by Cullingworth argued that the most important deterrent to voluntary improvement was the inadequate level of financial assistance.[106] The 1969 Act embodied the minority view retaining the emphasis on co-operation but raising the grant ceiling.

Higher grant limits had an immediate effect on performance which the introduction of 75 per cent grants in assisted and intermediate areas increased still further. Total grants approved rose from 156,000 in 1970 to 361,000 by 1973. However, very few of these grants were applied for systematic improvement of areas of older housing as the 1969 Act intended. Grants approved for dwellings in declared general improvement areas numbered only 32,600 in 1973, less than 10 per cent of the total. In the same year work was completed on only 15,100 dwellings in declared areas and fell away to only 13,000 in 1974. The effectiveness of the new housing action areas remains to be proven.

The history of government policy on older housing is at a turning point. Slum clearance has gone out of fashion but the alternatives based on large-scale improvement are not yet working effectively. After one hundred years of demolition the reduction of slum clearance in the early seventies resulted from the interplay of a variety of factors none of which provides a sufficient explanation on its own. The White Papers, circulars and Ministers' speeches stressed the unacceptable social consequences of clearance reflecting the findings of much academic work. Development of community action strengthened opposition to many individual local schemes and made the procedure less attractive to local officials. Conservative policy was to encourage alternatives to growing municipalisation of the housing stock through grants to private enterprise and the voluntary housing movement. Even the supporters of council housing experienced some disillusionment as the problems of new estates and multi-storey living emerged. The relative importance of these and other factors in swaying central and local government deserves a study to itself but all appear to have played some part in encouraging the recent withdrawal from slum clearance.

The fact remains that in many towns and cities the process of slum clearance and redevelopment has been a permanent backdrop to the lives of many thousands of citizens. Since slum clearance began in earnest in 1930 approximately 1½ million houses have been demolished or closed and approaching 5 million people moved. Slum clearance has been the cause of a major restructuring of cities and of the housing stock of the country. The procedures through which this has been achieved are considered in detail in the next chapter.

NOTES

1. For a detailed history of early legislation see Enid Gauldie, *Cruel Habitations: A History of Working-Class Housing 1780-1918*, Allen and Unwin, 1974, esp. Part 5.
2. Section 39 of the Act states that where a person is displaced by redevelopment 'and alternative residential accommodation on reasonable terms is not otherwise available to that person ... it shall be the duty of the relevant authority to secure that he will be provided with such other accommodation'.
3. Artizans' and Labourers' Dwellings Improvement Act 1875, Section 5.
4. In London, until 1919, the Local Government Board could not reduce the rehousing requirement below a number equivalent to half the persons displaced.
5. J.J. Clarke, *The Housing Problem*, Pitman, 1920.
6. Ministry of Health, *2nd Annual Report, 1920-21*, Cmd. 1446, HMSO, 1920, p. 71.
7. E.D. Simon, *How to Abolish the Slums*, Longmans, 1929.
8. Ministry of Health, *12th Annual Report, 1930-31*, Cmd. 3937, HMSO, 1931, p. 98.
9. For a full history of the inter-war period see Marian Bowley, *Housing and the State, 1919-1944*, Allen and Unwin, 1945.
10. House of Commons, *Official Report*, Vol. 238, Cols. 1806-1808.
11. Under Section 62(3) local authorities were to consider the extent to which sanitary conditions or repair of a house fell short of the requirements of local bye laws or the general standard of working class housing in the district. Sanitary defects included 'lack of space or of ventilation, darkness, dampness, absence of adequate and readily accessible water supply or sanitary accommodation or of other conveniences and inadequate paving or drainage of courts, yards or passages'.
12. Ministry of Health, *14th Annual Report, 1932-33*, Cmd. 4372, HMSO, 1933, p. 87.
13. Ministry of Health, *Housing Act 1930: Particulars of Slum Clearance Programmes Furnished by Local Authorities*, Cmd. 4535, HMSO, 1934.
14. House of Commons, *Official Report*, Vol. 473, Col. 1352.
15. 279,000 new houses in England and Wales and 39,000 in Scotland were actually completed in 1953.
16. Evidence of poor conditions and political pressure from professional associations and others accumulated from 1946 onwards. See D.V. Donnison, *Housing Policy Since the War*, Occasional Paper on Social Administration No. 1, Codicote Press, 1960, pp. 19-20; J.B. Cullingworth, *Housing and Local Government*, Allen and Unwin, 1966, pp. 33 and 36-37.
17. National Housing and Town Planning Council 'A Public Statement of the Council's Policy', *Housing and Planning Review*, Vol. 8, No. 3, (May-June 1953).
18. House of Commons, *Official Report*, Vol. 520, Cols. 173-194.
19. Cmd. 8996, HMSO, 1953.
20. House of Commons, *Official Report*, Vol. 521, Col. 817.
21. Central Housing Advisory Committee, *Report of the Sub-Committee on Standards of Fitness for Habitation*, HMSO, 1946.
22. The definition of unfitness under Section 4(1) of the Housing Act 1957, amended by Section 71 of the Housing Act 1969, is:

    In determining ... whether a house is unfit for human habitation,

regard shall be had to its condition in respect of the following matters that is to say —
(a) repair;
(b) stability;
(c) freedom from damp;
(cc) internal arrangement;
(d) natural lighting;
(e) ventilation;
(f) water supply;
(g) drainage and sanitary conveniences; and
(h) facilities for preparation and cooking of food and for disposal of waste water; and the house shall be deemed to be unfit as aforesaid if and only if it is so far defective in one or more of the said matters that it is not reasonably suitable for occupation in that condition .
The 1969 Act added the item 'internal arrangement' and deleted a reference to facilities for the storage of food from sub-paragraph (h).

23. Ministry of Housing and Local Government, Circular 30/54, *Housing: Slum Clearance*, HMSO, 1954.
24. Ministry of Housing and Local Government, Circular, 55/54, *Housing Repairs and Rents Act, Part I*, HMSO, 1954.
25. House of Commons, *Official Report*, Vol. 545, Written Answers, Col. 176.
26. House of Commons, *Official Report*, Vol. 604, Written Answers, Col. 101.
27. Ministry of Housing and Local Government, *Slum Clearance (England and Wales): Summary of Returns by Local Authorities*, Cmd. 9593, HMSO, 1955.
28. See J.B. Cullingworth, *Housing Needs and Planning Policy*, Routledge and Kegan Paul, 1960, p. 51; Raphael Samuels, James Kincaid and Elizabeth Slater, 'But Nothing Happens', *New Left Review*, January 1962.
29. House of Commons, *Official Report*, Vol. 545, Col. 791.
30. House of Commons, *Official Report*, Vol. 585, Col. 1006.
31. J.B. Cullingworth, *op. cit.* (1960), p. 53.
32. *Housing in England and Wales*, Cmnd. 1290, HMSO,, 1961.
33. House of Commons, *Official Report*, Vol. 640, Written Answers, Col. 169.
34. House of Commons, *Official Report*, Vol. 644, Written Answers, Col. 166.
35. L. Needleman, 'A Long-term View of Housing', *National Economic Review*, No. 18, November 1961.
36. Raphael Samuels, James Kincaid and Elizabeth Slater, *op. cit.*
37. F.T. Burnett and Sheila F. Scott, 'A Survey of Housing Conditions in the Urban Areas of England and Wales, 1960', *Sociological Review*, New Series, Vol. 10, No. 1, March 1962.
38. *Ibid.*, p. 45.
39. *Ibid.*, p. 60.
40. *Ibid.*, p. 77.
41. For a critique of the data and techniques used in this article see T.L.C. Duncan, *Measuring Housing Quality: A Study of Methods*, Centre for Urban and Regional Studies, Birmingham, Occasional Paper No. 20, 1971.
42. P.G. Gray and R. Russell, *The Housing Situation in 1960*, Central Office of Information, 1962.
43. *Ibid.*, p. 37.
44. House of Commons, *Official Report*, Vol. 658, Col. 1143.
45. House of Commons, *Official Report*, Vol. 676, Col. 1326.
46. House of Commons, *Official Report*, Vol. 677, Cols. 652-654.
47. *Housing*, Cmnd. 2050, HMSO, 1963.
48. House of Commons, *Official Report*, Vol. 681, Col. 1088.

49. House of Commons, *Official Report*, Vol. 691, Col. 1419.
50. Ministry of Housing and Local Government, Circular 11/65, *Slum Clearance*, HMSO, 1965.
51. Unlike previous returns these figures were not published in full. However, selected figures and national totals were made public in the report of the Denington Committee. See Central Housing Advisory Committee, *Our Older Homes: A Call for Action*, Report of the Sub-Committee on Standards of Housing Fitness, HMSO, 1966, pp. 56 and 57 and map.
52. The original article, 'The Contribution of Research to Housing Policy', was reprinted in D.V. Donnison *et al.*, *Essays on Housing*, Occasional Papers on Social Administration No. 9, Codicote Press, 1964.
53. G. Penrice, 'Recent Developments in Housing Statistics', *Economic Trends*, No. 181, November 1968.
54. Myra Woolf, *The Housing Survey in England and Wales, 1964*, HMSO, 1967.
55. D.V. Donnison, *The Government of Housing*, Penguin, 1967, p. 176.
56. House of Commons, *Official Report*, Vol. 709, Col. 82.
57. Cmnd. 2838, HMSO, 1965.
58. House of Commons, *Official Report*, Vol. 738, Col. 790.
59. The list of criteria were set out in a ministerial circular of 31st March 1967. The list of English authorities is given in House of Commons *Official Report*, Vol. 738, Written Answers, Col. 262. The list of Welsh authorities appears in House of Commons *Official Report*, Vol. 740, Written Answers, Col. 95.
60. The 38 authorities singled out for special consideration in 1963 were located exclusively in the North-East, the North-West, West Yorkshire and the West Midlands. The 65 authorities given special consideration under the Housing Subsidies Act 1967 included 14 London boroughs and the GLC and 11 authorities in Wales.
61. Central Housing Advisory Committee, *op. cit.* (1966)
62. Ministry of Housing and Local Government, *The Deeplish Study: Improvement Possibilities in a District of Rochdale*, HMSO, 1966. For a critique of the methods of appraisal used in the 1967 survey and other studies see T.L.C. Duncan, *op. cit.*
63. The results of the 1967 survey are published in 3 separate places: Ministry of Housing and Local Government, 'House Condition Survey, England and Wales, 1967', *Economic Trends*, No. 175, May 1968; *Old Houses into New Homes*, Cmnd. 3602, HMSO, 1968; Ministry of Housing and Local Government, *Housing Statistics, Great Britain*, Nos. 6, 9 and 10.
64. Central Housing Advisory Committee, *op. cit.* (1966), para. 68.
65. House of Commons, *Official Report*, Vol. 741, Col. 753 ff.
66. Ministry of Housing and Local Government, Circular 69/67, *Housing Act 1967: Slum Clearance*, HMSO, 1967.
67. Cmnd. 3602, HMSO, 1968.
68. House of Commons, *Official Report*, Vol. 769, Col. 921.
69. But as early as May 1970 Frank Allaun suggested that landlords were making large profits by selling off improved houses: House of Commons, *Official Report*, Vol. 801 Written Answers, Col. 614.
70. *Fair Deal for Housing*, Cmnd. 4728, HMSO, 1971.
71. *Ibid.*, para. 56.
72. House of Commons, *Official Report*, Vol. 826, Col. 46.
73. House of Commons, *Official Report*, Vol. 826, Col. 33.
74. House of Commons, *Official Report*, Vol. 836, Col. 1945.
75. Department of the Environment, Circular 50/72, *Slums and Older Housing:*

an Overall Strategy, HMSO, 1972, para. 18.
76. *Ibid.,* Annex B.
77. House of Commons, *Official Report,* Vol. 847, Cols. 163-164.
78. Clare Ungerson, *Moving Home: A Study of the Redevelopment Process in Two London Boroughs,* Occasional Papers on Social Administration No. 44, Bell, 1971.
79. Norman Dennis, *op. cit.* (1972).
80. Shelter, 1972.
81. *Community Action,* from February 1972, provided a national magazine; an example of a local magazine is *West Midlands Grass Roots,* published by Community Planning Associates, Birmingham, from March 1972 to 1976.
82. Robert McKie, *Housing and the Whitehall Bulldozer,* Hobart Paper No. 52, Institute of Economic Affairs, 1971.
83. Simon Pepper, *op. cit.*
84. Alan Stones, 'Stop Slum Clearance – Now!', *Official Architecture and Planning,* Vol. 35, No. 2, February 1972.
85. *Development and Compensation: Putting People First,* Cmnd. 5124, HMSO, 1972.
86. *Widening the Choice: the Next Steps in Housing,* Cmnd. 5280, HMSO, 1973.
87. *Ibid.,* para. 49.
88. *Better Homes: the Next Priorities,* Cmnd. 5339, HMSO, 1973.
89. *Ibid.,* para. 15.
90. *Ibid.,* para. 16.
91. Jane Morton, 'Slum Clearance', *New Society,* Vol. 28, p. 74, 11th April 1974.
92. Leeds Metropolitan District Council, *Leeds Housing Strategy: Report of the Housing Working Party,* 1975.
93. Newcastle upon Tyne Metropolitan District Council, 'Older Homes – Policy and Progress', *Housing Monthly,* Vol. 10, No. 1 (July 1964).
94. *The Guardian,* October 19th 1974.
95. City of Birmingham Urban Renewal Conference, *Urban Renewal Policy: General Improvement Areas and Renewal Areas,* City of Birmingham, 1973.
96. Department of the Environment, Circular 13/75, *Housing Act 1974: Renewal Strategies,* HMSO, 1975; Circular 14/75, *Housing Act 1974 Parts IV, V and VI,* HMSO, 1975.
97. Para. 6.
98. Ministry of Housing and Local Government, *Report of the Committee on Housing in Greater London* (Milner-Holland Report), Cmnd. 2605, HMSO, 1965, p. 16.
99. City of Manchester Housing Department, *Housing Tenancy Statistics, 1969,* mimeo, 1970.
100. City of Liverpool Town Clerk's Department, *Report on the City's Housing Requirements,* mimeo, 1970.
102. Figures derived from successive issues of Ministry of Housing and Local Government, *Housing Return for England and Wales,* quarterly, Appendix; since 1967, Ministry of Housing and Local Government, *Local Housing Statistics,* quarterly.
103. D.N. Muchnick, *Urban Renewal in Liverpool,* Occasional Papers on Social Administration No. 33, Bell, 1970, pp. 38-48.
104. To meet the 12-point standard a house must, as well as being fit for human habitation, possess a full range of amenities, including a bath, internal w.c., hot water and adequate facilities for heating and artificial lighting. The

Denington Committee considered this to be a standard of 'satisfactory' housing. See Central Housing Advisory Committee, *op. cit.,* (1966), p. 11.
105. K.M. Spencer, 'Older Urban Areas and Housing Improvement Policies', *Town Planning Review,* Vol. 41, 1970.
106. Central Housing Advisory Committee, *op. cit.* (1966), pp. 37-39.

3 SLUM CLEARANCE IN PRINCIPLE AND IN PRACTICE

The detail of slum clearance procedure merits attention both because it embodies an important segment of the rules of access to better housing and because it provides the basis of job definitions for local government staff. For many residents in older housing, particularly in the inner city, the procedural rules governing implementation of clearance programmes are an important determinant of housing opportunities. As Rex and Moore have argued, where slum clearance provides the main route to council housing a local authority's decision whether or not to declare a slum clearance area may be the crucial determinant of housing chances for those who aspire to a council house.[1] For all residents, whether welcoming or opposed to clearance, the rules on compensation, good maintenance and rights of appeal and objection in part determine the nature of the deal they can get out of it.

For officials, the same procedures provide the basic structure within which their jobs are defined. Most of the tasks, at least at the early stages of clearance, are required by law; completing them routinely to satisfy legal requirements provides a minimum job definition for staff and encourages a legalistic interpretation of the clearance process. The routinisation encouraged by conformity to rules which is common to any large bureaucracy[2] may also have been reinforced by the long established continuity of slum clearance procedures. These have developed the inertia of almost twenty years in operation without major change. At both central and local government levels specialised slum clearance units have developed the rigidity of organisations within which men have built careers and the dead weight of set patterns of paperwork negates change.

This chapter begins with a brief exegesis of the powers available for slum clearance and of the legal and definitional points governing their application in principle. The practice, discussed in the second section, resolves overwhelmingly into a process of compulsory purchase under Part III of the Housing Act 1957 and the application of this particular mode of clearance is considered in some detail. The third section examines the performance of the administrative structure through which slum clearance is processed, noting particularly the consequences of the protracted time scale involved and of the job interpretations adopted by key officials.

The Powers Available

The powers under Part II of the Housing Act 1957 are designed to secure the repair, closure or demolition of individual unfit houses rather than clearance of areas of unfit housing. Unfit houses are classified according to whether or not they are 'capable of repair at reasonable cost'. If they are capable of repair the local authority can enforce the necessary action at the owners' expense; if not, unfit houses must be demolished by the owner under a demolition order or closed following a closing order. Only unfit houses can be dealt with under this part of the Act and only buildings containing dwellings can be unfit for human habitation. An appeal against local authority action is heard by the county court.

Part III of the 1957 Act provides for the clearance of areas of unfit housing rather than individual houses. The first step is for the council to resolve to declare a clearance area; they must then secure its clearance either by making a compulsory purchase order or, until 1974, a clearance order.[3] A clearance area may include only: (1) unfit houses, (coloured pink on the statutory map and therefore referred to as 'pink' land); (2) other buildings, whether or not houses, which are 'by reason of their bad arrangement . . . injurious to the health of residents' (referred to as 'pink hatched yellow' land). This second category is little used and few clearance areas include buildings under this criterion.

A compulsory purchase order (CPO) transfers to the local authority all property and land in a clearance area and responsibility for demolition. It may also include any adjacent land which is reasonably necessary to secure a site of convenient dimensions for redevelopment ('grey' land). The acquiring authority has wide discretion in deciding what to do with the land. Frequently it is appropriated under Part V of the 1957 Act to build council houses but it may alternatively be sold or used for other purposes such as highways. Appeals against a CPO are made to the Secretary of State for the Environment (formerly the Minister of Housing and Local Government) and are heard at a public local inquiry by full-time inspectors from the Department of the Environment. The decision whether or not a CPO should be confirmed is made by the Secretary of State.

Apart from action under the Housing Acts local authorities also have power to acquire land compulsorily under the Town and Country Planning Act 1971 (formerly the Town and Country Planning Acts 1962 and 1968), if the Secretary of State is satisfied that the land is required to secure the development, redevelopment or improvement of an area. This can be a means of slum clearance when areas including unfit houses are acquired. Under the Town and Country Planning Act and certain other legislation[4] unfit houses may be subject to declaration of unfitness orders made under the Land Compensation Act 1961. Unfitness orders result in compensation being reduced to the level that would be payable for unfit houses under the Housing Act. Some unfit houses have been acquired and demolished under these powers, but this has usually been incidental to more general schemes of redevelopment and local authorities in England and Wales, in contrast to those in Scotland, have not used planning procedures as a major means of securing slum clearance.

Local authorities also have the option of acquiring property for slum clearance by agreement with the owner and without the use of compulsory purchase powers, thereby avoiding administrative expense and public resentment. Although many authorities buy up property which will be required for slum clearance as the opportunity occurs very few use it as a main instrument of policy. Dewsbury adopted purchase by agreement in 1954 because of a shortage of public health inspectors to process formal orders and came to prefer it.[5] In Bristol it has been stated Corporation policy since the early sixties to purchase property by agreement rather than by compulsory purchase.[6] This was a political decision reflecting concern for the financial interests of the property owner.[7] As houses were not formally declared unfit they were purchased at full market value rather than site value. But these authorities are exceptions and in general the reluctance of many owners to sell their property and the slow, piecemeal progress of acquisition by agreement are sufficient to ensure that compulsory procedure is adopted, particularly where land is urgently required for redevelopment.

Until the Land Compensation Act 1973 introduced a general rehousing obligation regardless of the form of procedure which displaces occupiers, the duties of authorities under different procedures were confused. There was a duty to rehouse under Part III of the 1957 Act and a similar duty under the Town and Country Planning Act 1971.[8] But there was no duty to rehouse under Part II of the 1957 Act, nor was there an obligation under Part V of the same Act, which is concerned with the provision of council housing. It has been suggested that some local authorities in Greater London may have preferred to promote CPOs under Part V of the 1957 Act for the purpose of *de facto* slum clearance because of the greater freedom it gave them to operate restrictive eligibility rules for rehousing.[9] There is little doubt that a certain amount of slum clearance is undertaken under Part V, though the usual reason is probably convenience in areas where the main purpose of redevelopment is housing gain and it might be difficult to prove that a substantial proportion of the houses is statutorily unfit.

Use of Different Procedures

Of the various procedures available to local authorities for slum clearance the most widely used in England and Wales is compulsory purchase following the declaration of a clearance area under Part III of the 1957 Act. During the post-war clearance drive the proportion of total houses dealt with in any year which were included in clearance areas increased from roughly 50 per cent in 1957 to around two thirds in the mid-sixties, and had reached 77 per cent in the survey year of 1970. During the cut back in clearance activity since 1971 the proportion cleared within clearance areas has continued to rise reaching almost 90 per cent in 1974.

The breakdown of figures for the years 1969 and 1970 in Table 4 includes the 18 months prior to the survey. Almost all of the houses dealt with outside clearance areas came under Part II of the 1957 Act and only a handful under unfitness orders.

Table 4: Houses demolished in 1969 and 1970 by whether or not in clearance areas

	1969		1970	
	No.	%	No.	%
Houses demolished in clearance areas				
Unfit	46,746	67.5	47,259	69.7
Others	6,653	9.6	5.279	7.8
Total	53,399	77.1	52,538	77.5
Houses not in clearance areas				
Demolished	8,499	12.3	8,591	12.7
Closed	7,335	10.6	6,675	9.8
	15,834	22.9	15,266	22.5
Total houses demolished or closed	69,233	100	67,804	100

Source: Department of the Environment, *Housing And Construction Statistics,* quarterly, Table 32.

Available figures giving the breakdown between different procedures under Part III of the Act are on a slightly different basis from the overall figures of houses demolished and closed. They refer to houses included in CPOs and clearance orders confirmed during the year and houses purchased by agreement in clearance areas, rather than to houses actually demolished. As there is always some delay in demolishing properties after a CPO or clearance order has been confirmed the numbers of houses in orders confirmed give some indication of the number of demolitions to be expected within the following year or so. But at a time of relative stability as in the years up to 1970 this time lag does not involve any serious distortion of annual figures. The breakdown between procedures under Part III of the 1957 Act in 1969 and 1970 is given in Table 5. Roughly nine-tenths of all houses cleared under Part III of the Act were compulsorily purchased at the time of survey and the proportion had risen to 94 per cent by the time clearance orders were abolished in 1974.[10]

Table 5: Houses included in CPOs and clearance orders in 1969 and 1970

	1969		1970	
	No.	%	No.	%
Houses included in:				
CPOs confirmed	50,030	89.8	39,129	88.9
Clearance orders confirmed	3,494	6.3	3,174	7.2
Houses purchased by agreement in clearance areas	2,175	3.9	1,747	3.9
Total houses in confirmed orders or purchased by agreement	55,699	100	44,050	100

Source: Department of the Environment, *Housing And Construction Statistics*, No. 12, 4th. Quarter, 1974, Table VII.

Bringing these two sets of figures together, on the assumption that the breakdown by form of action was stable at the time, about 69 per cent of all slum clearance in England and Wales in 1969 and 1970 was accounted for by Part III CPOs. On these assumptions a total of about 48,000 houses in 1969 and about 47,000 in 1970 were demolished under this procedure including some fit houses adjoining clearance areas.

Slum Clearance in Principle and in Practice   55

From the point of view both of residents affected and of the local authorities pursuing clearance programmes compulsory purchase under Part III of the 1957 Act was at the time of survey and still is by far the most important of the available procedures.

Slum Clearance in Practice: Compulsory Purchase and Compensation

Apart from their obligation to rehouse people displaced by slum clearance, recently extended by the Land Compensation Act 1973, local authorities are not constrained by the law when rehousing residents from clearance schemes. The activities of local housing departments are largely outside the control of legislation and reflect particular administrative arrangements and local circumstances. This is not true, however, of the other departments involved in the process of slum clearance; the early stages from declaration of a clearance area to the acquisition of property and settlement of financial compensation are closely controlled by legislation and procedural rules.

Clearance Area Declaration

The decision to deal with a particular area of inadequate housing may involve complex considerations of policy and political expediency as well as the condition of the property itself. In particular, the local authority must consider priority between the claims of waiting list applicants and slum clearance rehousing and frequently between the competing claims of several areas for redevelopment. However, in towns and cities with large-scale clearance programmes decisions regarding particular areas may become routinised as a result of long-term pressures of working to annual clearance targets, often set years before on the basis of a house condition survey, and usually conforming to the public health inspector's principle of 'worst first'. Whatever the nature of the decision to declare a clearance area, once the local authority have decided to take action the procedure to be followed is laid down in detail in the 1957 Act.

A clearance area must consist entirely of houses which are unfit for human habitation or of houses or other buildings which, because of their bad arrangement, are dangerous or injurious to the health of the inhabitants of the area. Therefore the first step in the entire process is for a public health inspector (PHI) to visit each house in a potential clearance area to decide whether or not it is unfit. Until reorganisation of the health services in 1974, inspection by a PHI was often also briefly checked by the Medical Officer of Health or one of his staff to satisfy themselves that the area justified an 'official representation' as suitable for clearance.[11]

Although the initial steps towards a clearance area depend on technical questions of housing conditions the initiative subsequently lies with the councillors. If the relevant committee are satisfied that the conditions in an area justify clearance area action they must declare the area a clearance area. The two essential conditions to be fulfilled are first, that in fact the houses in the area are unfit or badly arranged and that any other buildings in the area are badly arranged; and second, that the most satisfactory method of dealing with conditions in the area is by demolition of all the buildings. They must also be satisfied that suitable alternative accommodation is available for the residents who will be displaced and that the authority have sufficient resources to carry through the scheme. Normally these matters will have been considered well in advance of any recommendation coming to the committee and its consideration at this stage is usually a formality. But there is clearly an important element of judgement involved and occasionally committees have not accepted recommendations from their officers.

When, in the normal case, the council accept that clearance area action is justified a formal declaration of a clearance area is made. The local authority must then send a copy of the resolution to the Secretary of State for the Environment together with a statement of the number of persons occupying buildings in the area on a specified day. Details of clearance areas declared by each authority are logged centrally. The local authority must then secure the clearance of the area by purchasing the land, usually compulsorily, and demolishing the buildings.

A CPO relating to land within a clearance area must normally be submitted to the Secretary of State within six months of declaration of the clearance area. If the local authority also wish to purchase land surrounded by or adjoining a clearance area as 'added lands' (or 'grey' land) to ensure satisfactory redevelopment of the site they must submit a CPO for this land within twelve months of the clearance area resolution. In practice most authorities include all the land comprised in one clearance scheme in a single CPO. Many also submit CPOs at the same time as clearance area resolutions. On the other hand, some authorities initiate clearance area action well ahead of submitting CPOs and require extensions of the 6 month time limit.

The preparation of CPO documents involves collection of a good deal of information since all properties within or adjoining a clearance area have to be separately listed together with the names of the owners and lessees. To facilitate the service of notices local authorities are empowered, by Section 170 of the 1957 Act, to require the owners and occupiers of property to specify their legal interest and it is standard practice to circulate a questionnaire at least to known interested parties to clarify details of ownership and leases. The forms to be used are not standardised and it is not necessarily the case that a request for information is specifically related to a clearance area declaration or the preparation of a CPO. However, where the local authority do specifically link their request for information with clearance area progress and distribute questionnaires widely this may be the first clear indication to residents that their area is to be acquired and cleared.

Submission and confirmation of a CPO
Until submission of a CPO the residents of a clearance area and the owners of land and property in the area are not involved in the process in any way except for giving information required under Section 170 of the Act. Apart from the visit of a PHI residents may be totally unaware of the process leading to declaration of a clearance area. The local authority are not required to canvass local opinion nor to publicise their intention to declare a clearance area. On the contrary, the fear of blighting an area is an encouragement to secrecy. But when the local authority reach the stage of preparing and submitting a CPO individual residents and owners of property become directly involved. The 1957 Act specifies in detail how people affected by a CPO must be informed of the action which is being taken and of their right to object. At this stage the process becomes public whereas the declaration of a clearance area itself, although formally minuted by the council, is a largely internal matter. Involvement of the public at this stage is, however, a selective process. The procedure for informing residents of their rights can only be understood once a clear distinction is made between people who are and are not deemed to have an interest in the land; only the former have the right to have their objections to compulsory purchase considered. Others may raise objections but these are of doubtful legal standing.

Persons with an interest in the land are defined as 'every owner, lessee and occupier (except for tenants for a month or a less period than a month) of any land to which the order relates' and, insofar as they can be ascertained, every mortgagee.[12] The proviso 'except tenants for a month or a less period than a month' is of crucial importance. It refers not, as is often supposed, to the length of time for which a tenancy has existed but to the terms under which the tenancy is held. A long term resident in an area having an ordinary weekly tenancy is therefore regarded as having no interest in the land and is excluded from receipt of statutory notices and formal right to objection. This is the case for the majority of residents in most clearance areas; it is the minority of owner occupiers, or tenants with unusual tenancies, whose interests are formally protected by the procedure for compulsory purchase.

Before submitting a CPO to the Secretary of State the local authority must publicise the making of the order in one or more newspapers circulating in their district. The form of notice is laid down in *The Housing (Prescribed Forms) Regulations*[13] and must specify a place at which the CPO may be inspected. The authority must also service a notice on every person with an interest in the land stating that a CPO on their property is about to be submitted to the Secretary of State for confirmation. This is a 'Personal Notice of the Making of a Compulsory Purchase Order in respect of Land Comprised in a Clearance Area and the Land Surrounded by or Adjoining the Area'. The notice, Form 26 of the Prescribed Forms, is particularly important as the main statutory source of information available to residents specifying their rights to objection, compensation and well-maintained payments. However, it is important to remember that such a notice is required to be served only on persons with an interest in the land. In 1975 local authorities were requested to include with Form 26 a statement of their reasons for having declared a clearance area. Form 26 and its attached notes are reproduced (in the 1966 version) in Appendix D.[14]

If an objection is made by 'any of the persons on whom notices are required to be served', in other words persons with a recognised interest in the land, a public local inquiry (PLI) must be held. Alternatively, the Secretary of State may hold a private hearing to give objectors an opportunity of appearing before one of his inspectors. If an objection is made on the ground that a building is not unfit for human habitation the local authority must state the principal grounds of the alleged unfitness in a 'principal grounds notice' summarising the findings of the PHI's report on the property. Where such objections are made the PLI must not be held earlier than fourteen days after principal grounds notices have been served on every objector. The Secretary of State may require an objector to state in writing the basis of his objection and may disregard an objection if he is satisfied that it relates exclusively to the assessment of compensation. Questions of compensation are dealt with later, if and when the CPO has been confirmed, and disputes are settled by the Lands Tribunal.

The purpose of a PLI is to enable the parties involved, the local authority on the one hand and owners, lessees or mortgagees on the other, to present evidence and arguments to an independent inspector. Objections may be based on legal arguments regarding the authority's fulfilment of their statutory obligations or on the reasonableness of proposals which is essentially a matter of judgement.

Every objector is notified of the time and place of the PLI by the Department of the Environment and the local authority is required to post notices of the inquiry in the streets to which the CPO applies. The PLI need not be advertised in local newspapers but local authorities are expected to inform the press about it. These requirements are a matter of departmental practice rather than statutory duties.

After a PLI the inspector provides a formal report for the Secretary of State incorporating his findings and recommendations. On the basis of the report the Secretary of State may confirm the CPO, reject it or confirm it with modifications. The most common modification of a CPO involves the transfer of some houses from the unfit ('pink') category in the clearance area to the fit ('grey') category in added lands. It is not permissible for the Secretary of State to modify a CPO so that it becomes less favourable to the owners than the original either by transferring houses from the fit to the unfit category or by including in the confirmed order land lying outside the boundaries of the original order as submitted. The final decision is conveyed to the local authority and to objectors in a formal letter summarising the main points of the PLI and the findings and recommendations of the inspector. If, as occasionally happens, the Secretary of States does not accept his inspector's recommendations the decision letter will give his reasons; objectors can obtain a copy of the inspector's full report by writing to the Department.[15]

When a CPO has been confirmed by the Secretary of State the local authority must publish in a newspaper a notice in the prescribed form stating that the order has been confirmed and naming a place where it can be seen. They must also serve a personal notice of confirmation on all persons with an interest in the land. The CPO becomes operative six weeks after the publication of the notice of confirmation. During this period the validity of the order may be challenged in the High Court on the ground that it is not within the powers of the 1957 Act or that some requirement of the Act has not been fulfilled. In most cases there is no such challenge and the local authority proceed with negotiations for the purchase of the land.

Compensation and Well-Maintained Payments
The details of procedure for settling a purchase price and transferring

ownership of the land are also laid down by statute, mainly the Land Compensation Act 1961 and Compulsory Purchase Act 1965. Negotiations are often protracted and may continue well after the property has been demolished and residents have moved.

For fit property demolished under slum clearance the general law of compulsory acquisition applies. Owners are entitled to full compulsory purchase value compensation just as if the houses had been acquired for road widening or the building of a school. The more commonly used shorthand for full compulsory purchase value is full market value. Very broadly it means either the current market value of the buildings and land, or the potential value of the land for a different use for which planning permission either exists or might reasonably be expected to be granted, whichever is the greater. The legal framework for the assessment of compensation is mainly contained in the Land Compensation Act 1961. The valuation of buildings and land and the assessment of compensation is a complex process which cannot be briefly described. However, although owners may be dissatisfied with the adequacy of compensation in particular cases — it may not be sufficient to purchase an equally satisfactory alternative house — the intention is that the sum should reflect the ordinary market value of the property.

There is, however, a special code of compensation for unfit houses under slum clearance. The law of compensation for slum clearance has its origins at the end of the nineteenth century when virtually all the houses affected by slum clearance were owned and let by landlords. The rule was then established that an unfit house has no value. Therefore when an unfit house was compulsorily purchased the owner was entitled to receive only the value of the land as a cleared site. The important changes that have been made over the years to slum clearance compensation have all been in terms of modifications and exceptions to this site value rule. The rule remains formally intact though it is of diminishing practical importance.

The crucial breach in the site value rule was made by the Slum Clearance (Compensation) Act 1956. Over the years, and certainly since the Second World War, the context within which slum clearance was taking place had altered in two important ways. First, the proportion of houses affected by slum clearance which were owner occupied substantially increased. Whereas landlords could be seen as profiting irresponsibly from slum housing, owner occupiers might have spent their savings on houses that were being cleared and it seemed inequitable to dispossess them with only nominal compensation. Second, as slum clearance progressed the general standard of houses cleared became

Slum Clearance in Principle and in Practice 61

better. Both these trends combined in 1956 to persuade the government to suspend the site value rule in respect of certain owner occupiers.

Owner occupiers of unfit houses which had been purchased between September 1939 and December 1955 (when the concession was announced) would, until December 1965, receive supplementary payments to bring their compensation up to full market value. These were people who, during and since the war, had been forced by the housing shortage to buy unfit houses. The provision was due to expire after ten years but the Slum Clearance (Compensation) Act 1965 extended it until 1970 for owner occupiers who had had less than fifteen years' occupation. This was an interim measure and it was clear that action would have to be taken to end the essentially arbitrary differences in the treatment of owner occupiers of unfit houses.

The first concession to owner occupiers in general was made by the Land Compensation Act 1961, which provided that the total compensation for an unfit house should not be less than its gross rateable value. The basis of compensation for owner occupiers was fundamentally altered by the Housing Act 1969. In the case of clearance areas declared after April 1968 the equivalent of full market value compensation was payable, provided that the house had been continuously owner occupied, not necessarily by the same person, since that date. Since April 1970 the requirement has been for two years' owner occupation to prevent collusive sales of tenanted houses for the purpose of obtaining increased compensation.

Well maintained payments (WMPs) can be made where unfit houses have been kept in reasonably good condition. Good maintenance has never been statutorily defined in the same way as unfitness for human habitation, but in 1975 the Department of the Environment issued guidance to local authorities on the circumstances in which WMPs should be paid.[16] WMPs are payable both for owner occupied and tenanted houses which are unfit except where an owner occupier receives a supplementary payment to bring his compensation up to full market value. Since the Housing Act 1969 almost all owner occupiers of houses in clearance areas declared after April 1968 have been eligible for full market value and WMPs now mainly affect landlords and tenants.

A WMP is equivalent to three and one eighth times the rateable value of the house, provided that the total compensation does not exceed the value of the house were it fit. This ceiling affects only areas of exceptionally high land values. The amount of the payment is not large but the crucial point is that a tenant may be awarded all or part of it.

At the time of the survey this was the only sum of money that a tenant could claim other than a discretionary removal grant although additional payments have been introduced by the Land Compensation Act 1973. A WMP is payable to the landlord as the person responsible for the maintenance of the house 'provided that, if any other person satisfies the local authority that the good maintenance of the house is attributable to a material extent to work carried out by him or at his expense, the local authority may . . . make the payment, in whole or in part, to him'.[18] Since the Housing Act 1974 local authorities themselves decide on good maintenance[19] but at the time of the survey a Department of the Environment inspector (or district valuer in the case of late claims) determined whether a house had been well maintained. Only the apportionment of any payment between landlord and tenant was a matter for the local authority. Paradoxically if a house is found to be fit a tenant cannot receive a WMP even though its good condition is the result of work done by him.

Before 1956 Ministry of Housing inspectors visited all unfit houses included in clearance schemes to decide whether a WMP should be awarded but practice was then changed[20] and between 1956 and 1974 it was necessary for a landlord or tenant to claim a WMP. Houses in respect of which there had been no claim or objection were still sometimes visited by inspectors and WMPs might be awarded, but there was no certainty of this happening. Therefore it was important that those who were entitled to claim WMPs should be aware of them.

Prior to the Housing Act 1974 the only information that local authorities were required to provide about WMPs was contained in the Notes to Form 26, but this was of direct benefit only to owner occupiers and landlords as Form 26 is not sent to ordinary tenants. The Department seemed to envisage tenants being informed of their right to claim a WMP in two ways. First, the Notes to Form 26 included this sentence: 'persons on whom this notice is served who have tenants on a monthly or lesser tenancy or statutory tenants . . . are requested to bring . . . [WMPs] to the notice of those occupiers.' In short, the onus was on landlords to inform their tenants. This proved inadequate as a means of informing tenants.[21] Second, in 1967, Circular 69/67 noted that some authorities sent a letter to all occupiers whenever tenants might be entitled to claim WMPs and commended this practice for general use. This advice was repeated in 1969, when Circular 68/69 stated that, with the additional benefits available under the 1969 Act, it was 'even more desirable for authorities to consider the advice' given in the previous circular. Nevertheless, many authorities had not accepted

Slum Clearance in Principle and in Practice 63

this advice in 1970.

The Rights of Residents

Compulsory purchase procedure is designed to safeguard the right of the individual to receive information and to object to the proposals of the local authority. This right, however, is restricted to persons who are deemed to have an interest in the land so that almost all tenants, who formed nearly three quarters of the residents of the areas surveyed, are excluded. Whether residents other than owner occupiers receive any information is a matter for the initiative of particular local authorities. Some survey authorities were imaginative in producing non-statutory letters and booklets — for example, Liverpool — but many did little or nothing. Not all authorities had even followed the repeated official advice to inform tenants of their right to claim a WMP. Table 6 lists the standard notifications required under CPO procedure in 1970 separately for objectors, other owners and ordinary tenants. Whilst objectors received all official notifications and other owners received the basic documents tenants did not necessarily receive any information at all except what they were able to pick up from newspapers, friends and neighbours.

Tenants are similarly excluded from the right to object. Anyone can 'object' but the 1957 Act only requires the Secretary of State to recognise objections from persons deemed to have an interest in the land when deciding to hold a PLI. Compulsory purchase procedure can only be understood as a process for expropriating property rights. Ordinary tenants, or 'tenants for a month or less period than a month', have never been regarded as having, in the legal sense, an interest in property. The government even took the trouble to insert a clause in the Housing (Repairs and Rents) Act 1954 to the effect that a statutory tenant, that is a tenant remaining in occupation by virtue of the Rent Acts, should be deemed to be a tenant for a period of less than a month. This was to reverse the effect of a court decision that statutory tenants were 'occupiers' and therefore entitled to receive statutory notices.[22] But most tenants, enjoying the protection of the Rent Acts, obviously may have a good deal to lose from the demolition of their houses.

Compulsory purchase law, then is concerned with property rights and their protection, and ordinary tenants are not recognised as having any such rights. The Land Compensation Act 1961, the Compulsory Purchase Act 1965 and the 1957 Act are designed to ensure that expropriation can take place only if certain conditions are fulfilled and that proper compensation is paid. The Law is unconcerned with the resident *per se.* It is really a matter of chance that a substantial section of residents, owner occupiers, are both residents and property owners. It is as property owners that they have rights, in exactly the same way as absentee landlords. Indeed, the assumption of the law in the past seems to have been that residents and owners were generally not the same people.

Table 6. Notices issued under the Housing Act 1957

Type of Notice	In Press	Street Notice	Sent to:		
			Objectors only	Other owners, etc.	Tenants
1. Form inquiring about ownership of property (Section 170 Notice used at discretion of local authority)			x	x	x
2. Notice that CPO is about to be submitted to Secretary of State (Form 26)	x		x	x	
3. Notes on objections compensation and WMPs (Sent with Form 26)			x	x	
4. Principal grounds notice			x		
5. Notice of PLI		x	x		
6. Notice of confirmation of CPO	x		x		
7. Copy of CPO as confirmed				x	x

There are very few references in Part III of the 1957 Act to residents in general though tenants are given, by implication, a right to claim WMPs. When they were introduced in 1935 WMPs were justified in terms of equity to landlords; the 1957 Act merely provides that 'any other person' apart from an owner can try to persuade the local authority that he has been responsible for the good maintenance of a property. In the 1957 Act the only reference to residents as such relates to responsibility for rehousing when suitable accommodation is not otherwise

Slum Clearance in Principle and in Practice 65

available which, of course, is normally the case.

The opportunity to be rehoused by the local authority is the main right enjoyed by all residents, including tenants, under slum clearance procedure. In practice the responsibility to rehouse displaced residents is often limited by rules which limit eligibility. Local authorities have received a good deal of official advice about eligibility and the legal requirements have been tightened up by the Land Compensation Act 1973. Nevertheless, the rules seem to be, in the last resort, largely a matter for local authorities themselves.[23] There is a marked contrast with the very detailed specification of compulsory purchase procedures.

Slum Clearance in Action: Departmental Responsibilities and Time Scale

Compulsory purchase procedure under Part III of the Housing Act 1957 has been the backbone of the post-war slum clearance programme. A clear measure of the administrative burden involved for national and local government is the absolute number of CPOs submitted and confirmed. In the survey year, 1970, 918 CPOs were submitted for decision and 825 CPOs were confirmed; the figures for 1969 were 824 submissions and 855 confirmed.

A programme of this scale involves a steady stream of work for specialist staff whose only job is to scrutinise the maps and documents required for a CPO and to chase progress through the stages of PLI, inspector's report and ministerial decision. In 1970 at central government level there were approximately sixty staff allocated to processing Housing Act CPOs and similar orders. On average there were 380 CPOs outstanding for decision at any time during 1969 and 1970.

Locally, the annual targets of individual authorities often require a steady flow of CPOs and there will be orders at all stages of preparation and implementation at any one time. The survey authorities were selected as a result of a systematic sampling process and can be taken as a rough cross-section of all local authorities following slum clearance CPO procedure. Table 7 summarises details of the CPOs confirmed during 1970 for each of the fifteen authorities. Leeds and Liverpool both had more than twenty CPOs confirmed during the year — one every two or three weeks. Newcastle-upon-Tyne, Manchester and Stoke-on-Trent each had ten or more orders confirmed. Because of the protracted nature of the clearance procedure, even the authorities such as Gravesend or South Shields with only two confirmations during the year will have had several CPOs in progress at any time.

Manchester serves as a well documented example of an authority with a large, long-term clearance programme. By the end of 1969

Table 7. CPOs confirmed in Survey Authorities during 1970

Area	Total CPOs confirmed	Houses which were:			Total Houses
		'Pink'	'Pink hatched Yellow'	'Grey'	
Newcastle	11	1012	–	272	1284
Leeds	28	1655	–	170	1825
Liverpool	22	3271	–	358	3629
Manchester	10	2790	–	82	2872
Tower Hamlets	6	790	–	179	969
S. Shields	2	147	–	6	153
Bingley	3	95	23	9	127
Doncaster	3	305	–	56	361
Stoke	11	255	–	67	322
Warley	9	440	21	149	610
Wolverhampton	3	116	–	11	127
Haringey	4	102	–	47	149
Gravesend	2	130	–	12	142
Portsmouth	6	396	116	115	627
Norwich	5	512	–	87	599

Source: Department of Environment central register of CPOs confirmed.

Manchester had submitted 146 CPOs altogether since resuming slum clearance in 1951.[24] Those orders accounted for 41,925 houses in all giving an average of 287 houses per order. Six of the orders submitted, covering 2,581 houses, were still outstanding awaiting decision. A further thirty-four clearance areas containing 8,701 houses were in the pipeline awaiting CPO action. A similar summary published in Hansard in 1962[25] showed nine CPOs outstanding in Manchester covering 3,870 properties and a further 4,143 properties in declared clearance areas awaiting action. An analysis of clearance areas being processed in Stoke-on-Trent, published in April 1962, similarly confirms that the 1970 figures for Stoke are not unrepresentative of earlier years.[26]

Causes and Consequences of Delay

CPO procedure is not a process which can be quickly completed. The formal procedure laid down by legislation entails some small lapses of time but these are trivial compared with the time taken to collect large amounts of detailed information on housing conditions and the ownership of property, for the Department to scrutinise the CPO documents and arrange a PLI, and for the inspector to prepare his report. The timetable of events for the fifteen CPOs involved in the survey areas is set out in full in Table 8.

Table 8. Timetable of events in Survey Areas (month and year of key events)

Survey Area	Public Health Inspection	Clearance Area Declaration	CPO submission	Months elapsed from inspection to submission	Public Local Inquiry	CPO Confirmation	Months elapsed from submission to confirmation	Total Months elapsed
Newcastle	2 – 67	1 – 69	3 – 69	25	9 – 69	2 – 70	11	36
Leeds	3 – 68	7 – 68	5 – 69	14	9 – 69	12 – 69	7	21
Manchester	3 – 67	5 – 67	2 – 69	13	7 – 69	12 – 69	10	33
Liverpool	6 – 66	8 – 66	8 – 68	26	1 – 69	6 – 69	10	36
Tower Hamlets	11 – 67	12 – 67	10 – 68	11	4 – 69	1 – 70	15	26
South Shields	12 – 68	3 – 69	8 – 69	8	12 – 69	2 – 70	6	14
Bingley	9 – 68	11 – 68	5 – 69	8	9 – 69	1 – 70	8	16
Doncaster	2 – 69	5 – 69	6 – 69	4	10 – 69	2 – 70	8	12
Stoke-on-Trent	10 – 68	10 – 68	2 – 69	4	8 – 69	1 – 70	11	15
Warley	9 – 68	4 – 69	9 – 69	12	11 – 69	3 – 70	6	18
Wolverhampton	8 – 68	10 – 68	9 – 69	13	1 – 70	3 – 70	6	19
Haringey	6 – 68	10 – 68	4 – 69	10	8 – 69	3 – 70	11	21
Gravesend	12 – 68	4 – 69	9 – 69	9	11 – 69	3 – 70	6	15
Portsmouth	12 – 68	2 – 69	8 – 69	8	12 – 69	2 – 70	6	14
Norwich	3 – 69	7 – 69	8 – 69	5	11 – 69	2 – 70	6	11

Source: Compulsory purchase order documents.

Up to the stage of submission of a CPO the progress of events is entirely in the control of the local authority but at later stages, from submission of a CPO to the making of a decision, central government is responsible for the timetable. Table 8 shows that by far the most variable elements of the total lapse of time occur in those phases controlled by the local authorities prior to submitting a CPO to the Department for decision.[27]

In most cases the delay between inspection of properties and a council resolution declaring a clearance area was very short; Newcastle was exceptional with almost two years elapsing at this stage. At the next stage some authorities preferred to make and submit a CPO at the same time as they declared a clearance area — as happened in Newcastle and Tower Hamlets. Others might delay months or even years before acting and it was common practice for authorities to obtain an extension of the six month time limit. A lapse of two years, as in the Liverpool case, is unusual but not unique and intervals of eighteen months or more are common.

At the stage of departmental decision there is a regular review of progress to ensure that CPOs are not unduly delayed. The main cause of delay is the consideration of objections at a PLI and preparation of a report. In the first nine months of 1969[28] (after which a regular analysis was no longer made), the average delay from submission to confirmation was eight months for CPOs involving objections and a PLI. For unopposed CPOs the average delay was only two months; however, only a quarter of all CPOs were unaffected by objections[29] and virtually all of these covered very few houses. Amongst the fifteen survey area CPOs all but the Tower Hamlets CPO were confirmed within a year of submission.

Taking the process as a whole the delay from initial inspection by a public health inspector to confirmation of the ensuing CPO was three years at the worst (Newcastle and Liverpool) and slightly over a year at best (Portsmouth and Norwich). But it is worthwhile recalling that CPO confirmation is only the beginning of the rehousing stage during which households are moved to council houses or rehouse themselves. This final stage usually adds years rather than months to the total lapse of time before clearance of an area is complete.

The long delay often involved in clearance area action has important consequences. Few of the residents of a clearance area will have any formal knowledge of the legislation, departmental circulars and prescribed forms itemised in the previous section. They may be fortunate in having some sort of citizens' guide to slum clearance distributed by the local authority but most will be dependent on their memory of a friend's similar experience elsewhere or a distillation of local gossip. Their own direct experience of compulsory purchase procedure will be as a series of intermittent visits from officials or letters through the door. But when these sporadic events are spread over a period of two or three years it is difficult to link the parts together into some sort of cohesive whole which would give residents an adequate grasp of the legal and political significance of each step.

Bureaucracy and job definitions

Both the scale of clearance programmes and the demands of long-term continuity involved in the CPO process encourage bureaucratisation. A specialist section of clerical staff and inspectors in central government is mirrored by full-time housing inspectors in local public health departments and compulsory purchase specialists within town clerks' departments. Although this is the expected pattern of organisational development it is important to note the consequences for clearance area residents of the scale of CPO negotiation.

For most households clearance will be a 'once and for all' event which engages their interest only because of its immediate impact on their own life chances; they are not interested in questions of general principle but in the outcome of their particular circumstances. But for the central and local government departments involved the unique position and requirements of an individual household are appreciated only as one small part of a large and continuous process with its own organisational and procedural regularities. The responses of officials to what may be seen by individual households as reasonable requests for help or information can only be understood against the background of routinisation which a large-scale, long-term process is bound to involve.

Difficulties for clearance area residents may well be exacerbated by the interpretation of their job requirements which local officials apply. Put simply, none of the departments involved in CPO procedure has a general advisory or informative role. On the contrary, the quasi-judicial nature of the CPO process and the stress on legal correctness encourages officials not to commit themselves to hard information and, as first priority, to protect the legal interests of their council. This can be illustrated for both the key officials involved in compulsory purchase, the PHI and the town clerk.

Usually the first sign a resident will have of the impending demolition of his house is a visit from the PHI to classify the property as fit or unfit.[30] If the property is in a poor state of repair the PHI may already be a well-known figure who has called in the past to inspect drains or leaking gutters. But he may well be very cautious of giving firm information about the date of compulsory purchase or rehousing; strictly speaking the process which an inspection initiates could be terminated at any of several points. In the first place the Health or Housing Committee may not declare a clearance area. Even if a clearance area is declared a CPO may not be submitted for some time and even when submitted it is liable to be modified by the Secretary of State or even rejected entirely. Although the vast majority of clearance areas and CPOs do go ahead as planned a strict interpretation of the legal situation discourages any certainty of the outcome.

The most effective step that the PHI can take to ensure that events do run smoothly for the local authority is to concentrate on a detailed and careful inspection of the physical fabric of the property and to say nothing of substance.[31] As a good professional his main concern is to see that the information on which his report is based is detailed and accurate enough to withstand scrutiny; first the possible scrutiny of councillors who may not be prepared to take his recommendations on the nod; second, the scrutiny of individual house owners who may object to the CPO and require a detailed notice of principal grounds of unfitness; and, third, the scrutiny of an inspector from the Department at a PLI. Properties which are the subject of objections often receive particular attention involving several visits from PHIs including senior inspectors. All such properties will be visited by a Department inspector at the time of the PLI. The recommendations of Department inspectors are the only indication a local PHI has that his judgement of what is or is not an unfit house is being correctly applied according to a rough common standard. Individual public health departments pride themselves on how few houses in their clearance areas are reclassified[32] and how few CPOs are ever turned down.

These two considerations, the conditional nature of house inspections and the stress on detailed physical items of information generally discourage a discussive role for the PHI. The essential element in the PHIs job is to itemise physical conditions. Some authorities issue a list of the areas to be included in the next year or two of the clearance programme but rarely with much publicity and longer-term forward programmes usually remain confidential for fear of creating blight in advance of clearance action. Some authorities who were contacted were sufficiently confident of the outcome of their programmes that PHIs were allowed to give fairly precise dates to residents, for example, in Nottingham[33] and Liverpool. In other authorities, public health staff were instructed not to commit themselves to any hard information about the future of property.

Apart from the public health department the other main department concerned with compulsory purchase procedure is the town clerk's department. The clerk's department is responsible for ensuring that all the statutorily required steps of the process are fulfilled so that a CPO cannot be upset at any stage on the basis of legal niceties. The department is largely responsible for drawing up the CPO document and the attached schedule of property and its owners and lessees. In cities where a managerial and co-ordinating role is adopted the clerk's department also attempts to keep the other departments involved at all stages of clearance and redevelopment working to a common programme.[34]

For residents, contact with the clerk's department is exclusively through letters from the town hall and a principal concern of the clerks' department is to ensure that all the people entitled to receive notices are identified. On the face of it the occasions on which the clerk's department is required by law to write to at least some of the residents of an area (those who have an interest in the property) could be regarded as an excellent opportunity to inform residents as widely as possible of future developments. In practice this rarely happens.

The whole emphasis of the town clerk's involvement in compulsory purchase procedure is on the importance of legal formalities. The exact wording of forms and notices is laid down in the prescribed forms regulations and the 1957 Act specifies to whom they must be sent. It is important to observe legal exactitude not only to ensure that the local authority have acted properly but because the statutory notices specify the legal rights and obligations of recipients. For example, a Section 170 notice requiring details of ownership of properties within the area to be covered by a CPO has to be completed on request and recipients may be liable to a fine if they do not comply. Notes accompanying a notice of submission of a CPO to the Department (Form 26) specify rights to compensation, to WMPs and to objection. It is hardly surprising that clerks' departments see it their duty above all to communicate only with persons having a legal interest in property and strictly in terms of the prescribed legal wording. It is not the fault of the local authority if prescribed forms are designed to be understood primarily by lawyers and appear both peremptory and obscure to the general public.

But there is no reason why, having fulfilled their legal obligations under slum clearance procedure, the town clerk's department should not expand the information available to residents in additional letters or notices. In respect of WMPs local authorities were advised by the

Ministry of Housing to send out a general circular letter to all clearance area residents regardless of whether they had a legal interest in the property. But even this mild extension of the authorities' obligations was not accepted universally. Of the fifteen survey area authorities, eight complied with Ministry advice by issuing informal letters, one sent out Form 26 and the attached notes in prescribed form to all occupiers, and the other six issued no information about WMPs directly to tenants. Variation between authorities in this respect was very considerable. In Liverpool, for example, all occupiers received a letter from the town clerk after declaration of the clearance area and in advance of the CPO being submitted. A claim form for WMPs together with an informal letter was also sent to all occupiers. But Liverpool was exceptional in this respect; for the most part, excepting letters about WMPs, additional non-statutory letters from the clerk's department were concerned with completing the register of owners and those with a legal interest in clearance area property. Apart from the stress on legal correctness, the main reason for restricting the town clerk's role in this way appears to be a reluctance to give residents grounds for believing that the local authority is committed in any way beyond the minimum legal requirements, either to compensation payments or rehousing of residents.

Translated into action the compulsory purchase procedure embodied in legislation must be seen as a continuous large-scale process operating on a turn round time of two or three years. It is a process institutionalised in bureaucratic forms which, after nearly twenty years of operating the same procedures may have acquired an organisational inertia discouraging flexibility or new approaches. For residents caught up in the process, slum clearance in action means an intermittent series of contacts with the bureaucracy either through visits from officials or letters through the door, mainly from the local public health and town clerk's departments. Authorities vary considerably in the extent to which the statutory procedure itself is amplified to fulfill a generally informative role but in general the salient requirements of the process discourage such initiatives. The quasi-judicial nature of compulsory purchase procedure and the stress on legal exactitude discourage a discussive or advisory role for either the PHI or the town clerk's department. As good professionals officials are clearly aware of their overriding obligations to collect detailed information on physical conditions and to fulfill precisely the letter of the law. Both are alive to the possibility that their actions may not have the expected outcome in the long run and may thereby be unwilling to commit themselves to information which may turn out to be wrong. These aspects of the interpretation of their roles which officials are encouraged to adopt may well compound the fundamental weakness of the legal framework as a source of information to everyone affected by compulsory purchase. The principal concern of compulsory purchase procedure remains the protection of property rights.

NOTES

1. John Rex and Robert Moore, *op. cit.* Chap. 1.
2. Michael J. Hill, *The Sociology of Public Administration*, Weidenfeld and Nicholson, 1972, Section 7.
3. The alternative of making a clearance order was abolished by the Housing Act 1974. A clearance order required owners themselves to demolish property and they retained ownership of the land. As clearance orders could only apply to unfit houses they were often impractical in areas which included a sprinkling of fit houses and other premises. CPOs also achieve unified ownership of sites, but clearance orders were sometimes used where, for example, a firm wanted land for expansion.
4. The other legislation is Town Development Act 1952; New Towns Act 1965; Part II of the Housing Act 1969.
5. Personal communication.
6. *Bristol Civic News No. 40*, Corporation of Bristol, February 1961.
7. In Parliament a Bristol M.P., Mr. S. Awbery, was a principal spokesman in favour of more liberal compensation for owner occupiers. See, for example, House of Commons, *Official Report*, Vol. 612, Written Answers, Cols. 29, 30.
8. Previously Town and Country Planning Act 1968.
9. R. Haddon, 'A minority in a welfare state society: the location of West Indians in the London Housing Market', *The New Atlantis*, Vol. 1, No. 2, 1970.
10. Department of Environment, *Housing and Construction Statistics No. 12*, HMSO, 1975, Supplementary Table VII.
11. With the transfer of the local authority health services to the re-organised National Health Service from 1st April 1974 medical officers of health ceased to exist. Public Health Inspectors have generally been renamed Environmental Health Officers following local government reorganisation in 1974. For convenience the old title will be used throughout this text in both the past and present tense.
12. Housing Act 1957, Third Schedule, para. 2(1) (a).
13. *The Housing (Prescribed Forms) Regulations 1966*, SI 253/1966, were in force in 1970. They were replaced by new regulations in 1972 (SI 228/1972); amendments relating to well-maintained payments were made in 1974 (SI 1511/1974).
14. Department of the Environment, Circular 77/75, *Clearance of Unfit Houses – Procedural Requirements*, HMSO, 1975, paras. 30-34. The 1974 version of Form 26 is substantially the same as the 1966 version. The notes have been modified following the extension of full market value compensation to most owner occupiers under the Housing Act 1969. At the time of the survey the notes were inaccurate in this respect and were the cause of some additional confusion beyond the general difficulty of understanding

15. a lengthy and complex document.
15. Housing Act 1957, 4th Schedule.
16. 'In considering whether a house has been well-maintained, regard should be had to its age, situation and character, bearing in mind that since the house has been found unfit, it is bound to have serious defects . . . [but] minor items of disrepair can be overlooked . . . When considering the maintenance of the exterior, the authority should be satisfied that the house is in a reasonably sound and weatherproof condition of repair . . . When considering the maintenance of the interior, any necessary maintenance should have been carried out to such items as plaster and woodwork, in order to maintain the house or dwelling in reasonably good repair. Account may also be taken of any improvements, to the extent that they have eliminated items of interior disrepair, or work which, going beyond mere redecoration, has been undertaken to minimise the adverse effects on the interior of exterior disrepair.' Circular 77/75, *op. cit.*, paras. 18-20.
17. *The Housing (Payment for Well Maintained Houses) Order 1973*, SI 753/1973; this order takes into account the rating revaluation which came into operation on 1st April 1973. It replaces *The Housing (Payment for Well Maintained Houses) Order 1972*, SI 1972/1792, which applied a multiplier of eight times the rateable value from October 1972. At the time of the survey a multiplier of four was in operation under the Housing Act 1969, so that the value of WMPs was only about half the present level.
18. Housing Act 1957, Section 60.
    The Land Compensation Act 1973 introduced two new payments in addition to WMPs.
    Both tenants and owner occupiers displaced since October 1972, who have lived in their houses for at least five years, are entitled to a home loss payment equivalent to at least £150 and up to £1,500 depending on the rateable value of the dwelling (Land Compensation Act 1973, Sections 29 and 30).
    Both tenants and owner occupiers entitled only to site value compensation displaced since October 1972 are entitled to a disturbance payment equivalent to reasonable removal expenses (Land Compensation Act 1973, Sections 37 and 38).
19. The Housing Act 1974 made local authorities responsible for the initial decision on good maintenance. The council must now send a notice to all landlords, tenants and owner occupiers informing them whether a house has been well-maintained. Appeal lies to the Secretary of State for the Environment and is normally determined by the inspector at the time of the PLI.
20. Ministry of Housing and Local Government, Circular 44/56, *Slum Clearance: Simplification and Acceleration of Administrative Procedures*, para. 7.
21. See, for example: Ministry of Housing and Local Government, *Moving out of a Slum: A Study of people moving from St. Mary's, Oldham,* Design Bulletin No. 20, HMSO, 1970, para. 87.
22. The Minister of Housing and Local Government at the time, Harold Macmillan, justified the clause in terms of the burden on local authorities of complying with the court decision. He claimed that tenants had no difficulty in finding out about a CPO from the press. House of Commons, *Official Report*, Standing Committees 1954-55, Vol. II, Cols. 900-903.
23. Section 39 of the Land Compensation Act 1973 imposed a duty on local authorities to rehouse residential occupiers displaced under virtually all procedures including Part III of the 1957 Act. But the requirement will undoubtedly be subject to interpretation by local authorities. There has

already been at least one appeal to the Courts (Hendy *v.* Bristol Corporation, see *Times* 2nd November 1973). The Master of the Rolls stated that the local authority fulfilled their duty if they provided alternative accommodation 'as soon as practicable'. The right to be rehoused seems less than absolute.
24. Corporation of the City of Manchester, *Clearance Areas Progress Table to 31st March 1970,* mimeo.
25. House of Commons, *Official Report,* Vol. 656, Written Answers, Cols. 33, 34.
26. House of Commons, *Official Report,* Vol. 657, Written Answers, Cols. 73, 74.
27. A detailed timetable of events in a clearance area in St. Mary's Ward Oldham is given in Ministry of Housing and Local Government, *op. cit.* (1970).
28. Ministry of Housing and Local Government, *Slum Clearance Orders Monthly Statement,* mimeo.
29. House of Commons, *Official Report,* Vol. 762, Written Answers, Col. 221. 72% of CPOs submitted during the years 1963-67 were subject to an objection.
30. In some cases the receipt of a Section 170 notice requesting details of ownership of the property may precede the visit of a PHI.
31. For an example of the difficulties which may be caused by residents' mistrust of the public health inspectors' work see Norman Dennis, *op. cit.* (1970).
32. In the mid-sixties approximately 7 per cent of houses designated as unfit in CPOs were reclassified as fit. See House of Commons, *Official Report,* Vol. 762, Written Answers, Col. 222.
33. In preparation for more detailed study of local authority procedures visits were made to a total of twenty local authorities in advance of survey preparation. Details of the standard procedures followed were recorded in all cases.
34. Again, local government reorganisation has transformed Town Clerks in many instances into Chief Executives or Directors of Administration. But the old terminology is retained here.

4 HOUSING ALLOCATION IN CENTRALISED SYSTEMS — NEWCASTLE, MANCHESTER AND TOWER HAMLETS

Issues in Housing Management and a Framework of Analysis

Unlike the earlier stages of slum clearance the administrative arrangements for rehousing residents from clearance areas are not tailored to fulfill the requirements of legislation. As long as a local authority acknowledges a general responsibility to rehouse displaced residents there is no central government interference in the way this obligation is to be met nor is there a prescribed form of administrative machinery. Indeed, the lack of central government concern with such aspects of housing management has been a matter of both official and unofficial comment in recent years.[1]

Furthermore housing management is not yet sufficiently professionalised[2] to have established a 'normal practice' to be followed by all local authority housing departments. The wide variety of arrangements for dividing up housing responsibilities which existed under the old system of local government[3] has been only partly eradicated by reorganisation. There are not yet sufficient professionally qualified staff in local housing departments to establish firmly a corporate professional ethic from which a common definition of 'normal practice' might develop.[4] Nor is clear guidance to be obtained from the practice manuals available, particularly not on the special problems which may be encountered in rehousing residents from old-established areas affected by clearance. In a survey of the available literature on welfare aspects of slum clearance in 1967 David Bull pointed out that there was so little official guidance or expert opinion on the subject that the Director of Housing of Manchester C.B. felt obliged to make a postal inquiry amongst his colleagues and to commission Bull's study of clearance area problems in the city.[5] The situation has changed little since that time: a second edition of Macey and Baker's handbook on housing management issued in 1973 retains the same material on 'Practical Aspects of Slum Clearance and Rehousing' and on 'Allocations — Programme and Selection of Tenants' as the first edition published in 1965.[6] The Institute of Housing Managers is still issuing a management practice leaflet on 'The Allocation of Tenancies' first

Housing Allocation in Centralised Systems

published in the early sixties, reprinted in 1970[7] and still cited with approval in the profession's monthly journal. Yet, in the interim, both the Seebohm Report[8] and the Cullingworth Report[9] on council housing have been acknowledged as revolutionising the tasks of housing management and the approach which is required. For housing management the requirements of the Seebohm and Cullingworth Reports and local government reform appear to have been satisfied on the organisational side by the establishment of a 'comprehensive' housing service[10] with housing advice centres and on the 'social' side by the encouragement of tenant participation on council estates.[11] Most of the problems of clearance raised by academic research and by reports of the Central Housing Advisory Committee appear to have been ignored.

In this the housing management profession has shown a remarkable immunity to criticism which now spans almost twenty years of post-war slum clearance. Willmott and Young's attack on the fragmenting effects of housing allocation had its counterpart in advice issued in the Central Housing Advisory Committee's 1956 report on *Moving from the Slums*.[12] Where possible, neighbours who wished to move together should be rehoused in the same area and particular efforts should be made to rehouse old people near their relatives.[13] In general all households affected by clearance should be given full information about available housing early on in the process so that their negotiations with housing officials could be balanced and well-informed.

Commentators have inevitably directed attention to the part played by housing officials in the allocation process, and in particular, the role of housing visitors. Common sense dictates that the job of the housing visitor is bound to be central to the rehousing process and successive reports have reiterated the message that much depends on the calibre and effectiveness of these lowly officials. *Moving from the Slums* asserted the need for 'humane, experienced and well-qualified staff for . . . home visits and for . . . interviews given in the office'[14] and mapped out a one-week training course for staff newly involved in clearance work after the wartime hiatus. The Cullingworth Committee were more forthright in asserting the inadequacy of selection, training facilities and career structure for housing visitors.[15] Ungerson's study identified the housing visitor as the key point of contact in the clearance process and the training of visitors as a point of potential breakthrough for local authority housing policy.[16]

But despite the growth of a general interest in aspects of housing allocation and of a particular interest in the role of the housing visitor the conceptual groundwork for a study of allocation procedures is ill-developed and the promise of new theoretical formulations in urban sociology has not yet been redeemed in operationalised empirical studies. The researcher in the field is left very much to his own devices in developing the conceptual tools to be used.

In contrast with the early stages of clearance at which local authority procedures exhibit marked standardisation because of their basis in legislation, local variation in allocation systems suggests a comparative approach. In this and the succeeding chapter the problem is to compare the rehousing procedures of five large local authorities as they were organised in 1970-71 in a manner which permits some evaluation of their effectiveness. Such a comparison requires specification of, first, the criteria by which one system may be regarded as 'better' or 'worse' than another and, second, the relevant aspects of performance which must be compared.

Criteria of Evaluation

The overall requirement of the allocation system is that it should match houses and applicants so that new or relet houses are filled as they come available. Although, in the long run, this can be achieved to some extent by fitting the houses to the people — by new building, improvement or conversion — in the short run it is more realistic to regard the existing stock of houses as fixed so that the day-to-day problem for staff of a housing department is to fit people to the available dwellings. Inevitably, there is a tension between the demands of efficiency and those of humanity. While housing managers must concern themselves with loss of rent on vacant houses, with protection of their housing stock against careless users and with preventing bottlenecks in site clearance and building works they also generally recognise the need at least to 'minimise coercion'.[17] But whereas the relative efficiency of the system may be measured fairly unambiguously in money terms or time lost due to avoidable delays the criteria whereby an allocation system may be judged more or less 'humane' are not so simply specified. Although there may be general agreement that full and comprehensible information is a *sine qua non* of a good system, writers have otherwise selected a variety of characteristics of a 'humane' system. These may be categorised roughly as: justice, flexibility, self-determination and continuity.

Establishing a 'fair' allocation system requires at least a basic framework of rules and all writers have accepted the need for some allocation regulations. But the rules themselves must be 'fair' in that they do not involve gross disadvantages for any particular group of applicants. Residence qualifications and other restrictions on eligibility have been singled out for criticism because of their unfair effects on the rehousing chances of immigrant groups[18] and the exclusion of certain tenure groups from rehousing has been similarly attacked.[19] Other writers have been concerned that, whatever rules exist, they must be applied without prejudice and personal bias.[20] The difficulty of judging an applicant's housekeeping standards or cleanliness without depending heavily on the personal biases or class-based value judgements of interviewers is one reason why grading systems have been widely criticised.[21]

There is a general dilemma here. Whilst both the efficient running of a large bureaucratic concern and the imperatives of basic fairness require a degree of impersonality and routinisation, the rigid application of rules may result in a wooden uniformity in the treatment of applicants which is quite contrary to the spirit of fairness.[22] Although the exercise of administrative discretion is the obvious antidote to such ritualism its satisfactory exercise may require systematic training of a sort which is noticeably lacking at most levels in housing management.[23]

Flexibility and responsiveness of the allocation system is demanded by those who argue that groups of kin or neighbours should, if they so wish, be rehoused together or that special needs of, for example, the old or broken families, should be catered for. Catering for groups rather than individuals is, as Muchnick has pointed out, directly contrary to both the basic philosophy and administrative procedures of a system which treats each family as an equally independent unit. Further, it is not compatible with the essentially physical orientation of allocation processes which match applicants and dwellings primarily by size and type.[24] And catering for special needs at the margin involves a welfare role for housing staff about which the profession is ambivalent.[25]

Self-determination through the exercise of informed choice or participation in the control of change requires both information on the part of the applicant and a non-directive role for housing staff. As Norris puts it: 'The decision to accept a dwelling should be the tenants' deliberate choice, he should not be under pressure. If he is asking for the ideal he should be left to accept the real in his own time.'[26]

But, however self-effacing housing staff may be, the rules governing numbers of permissible offers or the grounds for a 'reasonable' refusal together with the urgency of impending demolition constrain the choices of a slum clearance applicant in ways which are outside staff control. While the restriction of offers to one only is clearly open to criticism, even in a system of multiple offers an applicant may still be under pressure to accept 'cod-offers' which are known by housing staff not to be what he wanted[27] or to accept the latest offer made to him because the time available is limited and he has no indication of when or what the next offer will be.[28]

Continuity of contact between staff and applicants and continuity over time have both been recommended by previous writers. Bull recognised the difficulties of applicants faced with an array of different officials on each visit and argued that people would welcome more discussion 'especially if they could speak to as few officials as possible',[29] and that lettings officers responsible for office allocations should also conduct home visits. Ungerson's emphasis on redevelopment as a process rather than an event stresses also the need for sustained contact over time. Since all other means of disseminating information are transitory she recommends the use of site offices as a base for trained housing visitors.[30]

In the present study the value judgements underlying comments on the relative merits of the systems which are compared place most emphasis on the need for continuity and self-determination. These values are encapsulated in the precept that the execution of rehousing activities should accommodate the requirements of residents as 'persons' and not simply 'process' them as disembodied 'particulars' recorded in categories designed for the convenience of the bureaucracy. From the resident's point of view his own experiences, his household needs and his aspirations are unique. Council housing, by contrast, is a highly standardised and easily categorised commodity. But the pressure to extend a matching categorisation and standardisation to the needs and circumstances of residents dehumanises the lettings procedure by denying the individuality of the applicant.

Conceptual Framework

Perceptions of the public with whom they are dealing are one aspect of the structure of meanings and day to day interpretations of reality which housing staff bring to the execution of their jobs. For purposes of comparative study these aspects of the work situation are conveniently conceptualised as aspects of the occupational ideology of housing staff. In this study the term 'occupational ideology' denotes the set of beliefs, factual claims and objectives by which housing staff justify their actions to themselves, their competitors and their detractors.[31] Although the term is often used to describe the legitimating beliefs of an occupational group spanning many different organisational contexts[32] the present usage recognises that, particularly within an occupational group as poorly professionalised as housing management, the set of ideas providing the basis of group cohesion within any department may owe little to the wider influences of ideas common to the occupational group as a whole. The influence of external ideas is itself dependent on the orientation of staff towards wider horizons; hence an important aspect of the investigation of ideology is the degree to which staff articulate their interests in terms of extending professional membership and control over housing activities by establishing the claims of professional expertise.[33]

While higher levels of management may be required to justify a wide range of policies and practices both to committees and to professional colleagues in other departments, staff involved full-time in day-to-day allocations require only a set of operational rules for matching houses and applicants or recognising problems that cannot be routinely treated. At this level the background of meanings is better conceptualised in terms of operational stereotypes[34] rather than in terms of a fully-fledged occupational ideology.

The incorporation in any system of a more or less 'personal' treatment of applicants will depend also upon purely organisational factors. There is a complex interplay of ideological commitment and organisational constraint. Ungerson has pointed out how the ideological commitment of individual housing visitors can make a considerable difference to the way they do their job within a given set of rules and responsibilities.[35] On the other hand, a particular ideological approach can be either enhanced or frustrated by the organisational structure.

Blau's study of case workers in an American public welfare agency describes the conflict between commitment to clients and the administration of complex rules in a work situation analagous to the lettings section of a housing department. Untrained staff administer a set of rules for the allocation of resources where the application of criteria of eligibility provides a minimum definition of the job requirement which they could adopt as a substitute for meaningful case work.[36] His findings show, first, that complex rules of access to resources diverted case workers' energies away from service to the client until the worker was sufficiently experienced to 'know the ropes' fully. Second, the study shows up clearly the importance of higher grades of staff in 'setting the tone' of a department. Blau found that the stress on case work rather than mere application of rules varied directly with the emphasis placed on these two aspects of the job by supervisors. Finally, Blau identified the mutual support of the work group as an important factor in determining case work orientations, particularly where there is no professional training to provide an articulated ethic of service.

Evidence from Blau's study indicates that commitment to clients by staff of a bureaucratically organised department will be achieved more effectively the simpler the rules and the more clearly articulated the occupational ideology of service amongst managers and supervisors thereby providing a basis of group cohesion amongst junior staff.

The division of responsibilities between different categories of staff will also have an important effect on the quality of performance, particularly through its effect on continuity of contact between officers and applicants. In describing the staff structures of housing departments we distinguish between categories of staff, identified by grade and title, and four roles which are 'manned' by these staff categories — the roles of 'senior manager', 'middle manager', 'allocator' and 'interviewer'. This conceptual distinction discourages the assumption that the boundaries of the decision making which processes individuals through the allocation system are necessarily coterminous with the formal structure of grades and labelled posts. It allows that differently named sections within one organisational structure stand in the same basic relationship to applicants and hence can be regarded as fulfilling the same role; also that similarly named staff in different organisations do not necessarily fulfil similar roles.

Senior managers carry overall responsibility for organisation and running of the housing department and for setting the rules and job specifications which guide or control other staff. They are responsible for committee work, the preparation of policy documents and for co-ordination and liaison with other departments. For the council tenant or applicant they are the ultimate authority for appeal or complaint. Middle managers run specialised sections, such as the lettings section, with responsibility for detailed organisation and personnel arrangements subject to approval of senior management. They settle standard points of appeal in the daily running of the section by application of the rules and policies elaborated by senior management.

The role of allocator is occupied by staff responsible for standard decision taking on individual applications. The house eventually accepted by an applicant may be very different from his original expectations; his expectations are mediated by the day-to-day decisions of staff who classify him, interpret his recorded circumstances and preferences in terms that are recognised by their administrative machinery and apply their own interpretations of what would be 'suitable' or 'best' for him given the constraints of supply and demand for housing.[37] Allocators operate usually from written records of the characteristics of individual applicants rather than from direct knowledge acquired

Housing Allocation in Centralised Systems

through face to face contact with applicants themselves, particularly where letting is organised on a centralised system providing a full-time job for staff who do nothing but allocate houses. Allocators are thereby constantly involved in routine clerical work and the interpretation of their responsibilities will be closely reflected (and, in turn, constrained) by the filing and record keeping system through which they work. The position of allocators as gatekeepers of the stock of available public housing gives them considerable power over the life chances of applicants. However, because the detailed workings of allocation systems are not normally publicly known (and may be protected from public knowledge by secret points systems, covert grading and unpublished rules), the role of allocator is unlikely to be clearly identified by the public and little constrained by public expectations of behaviour.

The role of interviewer carries responsibility for face to face contacts with applicants or complainants and provides the normal channel of formal and informal communication between the public and the housing department. Conceptually we can separate the role of interviewer from that of allocator by the interviewer's lack of control of available resources; unlike the allocator he is not usually in a position to allocate a particular property to an applicant and may indeed protect himself from applicants' demands by the plea that 'it's not up to me'.

As regular contact with the slum clearance public is part of the job of interviewers, whether at an applicant's home or in the office, there tends to be a fairly well defined public identification of the interviewer role. In clearance areas, particularly in large cities where long-term programmes of slum clearance affect very large numbers of houses, the housing visitor becomes a fairly easily recognised figure although variously labelled as 'the housing lady', 'the inspector' or 'the investigator'. The right to gather information and pass it on, which visitors claim, and the disclaimer of control over the results seem to be widely accepted by clearance area residents even though the process is known by many to include an appraisal of their personal conditions and house keeping standards. Similarly, staff dealing with inquiries or interviews at the Town Hall or Housing Department occupy a conventionally recognised position of 'just clerks' who are not expected to have any immediate influence over the outcome of an application.

The distinction of these four roles amongst housing staff is a conceptual distinction which may not be clearly specified at the operational level of the day-to-day affairs of the department. Indeed, it is an important aspect of this study to compare the distribution of detailed tasks which would be identified in a job specification or 'O and M' report with the broad strata of responsibilities, authority and values which are associated with the four roles. Although the terms chosen imply a position of rank within the hierarchy of local government, the four roles are distinguished partly also by differences of responsibility *vis-à-vis* the public served by a housing department. Compared with the roles of allocator and manager the role of interviewer is the most clearly structured by a normative framework of public expectations constraining the behaviour of incumbents.

The final element in the analytical framework of this study is a terminology of tasks which have to be completed during the rehousing process. In the following sections departments are compared by means of a series of charts which relate the actual categories of staff identified in each department to the execution of particular tasks. The first four tasks are, broadly, tasks of information collection and dissemination — completing application forms, giving advice and dealing with inquiries. The remaining five tasks are all tasks requiring decisions such as grading and vetting applicants and deciding on individual offers of accommodation.

The significance of this division is that the first four tasks are the main tasks connected with the interviewer role and the remainder are those connected with the role of allocator. A perfect consonance between the roles of interviewer and allocator and the structure of responsibility for tasks would involve no individual staff fulfilling tasks in both categories.[38]

To summarise: the burden of this and the following chapter is to compare the 'operational styles' of five housing departments in a manner which permits some evaluation of their effectiveness. Two aspects of the allocation processes of departmental operations have been singled out for study. First, on the ideological side, the perceptions of residents held by staff and their view of the benefits of a professionalised department; at the lower levels of the staff hierarchy this means investigating operational stereotypes rather than a developed occupational ideology. Second, on the organisational side, the study identifies four conceptually distinct roles, a set of tasks which in part define these roles and the categories of staff which are allocated differing responsibilities for these tasks and stand in varying relationships to the four roles. The detailed description of departments and procedures in the following section concentrates on organisational features and the division of tasks in centralised systems. In the final section of the next chapter, where direct comparison of authorities is attempted, the ideological emphasis of management is also brought directly into the analysis.

Centralised Systems: Newcastle, Manchester and Tower Hamlets

Three of the five authorities in 1970 operated a centralised system of allocations with a single central office from which interviewing and lettings were organised.

Newcastle-upon-Tyne C.B.

Interviewers. Three categories of staff, predominantly women, were normally involved in interviewing duties. Home visits were undertaken by seven lettings assistants. Interviews at the Civic Centre were the responsibility of eight interviewing officers who worked by appointment from their own suite of rooms. Incidental enquiries at the public counter were dealt with by reception assistants.

No appointments were made for home visits. Interviews averaged about half an hour, there were no evening interviews and households that could not be contacted during the day were left a standard letter asking them to contact the Civic Centre to arrange interview times. As an office interview was a standard part of the system for many residents, lettings assistants were not obliged to expand the advising and discussive aspects of the home visit, knowing that all residents would have the opportunity of a further discussion at the Civic Centre. Home visits in consequence tended to be identified as 'the Investigation'. Housing history was regarded as particularly important so that previous council tenants who had defaulted on rent could be identified. Rent books were inspected for arrears — 'its the first thing we ask for' — and date of marriage was a standard item to be recorded.

Grading required 'a quick look around the house', in particular at the bedrooms (because residents who may have had time to clear up when they heard the interviewer was coming would not have had time to wash dirty bedding). Although grading categories ranged from A to C- the crucial distinction was between B and B-; the B- category were thought to be 'able to do better' and were therefore likely to be excluded from post-war housing whereas better categories could expect post-war and possibly new accommodation. 'You picture people next door to a first class tenant and if the picture doesn't fit you don't recommend for that type of property.'

No standard information was carried by lettings assistants for distribution to residents nor did they carry maps of estate locations — 'most people know the estates better than we do'. On the other hand it was standard practice to inform residents about the rent rebate scheme

Chart 1. Newcastle upon Tyne C.B.

	LETTINGS ASSISTANTS	INTERVIEWING OFFICERS	RECEPTION ASSISTANTS	ASSISTANT LETTINGS OFFICER	LETTINGS OFFICER
Complete application form and report	Home visit. No appointment. Stress on housing history to find rent defaulters from previous council tenancy.	Tasks defined by office largely in case work terms. Known to be deficient and moving towards system of sustained contact. At present routinised.			
Advise and inform applicants	Advice on rent rebates. Other information limited. Full discussion of preferences.	Office interview by appointment on 2 weeks notice. Regarded as a standard part of educative process for applicants. Caller may request a particular interviewer but cases often swopped for support of second opinion.			
Interview at special home or office visits			Occasional second visits at request of lettings staff or to discuss change of preference.		

Task			
Answer routine office inquiries		Deal with all counter inquiries and make appointments for interview.	
Grade Applicants	Precedes discussion of preferences as guide to interviewer. Important decision. Grades A to C−		
Vet applicants for suspension			Eligibility unimportant
Decide household requirements		Families without children cannot get a *house*. Initial decision on house type and size required when cases enter system.	Day-to-day answering queries and setting individual queries on lettings.
Decide individual offers of housing		Routine allocation. Priority decided by length of time since clearance began.	
Monitor refusals of offers			

and to advise them that fuel bills were additional to the rent.

Several alternative preferences were recorded where possible. Households requesting an estate which the lettings assistant knew they would not get because of their low grading would be put off with an excuse such as the high rent or the cost of central heating — 'You can't tell someone they're dirty'.

Interviewing officers conducted all office interviews by appointment made two weeks in advance by a reception assistant. Interviews were spaced at 15 minute intervals but exchange of cases between staff permitted a degree of flexibility so that interviewers could extend their interest in a case where necessary. Office interviews were seen as an important part of the process of educating applicants to make 'realistic' assessments of their housing opportunities. Applicants were encouraged to widen their range of alternative choices so that they could speed up their chances of rehousing. Alternatively, they might have to be persuaded to adjust their preferences to accommodate the hard realities of the system, in particular the poor prospects of a low grading. Interviewing officers explained the situation by exploiting the division of responsibility between home and office interviews and placing the onus on the lettings assistants — 'in their opinion you will not be considered for a new property'.

Case files were not exclusive to individual interviewers although persistent callers might specifically ask for the same interviewer on each occasion. Interviewing officers themselves saw advantages in applicants seeing more than one interviewer, first, because it gave them the support of another opinion and, second, because a persistent caller would be encouraged to accept what he or she was told if she heard it from more than one person.

No standard information was distributed at office interviews and the interviewing officers were dependent on the office grapevine rather than systematic briefing to keep themselves informed about the availability of houses.

In this system the interviewer role could best be described as divided between home and office interviewing staff. Continuity of contact could be achieved only if an applicant used his own initiative to seek out the same interviewing officer on visits to the Civic Centre. The division was also exploited by the staff who appreciated the advantages of the mutual support which second opinions offered. But staff recognised that the division of responsibility caused an unfortunate discontinuity of contact. One lettings assistant welcomed a recent move from the Housing Management section to the Lettings section because it allowed her 'to put the case more strongly to the Lettings staff who were the final arbiters'. Amongst the interviewing officers there was some dissatisfaction that they could not also undertake home visits like the lettings assistants. Separation from the actual process of allocation meant that 'you don't see the end of a job. You don't see how people have ended up. If you do you only hear by chance.'

Rules of access and the Allocator role. Although in principle the department housed only those people who were resident in a clearance area at the date of confirmation of a CPO, in practice latecomers were rehoused as well without being penalised by inferior offers. The principal letting restriction was the exclusion of childless couples from allocation of a house rather than a flat. Since the department also followed a policy of making unlimited offers the allocation system did not require initial scrutiny of records for suspension nor a careful monitoring of refusals although, as elsewhere, details of offers made to each household were logged.

The essential initial decision was the size and type of house required and the areas preferred. There was some scope for the assistant lettings officer making this decision to modify the recorded preferences of applicants by ignoring those which he thought were inconsistent with the grading and likely rent paying capacity. Additionally, an applicant might be put down for an area which he had not considered if it was thought suitable. The basic decisions having been made, the reference number of each applicant was entered on ledger cards made out separately for each type and size of house on each estate. Each ledger card contained the case numbers of all applicants expressing a preference and/or considered suitable for that type, size and location of accommodation. Priority was simply established by serial number — those with the lowest numbers having waited longest. As each applicant was entered on a number of alternative cards he was automatically considered for houses in several areas of the city at the same time. Clearance area cases were given priority over waiting list cases on the card and a tie between two cases equally suitable in all other respects was resolved in favour of the applicant with the longer length of residence in a clearance area.

In this system the main tasks for the Assistant Lettings Officers were deciding on household requirements and making individual offers. Neither vetting for eligibility nor monitoring refusals were particularly important. In principle the process of offer and refusal, controlled mainly by one man, permitted the assistant lettings officer to build up cumulative knowledge of each applicant's circumstances and preferences encouraging a personal approach to letting. But working against this possibility, the very simplicity of the procedure meant that large numbers of offers could be handled in a short time encouraging routinisation. In fact the procedural rules for settling priorities and determining claims were stressed by the staff involved as an important means of minimising their use of discretion. The allocator role therefore, although manned in a simple one-to-one relationship by one category of staff, was interpreted in a restricted manner.

Manchester C.B.

Interviewers. In the Manchester system five different categories of staff were involved in interviewing duties of one sort or another although only three of them on a day-to-day basis. Home visits were completed by the inspectors of the Investigation and Disinfestation section, a separate unit responsible to the head of the Rehousing Division but located in its own offices a quarter of a mile from the main housing offices in the Town Hall. Four of the five inspectors were men and most had previously been rent collectors.

The purpose of the home visit was defined by inspectors exclusively in terms of information required by the Lettings section for determining eligibility and for subsequent allocation of houses. Visits were preceded by a standard letter giving residents a time of appointment and asking them to have ready a rent book, marriage licence, wireless licence, income tax notice or some other documentary evidence of their length of residence. 'Proof [of residence] is the main thing, plus details of the family concerned. After that we ask what areas they want. We don't put anything to them.' Fifteen minutes were allowed for interviews and housing preferences were noted without discussion, the only standard handout on housing alternatives being a leaflet on overspill schemes. The investigation required inspection of the whole house, partly to check on cleanliness and partly to check on the number of people sleeping there.

The investigation and disinfestation inspectors had a clear articulation of their limited objectives in home visiting. In contrast with the usual comment on the difficulties of dealing with old people one inspector remarked that old people were the easiest because they saved up their rent books which were clear proof of length of residence. In comparison with rent collection which most had done previously the inspector's job was seen as an improvement 'because it gets the bag off your back'. Because of their remoteness from the Lettings section and lack of information on housing opportunities inspectors were specifically briefed not to offer information or advice for fear of misleading residents.

A standard arrangement compensating for this very narrow interpretation of the home interview was a system of information points, opened in schools or church halls adjacent to each clearance area, to which residents were invited for a second interview. In large clearance areas the information points were normally staffed for three days from 3.0 p.m. to 7.0 p.m. Formal notification of the opening of an information point portrayed the interview as: 'an opportunity . . . for you to discuss the various areas in which property will be available without delay and to make inquiries regarding those areas where demand is already in excess of properties anticipated'. Four staff from the Lettings section attended the information points — the classification officer and three lettings officers from the Selection section. These meetings were primarily designed to readjust residents' expectations of rehousing. Lettings officers had lists of districts in which housing was available and could also draw on their own background knowledge when discussing residents' expressed preference. But the discussion often got off to a bad start with the lettings officer effectively ruling out the possibility of the resident getting what he had asked for at the time of home interview; for many residents it underlined the pointlessness of bureaucracy to have put down for the estate of their choice at the home visit only to be told shortly after at the information point that their choice was hopeless.

Two women housing visitors working under the classification officer made home visits to difficult or unusual cases. Their job had originally been to take out offers to people, particularly the elderly, who were unable to get to the office to collect keys. Although this job continued, the job definition had been extended to cover general information, welfare and trouble shooting tasks. Discrepancies in the information collected by inspectors or a failure to reply to letters might require a home interview. When a clearance area had been nearly cleared the visitors checked on the situation of remaining residents and the progress of demolitions, often discussing alternative choices in the hope of speeding up rehousing.

Office interviews were the special responsibility of six lettings officers (counter section) who staffed the general inquiry counter in the Lettings section. These officers were primarily concerned with recording the acceptance or rejection of offers of accommodation both from slum clearance and the waiting list and their work was primarily

Chart II. Manchester C.B.

	INVESTIGATION AND DISINFESTATION INSPECTORS	CLASSIFICATION OFFICER	HOUSING VISITORS	LETTINGS OFFICERS (Counter Section)	LETTINGS OFFICERS (Selection Section)	ASSISTANT SENIOR LETTINGS OFFICER
Complete Application form & report	Home visit. *With* appointment. Stress on proof of residence and arrears of rent.	Defined by office as redundant procedure but essential part of subsequent bureaucratic machinery. Office moving to additional case work section (for old people).				
Advise and inform applicants	Preferences recorded without discussion. Inspectors not equipped to advise.					
Interview at special home or office visits		Arranges *ad hoc* meetings as standard part of educative process of applicants.	Visitors follow up discrepancies in application forms. Standard revisits late in clearance process and to sort out	Deal with all routine enquiries. Task mainly acceptance or rejection of offers but may lead to extended office interview and discussion of preferences, etc.	Take part in rota at school meetings.	

Task					
office inquiries					counter as available.
Grade applicants	Good/fair/poor, but not very important				
Vet applicants for suspension		Decides eligibility on basis of complicated rules and corresponds with applicants.			
Decide on household requirements			Decides house type and size required on basis of household composition and qualification for separate rehousing.		
Decide individual offers of housing				Occasionally intervene with lettings officer to make a special case for an applicant.	Occasionally make on-the-spot offers of housing at the counter.	Routine allocation of only one house size. Priority given by length of time in clearance area.
Monitor refusals of offers				Follow up refusals or failures to reply to offers.	All refusals scrutinised and cases of three refusals referred upwards for decision.	Completes reports on all cases of three refusals in discussion with boss. May lead to committee decision for eviction.

geared to dealing efficiently with such routine decisions. But they also dealt with people wanting to change their stated preferences and with general requests for information. Counter staff could also make offers of accommodation across the counter and have extended discussions of household circumstances and preferences. However, working conditions were not conducive to very personal treatment. Staff were always subject to the pressure of other people queuing in the waiting area in front of the counter and the only private interview room was a small cubicle at one end.

In this situation the interviewer role may be described as fragmented. In his home a resident might see both an inspector and one of the housing visitors. At the information point he would meet a lettings officer or the classification officer. At the Town Hall he would normally deal with a lettings officer from the counter section. It would be a matter of extremely good fortune if he managed to see the same person twice. Only the housing visitors were likely to undertake an extended interview at a resident's home but such visits were confined mainly to cases which threw up an administrative problem. At the information points or at the Town Hall working conditions were unsatisfactory for personal interviewing even if staff had the time and commitment.

Rules of Access and the Allocator Role. At the time of interview the rules governing eligibility for rehousing in Manchester were very complicated. Any household resident in an area prior to its declaration as a clearance area was eligible. Households taking up residence between the date of declaration and the PLI were eligible only if they had lived in Manchester continuously for at least two years previously. Households moving into a clearance area between the date of PLI and date of confirmation of the CPO were eligible for rehousing only if they qualified by virtue of their position on the waiting list. Lodgers were not rehoused, regardless of length of residence, unless they were aged over 60.

It was the first job of the classification officer to scrutinise the application forms completed by the inspectors and to determine households' eligibility. When eligible cases had been sorted out they were classified according to the numbers of bedrooms required and their papers filed in the Lettings section. This set of decisions involved a good deal of personal judgement based on the officer's experience. Her commitment to the job derived from an avowed interest in the welfare of other people and she was concerned to be as generous as possible in applying the rules: 'I use every loophole I can to make people eligible because we *are* displacing them.' Nevertheless a close attention to the rules and a sound knowledge of precedent were important aspects of the job.

The papers of vetted eligible cases were filed in sequence of CPO and within CPO by CPO reference number which ensured that cases who had been waiting longest in a clearance area were in the front of the file and thereby given top priority for letting. As in Newcastle, all case numbers of households expressing an interest in an estate were listed on a chart for that estate thereby giving a clear indicator of demand. Anyone selecting several areas would be considered for each of them.

Six lettings officers (Selection section) allocated houses. They worked in three pairs each specialising in particular sizes of property: one and four bedroom accommodation, two bedroom or three bedroom accommodation. One of each pair dealt with slum clearance applicants and one with waiting list applicants. Properties coming available were accumulated by the assistant senior lettings officer and then divided up between the three pairs. All properties were considered first by the lettings officer in each pair responsible for slum clearance and only passed on for the waiting list applicants if they could not be let to a slum clearance case.

A formal policy of limiting the number of 'reasonable' offers of housing to three meant that refusals of property had to be carefully monitored by lettings staff. An important part of the counter section's job was to record reasons for refusing an offer of a house. Selection section scrutinised all refusals of offers before returning papers to the files and passed on all cases who had made two or more refusals to the assistant senior lettings officer. His task was to decide whether the grounds for refusal were 'reasonable' and to pass on to the senior lettings officer those cases in which preferences and offers matched closely. These were considered for presentation to an Appeal Panel of councillors and eventual eviction proceedings. In new clearance areas where it was standard practice to try a few 'fliers' or 'cod-offers' refusals of such unlikely offers was not taken into account. Despite the importance of scrutiny of refusals it was only rarely the case that the assistant senior lettings officer would have an opportunity of seeing applicants rather than taking the reports of the counter section or applicants' letters as the basis of his decision.

The subdivision of lettings into three house sizes introduced an unfortunate inflexibility into this system. Interest of individual lettings officers was narrowly focused and it was not possible for them to change the priority of a case by balancing the urgency of their predicament against the pros and cons of permitting them a smaller (or larger) house than would normally be permitted. On the other hand, the system distributed applicants amongst the available houses on a queuing principle rather than by a process of grading. At the stage of final allocation, grading was ignored and there was a good deal of uncertainty amongst lettings staff as to the significance of the different categories. But the process of classification and the discussions at information points did provide scope for the classification officer or the lettings officers to direct unsatisfactory applicants away from the better quality housing. Certainly the classification officer was very clear about the significance of the inspectors' reports on bedding. She reported that the inspectors inspected bedding 'by lifting up the mattress with the end of their pencil. I like clean beds to start off with. Beds are one thing I'd go for — I love clean bedding. I'd have clean bedding every day if I could.' However, the senior lettings officer insisted that a householder with a very poor report would be offered a brand new house if that is what he held out for.

The allocator role in this system was highly fragmented, with four categories of staff involved in routine decision taking for any particular case.

Tower Hamlets London Borough

In comparison with the other four authorities covered in this study Tower Hamlets London Borough administered a small stock of housing requiring only a small staff at head office. This permitted the head of the housing department, the housing officer, to be concerned with and involved in all aspects of the department down to the level of scrutinising all offers of accommodation. In many respects the head office thereby resembled the organisation of a district office in the decentralised systems of Leeds and Liverpool.

Interviewers. Home visits were undertaken by housing visitors working without appointments. Two men and one woman filled these posts at the time of interview and two posts were vacant. The limited purpose of the home visit was indicated by the housing officer's reference to the 'census' of residents and the housing visitors themselves had a restricted view of what their job was meant to achieve. Because of complex rules for eligibility, establishing a household's length of residence was an important part of home interviews requiring a check on rent books or, in doubtful cases, with the electricity board. Otherwise standard interviews were confined to collecting details of household circumstances, renting arrangements and housing preferences. The main distinction for rehousing purposes was between someone wanting a 'local' house and wanting to be rehoused by the GLC which required completion of a separate application form. No standard information was distributed by housing visitors. The housing officer expressed the view that applicants probably knew the possibilities open to them rather better than the interviewers themselves but one housing visitor argued that residents understood neither the amalgamation of the three previous boroughs into Tower Hamlets nor the relationship of the Borough to the GLC. Nor was there any special provision to cope with the difficulties of an area such as Spitalfields in which there was a high proportion of immigrants, many of them with language difficulties.[39]

Grading of applicants was not based on formal categories but depended on the housing visitors' informal assessment. The most important distinction was the category of households suitable 'for relet only'. In contrast to many housing visitors elsewhere those in Tower Hamlets were particularly straightforward about grading applicants, telling them directly if they were unsuitable for a new house and offering to return in six to eight weeks to see if there was any improvement. One housing visitor reported that if people refused to allow an inspection of their house, 'I tell them I can only presume it's dirty. Straight out, I never mystify.' The criteria applied, however, were not clear: 'My initiative tells me if it's a buggy house. You know when someone's buggy or going to be a problem on a new estate.' Except in cases of poor housekeeping or rent arrears, second visits were unusual.

Unlike either Newcastle or Manchester there was no back-up arrangement of specialised staff available for interviewing at head office or for further home visiting. If a situation arose which required a special interview the housing officer herself would frequently interview an applicant.

In this system the routine interviewer role was narrowly restricted by the job interpretations of senior management and the housing visitors themselves. Although they had a good deal of flexibility in working arrangements and their office was located next door to the lettings staff, permitting an extended interest in individual cases, the 'census' interpretation of the job was closely adhered to and the need to establish eligibility dictated priorities. As one housing visitor put it, 'Our job is to determine whether the family is entitled to be rehoused.' Unlike the Manchester system where a similar job interpretation prevailed for home visits there was not a back-up system of interviewing

Chart III. Tower Hamlets L.B.

	HOUSING VISITORS	COUNTER CLERKS	LETTINGS OFFICER (Decanting)	HOUSING OFFICER
Complete application form and report	Home visit. No appointment. Stress on proof of residence and arrears of rent. Defined by office as 'census'. Staff consciously limit their own role to routine collection of information.			
Advise and inform applicants	Information on GLC nominations. Little discussion of preference or possibilities.			
Interview at special home or office visits.	Second visits on request of lettings staff or to check up on improvement of a poor assessment.			Housing Officer easily available for office interviews.
Answer routine office inquiries		No specialised office interviewers.		

Grade				
Applicants	Not standardised. 'Only suitable for relet' is the usual comment.			
Vet applicants for suspension		Only one offer to ineligible cases.		
Decide household requirements			Decision on number of rooms required when cases enter the system.	
Decide individual offers of housing			Routine allocation. Cards filed alphabetically give no automatic priority.	
Monitor refusals of offers			Refusals are recorded by estate caretakers and reasons recorded on offer slips.	All offers checked by Housing Officer. Pattern of refusals is a better guide than initial statement of preferences.

staff with a more personalised job interpretation except for the housing officer who had many other duties besides.

Rules of Access and the Allocator role. Eligibility under the Tower Hamlets rules was divided into three classes. The only group fully eligible were those who could establish residence in a clearance area at the date of representation of the area. Households moving into the area between the date of representation and date of confirmation of the CPO were given only one offer either in less desirable estates or in acquired houses due for eventual demolition. Households moving into the area after date of confirmation were not considered eligible for an offer at all and were expected to make their own arrangements.

Forms completed by the housing visitors were subdivided according to the numbers of bedrooms required and standard letters sent to households who were not fully eligible. Within the bedroom requirement, the filing sequence was by alphabetical order of applicants' names which gave no automatic sequence of priority and was workable only in a relatively small-scale system. All allocations to slum clearance cases were made in the first instance by the lettings officer (decanting) whilst transfer and waiting list cases were each handled by another specialist lettings officer.

Formal policy was to make three offers of housing in the area of the applicant's choice but 'wild' offers in other areas did not count. As information on preferences was very limited the lettings system depended more on the pattern of refusals than on applicants' stated preferences. But arrangements for monitoring refusals relied on a very indirect flow of information. Applicants refusing accommodation were expected to inform the local caretakers, from whom they obtained keys to view, of their reasons for refusal. These were passed on to one of three local management offices and the local office managers passed them on to central office to be recorded on applicants' files. The routine system did not thereby permit even the restricted feedback interviews which occurred in Manchester. But dependence on the pattern of refusals encouraged a liberal policy on offers. This was also supported explicitly by the housing officer who pointed out that 'if the number of offers is limited it puts a dreadful responsibility on us'.

A unique aspect of the Tower Hamlets system was the checking of all allocations by the housing officer herself. Since only 40 to 50 offers were made each week this duplication of the lettings officer's job was a manageable burden. The housing officer estimated that she queried about one in seven of the allocations each week.

In this system the allocator role, as in Newcastle, was 'manned' by only one person, the lettings officer (decanting) whose work was partly duplicated by the housing officer. The relatively small numbers of applicants, a liberal view of numbers of offers for fully eligible cases, informal grading and the close proximity of housing visitors for discussion might be expected to encourage a personalised approach to the job. But dependence on the educative process of offer and refusal rather than detailed discussion of preferences and the very limited feedback through caretakers was not consistent with a personalised perception of residents. Nor was there any special provision, such as might have been expected in an acknowledged 'difficult' area like Spitalfields, for catering for the special needs of applicants with special problems.

NOTES

1. On the 'official' side the Cullingworth Committee in 1969 recommended that the housing management advisory functions of the then Ministry of Housing be strengthened by appointing additional staff to complement the one professional officer concerned with housing management see Central Housing Advisory Committee, *Council Housing: Purposes, Procedures and Priorities,* Ninth Report of the Housing Management Sub Committee, HMSO, 1969, p. 25. See also Mary E.H. Smith 'Housing Management in the Future: Problems and Opportunities', *Housing Monthly,* Vol. II, No. 1, January 1975.
2. This usage is consistent with the use of the term 'professionalisation' as meaning the development of certain key attributes which are 'essentially' professional. The terminology is, however, problematic: see T.J. Johnson, *Professions and Power,* Macmillan, 1972, Chap 2.
3. See J.B. Cullingworth, *op. cit.* (1966), Chap 3; also, Bryan Glastonbury, *Homeless Near a Thousand Homes,* Allen and Unwin, 1971.
4. Mary E.H Smith, *op. cit.*, p. 6.
5. D.G. Bull, *op. cit.* (1967), p. 9.
6. J.P. Macey and C.V. Baker, *Housing Management,* The Estates Gazette, 2nd Edition, 1973, Chaps. 14 and 17. The only substantial change in the text of these two chapters is the omission of three paragraphs in the section on disinfestation in the later edition.
7. *The Allocation of Tenancies,* Institute of Housing Managers, Housing Management Practice Pamphlet No. 1, 1962.
8. *Report of the Committee on Local Authority and Allied Personal Social Services,* Cmnd. 3703, HMSO, 1968.
9. Central Housing Advisory Committee, *op. cit.* (1969).
10. See *The Comprehensive Housing Service — Organisation and Functions,* Institute of Housing Managers, 1972.
11. See discussion in recent issues of the Institute of Housing Managers' *Housing Monthly;* e.g. Vol. 10, No. 1, July 1974.
12. Central Housing Advisory Committee, *Moving from the Slums,* Seventh Report of the Housing Management Sub Committee, HMSO, 1956.

13. *Ibid.*, p. 6.
14. *Ibid.*, p. 5.
15. Central Housing Advisory Committee, *op. cit.* (1969), p. 29.
16. Clare Ungerson, *op. cit.*, esp. Chap. 6.
17. 'Minimising Coercion' is the title of section xii of Macey and Baker's book, *op. cit.*, p. 210.
18. See Elizabeth Burney, *Housing On Trial: A Study of Immigrants and Local Government,* Oxford University Press for Institute of Race Relations, 1967.
19. Central Housing Advisory Committee, *op. cit.* (1969), p. 79ff.
20. The most thorough-going study of evidence for or against accusations of prejudice and discrimination in housing allocation in the slum clearance context is Christopher Duke, *Colour and Rehousing: A Study of Redevelopment in Leeds,* Institute of Race Relations, 1970.
21. See Sean Damer and Ruth Madigan, 'The Housing Investigator', *New Society,* Vol. 29, p. 226, 25th July 1974; also J. Tucker, *Honourable Estates,* Gollancz, 1966, esp. Chap. 5.
22. A useful discussion of this general issue is Olive Stevenson, *Claimant or Client? A Social Worker's View of the Supplementary Benefits Commission,* Allen and Unwin, 1973, esp. Chap. 2.
23. A recent study of bureaucratic behaviour argues that the discretion of the official cannot be eradicated from administrative procedures but that the imposition of standards inculcated through training can provide a measure of control over discretion by establishing the norms against which serious systematic deviations can be detected. See Michael J. Hill, *op. cit.,* Chap. 4.
24. D.N. Muchnick, *op. cit.,* p. 95.
25. Apart from the evidence mentioned by Bull, *op. cit.* (1967), that the available advice on welfare aspects of housing is inadequate there is a countervailing argument that the first requirement of local authority housing is that it should be effectively run as a business. See W.M. Brook, 'Housing – Humanity and Big Business', *Housing,* Vol. 4, No. 3, September 1968.
26. June Norris, *op. cit.*
27. D.N. Muchnick, *op. cit.,* p. 90.
28. Norris has argued that several offers of one property at a time does not present the applicant with a real choice:
    '... wherein does the choice lie? Not between alternatives, so that he can weigh up merits and demerits and choose the better (or if he sees it, the lesser evil). His choice is between accepting what is offered ... or refusing it. If he refuses it he does not know in any detail what will be offered to him next. His freedom of choice is therefore mainly illusory.' June Norris, *op. cit.,* p. 43. Norris's suggestion that two houses might be offered at the same time is touched on, but without clear guidance, in the Institute's practice notes:
    'To make two offers simultaneously may in some circumstances prove good policy.' Institute of Housing Managers, *op. cit.,* (1962), p. 7.
29. D.G. Bull, 'Housing Departments and Clearance Areas: Problems of Communication' *Social and Economic Administration,* Vol. 2, No. 4, October 1968.
30. Clare Ungerson, *op. cit.,* p. 90.
31. The term ideology is used with a wide variety of meaning. In another study of housing administration Harloe *et al.,* define ideology as 'a belief system about how society – or a significant part of it such as a housing market – does and should operate, about how it should distribute resources and "life chances".' M. Harloe, R. Isacharoff and R. Minns, *The Organisation*

of Housing: Public and Private Enterprise in London, Heinemann, 1974, p. 8.
32. For example in D. Foley, 'British Town Planning: One Ideology or Three?', *British Journal of Sociology,* Vol. XXI, No. 3, 1960.
33. Managers engaged in a 'professionalising strategy' may be regarded as attempting to influence *other people's* definitions of reality in a way which will justify the activities of the occupational group.
34. For an example of related work applying the concept of stereotype in the housing field see R.N. Morris and J. Mogey, *The Sociology of Housing,* Routledge, 1965, Chap. 1.
35. Clare Ungerson, *op. cit.,* p. 80.
36. P.M. Blau, 'Orientation toward Clients in a Public Welfare Agency', *Administrative Science Quarterly,* Vol. 5, 1960.
37. Detailed study of the 'interpretation' of residents' needs by housing staff is currently being undertaken in Birmingham. See John Lambert, Bob Blackaby and Chris Paris, 'Neighbourhood Politics and Housing Opportunities', *Proceedings of the Conference on Urban Change and Conflict,* Centre for Environmental Studies Conference Papers No. 14, 1975.
38. It must be stressed that the identification and subdivision of tasks is a theoretical convenience rather than a reflection of the way staff themselves see their jobs in practice — a set of categories imposed by the need to compare diverse organisational structures. In particular, it is unrealistic to expect the information gathering tasks of a housing visitor to exclude decision-making. The recording process by which family particulars, length of residence, rent-paying record and housing preferences are noted involves constant selection of some items and dismissal of others. Most important, some form of grading of applicants' housekeeping standards in the categories of office procedure (good/fair/poor or A.B.C.D.) is a standard part of most visitors' job. This may be a vitally important decision as a poor grading often severely restricts the applicant's access to new, or high standard, council housing or to a preferred area.
39. The clearance area in Tower Hamlets with which the present study was particularly concerned lay in the Spitalfields area of the borough. Experience of interviewing residents in this area showed that there was a special need for very careful interviewing, often requiring the help of an interpreter. For a general view of the slum clearance process in Tower Hamlets see E. Burney, *op. cit.,* Chap. IV.

5 HOUSING ALLOCATION IN DECENTRALISED SYSTEMS — LEEDS AND LIVERPOOL

It is the decentralised lettings procedure which principally distinguishes Leeds and Liverpool from the other three authorities which, at the time of interview, used local offices only for management of their stock. Leeds operated eighteen district offices, each one responsible for lettings, and Liverpool had nine. It was not possible to interview staff and establish procedure in detail in every office so interviews were confined to staff in those offices most likely to handle cases from the areas where our survey population lived.

Leeds

Under the Leeds system, initial home inspections and preliminary vetting of application forms was completed at head office and application forms then distributed to the area office within which the stated preference for rehousing was located.

Interviewers. Of the five authorities, Leeds placed the heaviest emphasis on initial home visits both as a source of information for guiding allocations and as a channel of information for residents. Five housing visitors (three women and two men) worked from the central office under the supervision of the chief assistant, slum clearance. He stressed that the visitors were free to organise their time to suit the needs of individual cases: 'As far as I'm concerned there is no limit to the length of the visit, it could be 1½ hours.' The ideal housing visitor was described as 'patient, understanding and prepared to go to great lengths to satisfy a person's need for information'. Housing visitors were expected to keep up-to-date on the housing available and to inspect new estates as they were completed. The application for tenancy listed municipal estates by postal district and also gave limited information about the levels of rent in flats and maisonettes and some details of tenancy conditions. The application form also included seven detailed questions establishing housing preferences both for area and type of accommodation — a more detailed approach than in any other of the five authorities.

This was required partly by the formal ruling that only one offer of accommodation would be made to each resident. Housing visitors appeared to have adopted a discussive approach to their task and were prepared to make several visits and evening appointments where necessary. Grading of applicants was informal, being based either on the categories of Good/Fair/Poor or A to C with variation between visitors. One housing visitor described 'a good B' as an average category sufficient to qualify a household for a new house if one was available. A lower category would only be offered a pre-war house in normal circumstances.[1] The significance of any grading depended heavily on the interpretation which district managers applied when allocating houses. Since eligibility for rehousing was liberally applied housing visitors were not encouraged to stress the investigatory aspects of their visit but to discuss rehousing alternatives fully. However, this did not necessarily involve a passive role for the housing visitors. The chief assistant expected them to discourage poor standard households from choosing new estates: 'You can't slot a very poor family into a brand new estate.'

Despite the emphasis on free discussion at the initial home interview conducted from the central office, home interviews were also undertaken by locally based staff in the district offices. District housing managers responsible for lettings reported that the categories used by housing visitors to grade applicants were often vague and provided a poor basis for allocation of applicants to an area where they would 'fit in'. In such cases, or on occasions when an applicant had a particularly poor assessment, the district housing manager might send out one of his own, locally based, welfare officers to make his own assessment rather than requesting an additional visit from central section housing visitors. This might be either to get 'a more impartial judgement' or to apply some sort of criteria which could be clearly understood by the district manager.

Office interviewing was largely a local matter. District managers were readily available for interviews on request and frequently invited applicants in for discussion, particularly after they had refused an offer of accommodation. As one district manager said, 'We are usually more successful with our second offer because we have had a chance of interviewing the person for ourselves.' District managers might also undertake home visits to applicants still occupying houses late on in the clearance of an area.

This system might best be described as one of duplication of the interviewer role. The organisation of the system and the interpretation of job requirements encouraged housing visitors to adopt a personal relationship with residents discussing their needs and preferences in full and sustaining contact by additional home visits where necessary. But

Chart IV. Leeds C.B.

	HOUSING VISITORS	DISTRICT HOUSING WELFARE OFFICERS	CENTRAL and LOCAL COUNTER CLERKS	DISTRICT HOUSING MANAGERS	CHIEF ASSISTANT SLUM CLEARANCE
Complete application form and report	Home visit. No appointment. Stress on details required to guide allocation officers. Office defines tasks as crucially important, case work nature. Allows sufficient flexibility and initiative to permit case worker definition by staff.				
Advise and inform applicants	Very full discussion of preferences and possibilities with comprehensive application form.				
Interview at special home or office visits	Standard revisits as clearance proceeds and on request of district officers. No provision for interviewing at central office.	Welfare officers may be asked by district managers to supplement housing visitors' record.		Visits to cases remaining late in clearance areas. Readily available for personal interviews.	
Answer routine office inquiries			Receive all standard inquiries centrally or locally. Locally pass on cases to district manager for interview.		

Task			
Grade Applicants	Not standardised. Good/fair/poor with variation between interviewers. Not very important.	Welfare officers may check central office grading at request of district manager.	Intervenes to check grading if central office grading is not clear.	All forms vetted at central office. Ineligible cases suspended until end of clearance area. Papers always sent to office of first preference.
Vet Applicants for suspension				
Decide household requirements				Classified by size of house required and filed alphabetically. Individual allocations involve carefully considered judgement rather than routine. Priority given by central section
Decide individual offers of housing				
Monitor refusals of offers	Check on refusals at request of district office.		Refusals interviewed at office and referred to central section if 'unreasonable'.	All difficult questions of priority and all cases of 'unreasonable' refusals referred to centre for decision. Loss of priority if refusal considered 'unreasonable'.

the lack of precise standardisation of information, particularly on grading, encouraged the district managers to initiate their own interviews.

Rules of Access and the Allocator role. Formally, eligible households were confined to those who had been resident in an area at date of confirmation; single men living in furnished accommodation were not eligible. In practice the department rehoused anyone who was still in residence when the area was ready for clearing. The principal restriction was the limit of only one offer of accommodation unless there were good grounds for refusing the first offer. The director of housing expected housing visitors to find out exactly where people wanted to go so that the first offer would be acceptable. This encouraged very close attention to the details of household needs by the district managers when making their allocations.

Before being passed to the district office of their choice, applicants' papers were vetted by the chief assistant, slum clearance, and ineligible cases temporarily suspended. Once applicants' papers were passed on to local offices the central office was involved only as a source of guidance on general questions of clearance area priority or particular cases of refusals of accommodation. As the applications were thenceforward handled by only one district office the initial choice of area was a very important decision under this system and seriously limited the range of possibilities for which an applicant might be considered.

The main advantage of decentralised lettings — a small file of applicants awaiting housing — means that the staff responsible for allocating housing can handle a good deal of information on applicants without depending heavily on the actual organisation of paper work to routinise individual decisions. In Leeds district offices, the district managers filed application forms in alphabetical sequence subdivided into sections according to number of bedrooms and house type required. The file of individual applicants for any house type and size of property available for letting was small enough for the manager to thumb through all applicants for that style of house and to balance their ages and requirements against priorities for clearance of their area and the length of time they had been awaiting rehousing. Because of the local background of district housing managers they were also likely to have a detailed knowledge of the particular house being let. A measure of the appreciation of local circumstances acquired by district housing staff was the comment of one manager that 'you have to make things socially harmonious. You have to have regard to the situation. For example, you can't put noisy men above a timid old lady.'

Despite the obvious care with which district managers matched applicants and houses there was a substantial proportion of refusals. Grounds for a 'reasonable' refusal were that the applicant had changed his mind about the type or location of house he would prefer or that he had realised that the fares to work would be too much for him. On the other hand, if a house was refused because it did not have a modern fireplace or if the manager felt that 'turning that one down means they're going to turn down the lot' it would be considered an 'unreasonable' refusal and would be referred to central office for advice. Despite the emphasis on acceptance of first offers which dictated many aspects of office procedure, there were some indications that consideration of offers by applicants was seen as a necessary part of the educative process for applicants. One district manager who regularly interviewed all applicants refusing offers argued that careful discussion with housing visitors was not necessarily adequate preparation for choosing a council house and accepted that it was reasonable in many cases for people to turn down their first offer because their original choice had been based on inadequate knowledge of the possibilities.

Under the Leeds system the allocator role was divided between central office and the district managers but the main burden of tasks fell on the local officers. Taking advantage of the relatively small scale of local operations, district managers were able to adopt a wide interpretation of their lettings responsibilities establishing a detailed and often personal knowledge of both applicants and available houses. The department had been organised on a decentralised basis since 1947 and the local office was seen as an important focus of contact and information. As the director of housing put it: 'the squire has gone, the doctor has gone and most people aren't bothered about the parson. The housing manager living and working among the people is an amalgam of these three worthies. People will go to the housing manager to discuss their problems.'

Liverpool C.B.

In Liverpool both lettings arrangements and slum clearance inspections were decentralised to district offices. Of the nine district housing management offices in the city only three were located in areas containing substantial numbers of houses likely to be demolished under slum clearance and at each of these a staff complement of four male CPO inspectors plus additional clerical staff were added to the normal recruitment. The three offices affected were North and South City

Centre and Walton/Club Moor. Interviews were undertaken with staff at each of these three district offices.[2]

Interviewers. The most important consequence of full decentralisation in Liverpool was a scaling down of the office situation so that staff responsible for home visits were part of a fairly small local team working in close proximity to each other and with a degree of informal overlap of task or interest which was missing in larger offices. The CPO inspectors working from the three central area offices were only a specialised section of the general office. Their involvement in other tasks than those formally allocated to them encouraged a wider interest in other aspects of office procedure which was likely to broaden their knowledge and experience of house letting arrangements. Concentration on a relatively small area of the city for which he was permanently responsible enabled an inspector to build up a detailed knowledge of his own patch.

Overall the emphasis in local offices stressed the purely administrative aspects of the home interview rather than its importance as a source of help and guidance for applicants. Details of family circumstances were particularly important because only families with children aged under 9 could expect to be offered a house rather than a flat; rent paying record and grading were also important items for administration of the lettings arrangements. For the inspectors, grading clearly featured as a prominent part of the job. The standard grading categories were A, B, C and D and it was normal practice for 'Cs' or 'Ds' to be excluded from *new* council housing. Inspectors reported that most people fell into the 'B' or 'A/B' category. Households graded 'C' were those who, in the inspector's opinion, 'haven't really made an attempt to better themselves'. General untidiness in the house was not thought to warrant a C grading. As one inspector put it: 'For C the bedding would have to be dirty and in a D your feet stick to the floor. An A would be given only for a place with fitted carpets and really clean.' Households receiving low grading were often visited again, to see whether they had made any improvement in their housekeeping standards and warranted a higher grading.

Discussion of preferences was administratively important in a decentralised system where applications had subsequently to be distributed to local offices for letting. But the inspectors' interpretation of their job requirements in this respect was a good deal wider than that required merely for administrative convenience. There was no limit put on the number of offers which could be made to each applicant and overall office procedure did not emphasise the need for detailed discussion of household preferences. Nevertheless, inspectors regarded the discussion of rehousing possibilities as an occasion to inform and guide applicants' preferences. 'We suggest what it might be reasonable for people to choose. For example, we've got to discourage them from asking for 1- and 4-bedroom accommodation in the central city.' Although receipt of an application form in advance of the visit encouraged applicants to think about their preferences, inspectors reported the need to press people to specify a precise locale rather than just 'Liverpool 5' or 'Everton'. At a second visit after six months inspectors would have knowledge of an applicant's refused offers to guide further discussion of housing preferences.

It was clear from discussion with inspectors that they were often able to pursue an interest in individual cases right through from initial inspection to final letting of a house. It is this last feature of the Liverpool system which was most unusual. The ledger of available properties at each district office was open for inspection by office staff; inspectors were able to approach the district manager if they saw a particular property which they knew would suit an applicant in one of their areas and, with his agreement, to take out details of that house to offer to them. Alternatively, when a clearance area was almost empty or was urgently required for demolition and redevelopment, inspectors might be asked by the district manager to take out an available house on offer and try to find someone in the clearance area who would like to move into it. This meant that the house could be offered several times in the same day to help clear remaining residents. In this way the staff who made first contact with applicants might sustain contact with those who required rehousing in the area covered by their district office through to the stage of accepting a council house.

In this respect Liverpool permitted the greatest cohesion of the interviewer role. All home visits were made by the CPO inspectors. Callers at the office would have a good chance of talking to their initial inspector if they wished. However, only a proportion of residents could be rehoused locally. The rest either chose, or were obliged, to move to a house elsewhere. Application forms for these people were sent to the district office covering the area of their choice. As residents were instructed to make all further enquiries concerning their application to the office where their papers were lodged, these people were discouraged from calling at the office where they might see the inspector who first called on them.

Chart V. Liverpool C.B.

	INSPECTORS	COUNTER CLERKS	OFFICE MANAGER	DISTRICT HOUSING MANAGER
Complete application form and report	Home visit. No appointment. Stress on proof of residence and arrears of rent.	Defined by office in largely bureaucratic terms. But staff themselves taking case work approach.		
Advise and inform applicants	Information on overspill whenever relevant. Discussion of preferences fairly full but anticipates more realistic discussion at second visit.			
Interview at special home or office visits	Second visits standard after 6 months or when clearance nearing completion. Office interviews not important but inspector may be involved.			Especially at Walton and South City Centre District managers frequently interview special cases.
Answer routine office inquiries	Occasional work on inquiry counter as available.	All grades of staff work on counter as available.		

Grade Applicants	A to D, important part of home visit.	
Vet Applicants for suspension		Standard vetting procedure suspends ineligible and arrears cases. Papers sent to district office requested.
Decide household requirements	Summary of requirements on basis of household size and house type.	Only families with children under 9 get *houses*. Given priority in allocation.
Decide individual offers of housing	Occasional interventions to secure particular property for known applicants.	Routine allocations with priority given by need for site clearance. Otherwise by length of residence in clearance area. District manager does all allocations in S. City Centre and checks all at Walton.
Monitor refusals of offers	Reasons for refusal checked at second visits.	

Rules of access and the Allocator role. Variation of procedure between district offices was greater for the tasks of allocation than it was on the interviewing side. In particular, the involvement of the district manager in allocations varied from advice on particular cases referred to him to complete control of all allocations that were made. On the other hand, arrangements for vetting application forms and passing them on to the district office of choice were fairly standardised.

Initial scrutiny of forms was the job of the office manager (distinct from the district housing manager). Three aspects of the applicant's characteristics were given most attention. Eligibility was determined by the date of confirmation of the CPO and all households moving in after this date were sent a letter suggesting that they should look for their own alternative accommodation. However, most of these households would be offered accommodation if they were still in the area towards the end of clearance. Families with children aged slightly under 9 were set aside for priority treatment. Unless they were offered a house quickly and the child passed its ninth birthday the family would lose its chance of being offered a house and would only be eligible for a flat. To avoid families feeling unjustly treated in this way the office manager might ring the district office of their choice to speed up the offer of a house. The third aspect of vetting requiring most attention was checking on arrears of rent for those cases who were former corporation tenants. Cases who had left a council house in arrears would be called into the office for issue of a rent book to pay off arrears before they could be offered accommodation. Several other features of the application form might lead to temporary suspension of a case. For example, lack of proof of residence noted by the inspector or doubt over the number of families living in the house. One office manager estimated that the proportion of 'suspended' cases whose papers would not enter the normal office procedure for allocation might be as high as 20 per cent in areas of multi-occupation.

Distribution of papers to district offices allowed office managers to try guiding applicants' choices by 'cod-offers' or 'try-ons'. Although in principle the papers would go to the district office of first choice the office manager might decide to send them to the office of second or third choice if he thought that this would lead to quicker rehousing. Some dissatisfaction was reported from people who objected to their papers being sent to a district they had not chosen but one office manager remarked that it was obviously not understood by these people that, in a situation of unlimited offers, they had lost nothing.

For lettings, each of the three central district offices dealt both with applicants currently living in their area and those living elsewhere who were hoping to move to a council house in the area. In one of the three offices the office manager made all allocations without reference to the district housing manager. At a second office all allocations were checked by the district manager and at the third office the district manager made all allocations himself in consultation with his inspector on local cases. Working from a card index system priority in all areas was given by date of CPO and within CPO areas according to the urgency of an area for development which was set by the programme co-ordinator under the director of housing. As there was no limit on the number of offers made to each family reasons for refusal were recorded only as a guide to inspectors making second visits.

Working in a relatively small area of the city enabled lettings staff to gain a close acquaintance with their housing stock. The close involvement of CPO inspectors in all aspects of office procedure enabled them to advise managers on particular cases and to make additional home visits to local clearance areas where necessary. Except in unusual cases where CPO inspectors allocated houses the allocator role was filled mainly by one category of staff who undertook both the initial scrutiny of papers and detailed lettings. Staff letting houses often took advantage of their localised responsibilities to operate a very personalised approach to making offers. This advantage was lost, however, where households opted for rehousing in an area which was not local as their papers were then passed on to another office.

A Comparison of Departmental Styles

Any static comparison of the operational styles of five housing departments is bound to suffer from the arbitrariness of selecting one point in time and freezing the evolution of ever-changing organisations. It is bound also to be unjust to some extent. In the present case, concentration on the system existing in 1970-71 was required by an overall research strategy relating residents' experience of the clearance process to the procedures in operation at the time of survey.

The criteria of evaluation of different systems, discussed in the first section of the previous chapter, place particular stress on two aspects of organisation which have also been promoted by other writers — continuity and self-determination. The broad precept of humane treatment requires that the system through which their rehousing is organised permits individual applicants to be treated as 'persons' rather than being merely processed as disembodied 'particulars'. It is argued that this is best accomplished if the system permits continuity of contact through the stages of clearance. Hence the stress on cohesion or fragmentation of interviewer and allocator roles in the previous sections. Further, treatment of applicants in personal terms requires that their particular needs, preferences and aspirations are not ignored during the rehousing process; self-determination requires that the outcome of rehousing is determined to the fullest extent possible by the interests of the applicant rather than the interests of the bureaucracy itself.

Two alternative conceptions of applicants which were implicitly adopted by at least some staff in the authorities examined, encapsulate these values. First, residents may be regarded as 'customers' requiring a service. This means recognising that they can make an adequate appraisal of their own requirements and need only further information on which to base a choice between alternatives. The 'customer' requires a service which will answer his queries, display as wide a range of alternatives as possible with their price tags (rent and likely delay for different types of property), pays due attention to his choice when he has made it and which does not penalise him when he changes his mind or shows himself to be particularly choosey. Second, the minority of residents who are ill-equipped to handle the decisions and disruptions of rehousing may best be regarded as 'clients' of a welfare service requiring sympathetic help, guidance and support. A common factor in both the 'customer' and 'client' conceptions of residents is the implication of sustained personal contact between housing staff and the individual resident. An ideal of 'personal service' implies that the customer is best served by the continued attention of one member of staff until his requirements are satisfied. The 'case work relationship' again implies the personal attention of one person able to build up and act upon a full picture of the client's needs and to establish a personal relationship strong enough to sustain the client through a period of difficulty. Both models involve maintaining the resident's identity during the process of rehousing and paying due attention to individuals' own preferences or needs.

A form of organisation of tasks which does not permit one category of staff to fulfill all aspects of the interviewer role or the allocator role is unlikely to establish the sustained personal relationship between staff and applicants which is required by either of these models. But a coherent distribution of tasks does not guarantee a personalised style of operation unless the ideological context of the department encourages staff manning interviewer or allocator roles to adopt a 'personal' approach to applicants with whom they have contact. This is an independent element of the system which closely reflects the views

Chart VI. A Summary of Departmental Styles

Area	Interviewer Role	Allocator Role	Departmental ideology
Newcastle	*Divided* responsibility between home and office interviewers limits continuity.	*Restricted* — fulfilled by one man. But heavy work-load encourages routinised job interpretation.	Stress on autonomy of applicants implies 'customer' orientation.
Manchester	*Fragmented* between investigators, home visitors, school and office interviews.	*Fragmented* between classification officer, lettings and counter staff. Heavy work-load and routinised procedure.	Limited prevailing interpretation of departmental responsibility.
Tower Hamlets	*Restricted* role due to narrow job interpretation rather than subdivision of tasks.	*Duplicated* by intervention of housing officer in lettings. Small work-load permits acquaintance with individual cases.	Restricted interpretation of departmental responsibilities minimising the load on housing resources. Paternalistic view of residents but without provision for case work arrangements.
Leeds	*Duplicated* role. Both central and local interviewers (and local managers) adopting customer/client view of residents with sustained contact.	*Divided* responsibility between local and central offices.	Stress on full information and discussion and return visits support customer view. But strict limit on offers inconsistent with customer orientation.
Liverpool	*Cohesive* role covering all interviewing (and some allocation tasks). Continuity encouraged by localised organisation.	*Diffuse.* Decentralised clearance inspections and frequent circulation of papers between district offices reduces continuity. But cohesive role *within* any district office.	Routinised view of job requirements apparently modified by the experience of localised letting and slum clearance system to accommodate a case work orientation by inspectors.

of senior and middle management who 'set the tone' of the department. In Chart VI the salient features of rules, organisation and ideology are summarised for each of the five authorities.

In Newcastle the strict division of responsibility between home and office interviewers restricted continuity of contact. With the back-up of office interviews home visitors tended to limit the discussive aspects of their job and stress the investigatory aspect. But office interviewers themselves tended to exploit the transfer of cases, further reducing continuity. In the process of allocation a heavy work-load encouraged a routinised job interpretation.

The system in operation at the time of survey was in many ways in conflict with the ideals expressed by management. At both levels of management there was a high level of commitment to the housing management profession and to training and managers actively promoted a 'customer' view of applicants. The director of housing explained the policy of unlimited offers explicitly in these terms:

> we can't say what is suitable for other people, suitable is not just a question of number of rooms and location. We must not dismiss what appear to be whims . . . People are seriously thinking about housing all during the clearance period. They make up their minds over a period of time.

Similar views were echoed at lower levels in the department and encouraged support for proposed new arrangements for home visiting. This ideological commitment heightened awareness of the unfortunate division of the interviewing role between lettings assistants and interviewing officers and senior managers had considered plans for amalgamating the two groups.

In Manchester the housing department had achieved independence from the architect's department only two years previously and very few staff were professionally qualified. Senior and middle managers did not present a clearly articulated work ideology. Although senior managers talked with approval of 'the Cullingworth approach' there was little evidence of commitment amongst staff involved in interviewing to a more extended personal approach. The fragmented organisational structure and application of complex rules dominated the style of the department. This fragmentation itself reflected the accretion of tasks and specialised sections intended to fill gaps in the system. Bull's report in 1967 had recommended local sub offices and more effective home interviews[3] and the information points and home visitors had since become a standard part of the system. But these innovations were superimposed on the old system and did very little to change its basic style. Within the Manchester system lack of continuity worked against a personal style of operation and there was no dominant countervailing ideology encouraging either customer or client orientation amongst staff. Strict rules on eligibility and offers combined with a very large, centralised work load and no countervailing management ideology produced a heavily routinised system.

A simple organisation of responsibilities and small-scale operation in Tower Hamlets were not matched by an ideology which would lead to an effectively personalised system. The potential burden on the housing department of the London housing situation was such that the responsibilities of the department were minimised by eligibility rules and restricted offers. A minimal interpretation of the job requirements of housing visitors and emphasis on the pattern of refusals rather than careful attention to preferences further restricted the potential of the Tower Hamlets system to accommodate individual treatment of residents.

The only qualified member of staff — the housing officer herself — accepted responsibility for personal involvement in tasks at all levels of administration rather than attempting to motivate all levels of staff by an explicit ideology. This practice itself reflected a basically paternalistic orientation towards the tasks of housing management and allocation.

Both the decentralised systems had the advantages of scaling down the operations of lettings staff and thereby opening up the possibility of treating cases with more individual attention than is possible in larger systems. The Leeds system, in which organisation of home visits was still based on central office, had the most fully developed ideology of individualised treatment of any of the five authorities. The director of housing asserted the need for training at all levels: 'Housing manager's assistants [rent collectors] are the front men. They must have an attitude of mind which cuts out the rule book mentality.' Deadlines for clearance of particular areas were not important compared with the need to match household preferences closely and both at the district offices and slum clearance section central office, management asserted the importance of humane treatment of residents. Referring to households left behind at the end of a clearance area one district officer remarked sympathetically: 'You've got to remember that these are people. They've lived there twenty years. All their friends and memories are there.'

But the job interpretation that this approach encouraged — stressing careful attention to individual circumstances of residents and full discussion of preferences — was dissipated in part by the essential drawback of a decentralised lettings system, that is, the circulation of papers between different district offices if the individual applicant changed preferences. In addition, the rationale for close individual attention was inconsistent with a 'customer' rather than a 'client' orientation. Housing staff expected to make one or, at most, two offers of housing. It was assumed that the investigations carried out by housing visitors and the information which they collected and gave out provided an adequate basis for lettings staff then to decide unequivocally what was best for each applicant.

In Liverpool a well-developed personalised approach to the problems of slum clearance and housing allocation appeared to have been fostered particularly by the introduction of a decentralised system and the influence of professional training rather than reflecting the particular ideology of the housing manager. He presented himself as an essentially practical man, sceptical of 'sociologists' and 'social' problems.

In a decentralised system of nine district offices there was a good deal of variation in approach. However, at the level of middle management, staff stressed the importance of a personal approach based more on an awareness of welfare considerations than on a 'customer' model of applicants. One district manager had become involved with a community development project in his area. Another stressed that 'If you forget you're dealing with the lives of people you're not entitled to this job'. The decentralised system and consequent small scale of operations permitted staff to follow through their commitment to a personal approach on their own initiative and the localised interest of the district offices encouraged a personalised job interpretation despite the overall bureaucratic manner of a very large housing department. Commitment of staff to a personalised approach was suggested by liberal rules on eligibility and unlimited offers.

There are two important general comments which can be made about the five authorities. First, they were all, except Tower Hamlets, large organisations. Liverpool, with 96,000 council houses in 1971 was the third biggest housing authority in the country and Leeds, Manchester and Newcastle were all in the top ten. Inevitably the scale of operation of organisations of this size places some limitations on the potential for a personal service. A centralised system as large as Manchester processing some hundreds of offers of accommodation each week is bound to introduce a narrower division of labour than in Tower

Hamlets where only 40 to 50 offers were made weekly. The obvious conclusion is decentralisation of lettings and interviewing and this was in the process of being adopted in Manchester. On the evidence of this study the 'best' authorities were Leeds and Liverpool where decentralisation had already been introduced. But size alone is not responsible for restricting the possibilities of personalised treatment. The organisation in Tower Hamlets was comparable in size with a district office in Liverpool but the job interpretations of staff and the manner in which lettings were organised produced a restricted and routinised departmental style.

Second, it was striking how, despite the advice of official reports and the emphasis of research studies, very little attention was paid to training or induction courses for home or office interviewers. At best, most housing visitors spent a week or so learning the ropes by working with a colleague. Many switched straight from other duties such as rent collection. Only in Leeds was training substantial with a period in the head office learning the operation of the slum clearance section before going out to work for a month with an experienced housing visitor. For the most part, therefore, interviewing staff were ill-equipped to exercise the discretion which can effectively counteract the routinisation of bureaucracy.

The limitations of bureaucracy are perhaps more serious at the stage of rehousing than at any other stage in the clearance process. Rehousing from a slum clearance area may provide the only opportunity that a household has of securing a house satisfying both their needs and their aspirations. If transfers and exchanges from council property are not easy to arrange the move may literally be 'the chance of a lifetime'.[4]

Following Blau's findings[5] one would expect commitment to clients or customers to be greatest where the rules of allocation are simple and an ideology of service is clearly articulated by managers. But, on the whole, housing departments do not provide this sort of work context. The level of professional training is low and the basis for group cohesion based on an ideal of service therefore generally weak. Complex rules of access prevail in most cases. In addition a common preoccupation with property rather than persons provides the background assumptions of housing management in general. The stress on 'protection of property' which is the guiding principle of compulsory purchase and compensation has its equivalent in allocation procedures based on grading, moral desert and a 'career pattern' for model tenants. The Cullingworth Committee reported that: 'we were surprised to find some housing authorities who took up a moralistic attitude towards applicants: the underlying philosophy seemed to be that council tenancies were to be given only to those who "deserved" them and the "most deserving" should get the best houses.'[6] In interviews with housing department staff a moralistic attitude was frequently made concrete in terms of a statement to the effect that 'it wouldn't be right to let inadequate tenants wreck good properties'. Management problems, of vandalism, rent arrears and the sheer demand of the backlog of applicants reinforce the moralistic interpretation of access to council housing which focuses attention on procedural rules rather than the personal requirements of individual applicants.

Housing management further restricts the legitimacy of personal commitment by staff by maintaining a partially covert system which puts staff attempting a personal approach in a position of bad faith. The public health inspector who avoids giving the details of his programme of clearance does so on the plausible argument of avoiding planning blight and of not anticipating a quasi-judicial decision. But secrecy about selection procedures for council housing has no equivalent justification. 'It should go without saying that details of selection schemes should be freely available. Yet we were surprised to find that over a quarter of the local authorities in our sample treated their detailed selection schemes as being confidential.'[7] Although, for slum clearance applicants, the points system applicable to the waiting list is not relevant, a general hesitancy in publicising selection methods helps set the tone of rehousing activities. On details of grading schemes housing departments were particularly sensitive with some notable exceptions. Even where the existence of grading itself was not denied by the department it was common practice for housing visitors to dissemble when inspecting people's homes. One described how he always looked up at the ceiling when asking to look around the house so that people thought he was inspecting the property. Another recorded grading details in a special note book so that applicants had no chance of seeing his comments on their application forms.

The 'closed' character of housing management can be further exacerbated by the actual physical arrangements of public reception areas in housing departments. Particularly in offices where rent collection and general complaints and inquiries are carried on in the same building the need for security works directly against the provision of informal, welcoming surroundings which might encourage open discussion. At its worst a local housing department office resembles an embattled fortress with wire mesh grilles at all windows, impregnable doors and an insurmountable inquiry counter. Even where security is less immediately important the inquiry counter can often function as a barrier between the public and private regions of the department and may explicitly be manned as a barricade heading off demands for access to managerial staff who could give definitive decisions on individual cases.

These important characteristics of the general style of housing management reinforce those tendencies in a bureaucratic organisation which work against commitment to applicants and help to maintain distance between staff and public.

NOTES

1. For comparison see Christopher Duke, *op. cit.*, p. 56.
2. A description of the Liverpool system when in transition to full decentralisation is given in D.N. Muchnick, *op. cit.*, p. 88ff.
3. D.G. Bull, *op. cit.* (1967), p. 170.
4. One respondent in Liverpool had exchanged her modern flat with an aunt living in a slum clearance area. This gave her a chance of being offered a council house when she was rehoused instead of a multi-storey flat. She saw no prospect of getting a house through the transfer system.
5. P.M. Blau, *op. cit.*
6. Central Housing Advisory Committee, *op. cit.* (1969), p. 32.
7. *Ibid.*, p. 26.

6 RESIDENTS' KNOWLEDGE OF THE SLUM CLEARANCE PROCESS

The appraisal of administrative procedures set out in the three previous chapters is continued in the present chapter by considering direct evidence of residents' knowledge and comprehension of the process affecting their lives. Reporting in 1969 the Cullingworth committee reasserted the need for adequate information which had been stressed thirteen years earlier in *Moving from the Slums*.[1] The committee reported that they had received:

> a great deal of critical comment on the adequacy of information, the difficulties facing households who could not find out when they were to be rehoused, the apparent shroud of secrecy which often surrounds selection procedures, and the lack of advice on what alternatives were open to those in need.[2]

This criticism of the existing practices of local authority departments is echoed in many other studies. Most researchers, whether or not they began with information needs as a major object of inquiry, have been impressed by the extent of ignorance and misinformation. Wilkinson and Sigsworth, reporting a survey concentrating on attitudes to moving, felt obliged to comment on the 'uncertainty and anxiety' resulting from the ignorance which existed in their survey areas in Leeds.[3] Bull's study of Manchester which began as an investigation of the need for welfare services in clearance areas concluded that 'the first improvement that needs to be introduced for clearance occupants is *not* social work for the few, but information for them all'.[4] In their report on slum clearance in 1974 Shelter commented: 'One of the most frequent complaints that one hears from people living in clearance areas is that there is little information available to them about what is going on.'[5] A recent research report from Glasgow quotes one respondent who said:

> Suddenly you get a letter to say you're moving. That's all you hear. You don't know when, or what's happening, and suddenly you notice that your place is not getting repaired. But you're still paying away rents. Then a burst pipe remains burst.

To me the worst thing is the lack of information.
They don't tell you anything.[6]

In response to the widespread dissatisfaction with available information many community action organisations have set up information and advice centres of one sort or another[7] and local and national community action journals have consistently instructed readers on their rights during the clearance process.[8]

Four principal lines of argument have been used in justification of more comprehensive information. The first is simply satisfaction of the felt need which has so impressed researchers in the field and is well documented in works cited. Second, improved information has been urged on grounds of public relations. Norris, in particular stressed that 'only if [the local authority] can convince its clients that its difficulties are genuine and not manufactured to spite them will it escape their hostility'.[9] Fuller information about clearance procedure and available housing would educate applicants to an appreciation of the limitations on their choice of housing and establish the legitimacy of the procedures followed. Jennings similarly argued that better information would reduce exasperation and resentment against the local authority.[10]

A third line of argument justifies better information as a prerequisite of meaningful choice. Particularly when offers of accommodation are strictly limited a meaningful choice from the complete available range is only possible where information is both comprehensive and clearly understood. While most writers on the subject have argued that housing staff must therefore be fully briefed on all aspects of the available stock, some have suggested that choice will only be meaningful where information is presented as concretely as possible through exhibitions or organised trips to housing estates.[11]

Finally, improved information has been urged as an essential basis for public participation and greater resident involvement in the redevelopment process. Bull, in particular, developed this approach.[12] The Cullingworth Committee approached the whole issue of advice, information and publicity, emphasising their support for the principle of public participation embodied in the Town and Country Planning Act 1968[13] and the emphasis on information in community action literature stems from a strategy of extending community control over the redevelopment process.[14]

Whatever the justifying arguments for more information they have inevitably directed attention to the part played by the officials responsible for managing the clearance process. Although in many cases it is local authority planners who have borne the brunt of popular and academic criticism the previous chapters indicate that the role of town clerks, PHIs and housing staff is far more relevant.

In this chapter the stages of the clearance process are considered in temporal sequence and the extent of residents' knowledge of key items of information is investigated in turn. Whereas knowledge and comprehension of the early stages of clearance is discussed for the sample as a whole the final section presents an analysis of residents' experience of the housing visitor by area to provide further material by which the relative strengths and weaknesses of the systems discussed in Chapters 4 and 5 may be evaluated.

One difficulty of such an approach is the problem of recall. Residents were asked to express opinions about events in the past or officials whose visits were long since over. The total time elapsing from initial inspection to CPO confirmation is normally two or three years for opposed orders. The CPOs in all fifteen survey areas were opposed and the timescale for each area is given in Chapter 3. By midsummer 1970 over three years had elapsed in some areas since the first visit of the PHI and at least 18 months had elapsed in most areas. As the survey included questions on the activities of the PHI it therefore covered a very long period of recall. But apart from the visit of the PHI the significant events in the clearance process from the residents' point of view follow the submission of a CPO to the Secretary of State. In all but two areas this had taken place less than eighteen months previously. In addition, the issues may have been reactivated in people's minds by the subsequent PLI and CPO confirmation and by visits to virtually all households from a housing department visitor within a few weeks of the field work. Interviewers were also briefed with a list of dates on which key events took place and were instructed to probe replies carefully before accepting that respondents had correctly identified the event or official in question. Further, the often bizarre behaviour of PHIs making an inspection helped to fix events in respondents' memories. An internal inspection usually means the PHI measuring rooms, testing walls for dampness with a meter, flushing the lavatory, jumping up and down on floors and stair treads to test their soundness and even rolling marbles to test whether surfaces are true. Many respondents were quick to identify the PHIs visit by reference to some such aspect of his behaviour despite the lapse of many months. In these circumstances and given the high level of interest which residents show in the information which does come their way, respondents' recall of the events investigated is likely to have been generally valid.

Official Visits and the Public Enquiry as Sources of Information

Public Health Inspector and Form 26

The PHI normally inspects all houses in a clearance scheme but the character of an inspection varies from area to area. In three of the survey authorities, Newcastle, Manchester and Liverpool, the PHI undertook a detailed inspection of all houses lasting between 40 minutes and one hour for each house. In Leeds and Tower Hamlets detailed inspections were undertaken only for properties which were the subject of objections.

This difference in local practice was reflected in the proportions in each survey area recalling the visit of the PHI. Overall the visit was recalled by 66 per cent of respondents but the variation was substantial from 32 per cent in Leeds and 44 per cent in Tower Hamlets to nearly 80 per cent in Liverpool.

Table 9. Recall of Public Health Inspector by area

Area	Per cent recalling PHI %	Base
Newcastle	72	161
Leeds	32	145
Manchester	56	135
Liverpool	78	192
Tower Hamlets	44	131
Pool	73	783
All areas	66	1547

Amongst respondents recalling the visit of the PHI there was a strong contrast between their opinions of inspectors' technical competence and their opinions of his helpfulness as a source of information. Whilst 72 per cent of all respondents recalling the inspection felt that the PHI had spent enough time to do a thorough job over half made critical comments on the lack of information available from inspectors. One quarter felt that the PHI definitely withheld information from residents and a further 14 per cent said that he was himself ill-informed. Not surprisingly the level of comprehension of the PHI's task was correspondingly low.

The basic purpose of the visit of the PHI is to determine whether the condition of a house is such as to make it statutorily unfit for human habitation. Only 16 per cent of respondents who remembered the visit of the PHI explained its purpose in this way. A further 10 per cent thought that he was concerned with compensation or well-maintained payments, which was true only very indirectly, and 29 per cent said merely that his visit was in connection with clearance. Altogether, therefore, only 55 per cent understood the purpose of the visit though in most cases only in very general terms. No doubt some of the 20 per cent who said that the PHI came to inspect conditions realised that this was connected with clearance but they gave no indication that they knew why he did so. In retrospect, it was fairly obvious to residents that the PHI had been concerned with clearance but few people seemed to understand more than this bare fact.

Table 10. Understood purpose of Public Health Inspector's Visit

Understood purpose of the visit	Per cent stating each purpose %
To decide fitness	16
About compensation	10
About clearance	29
To inspect conditions	20
Other reasons	6
Don't know	20
Base	1007

In summary, residents' perceptions of the PHI's role clearly reflected the heavy emphasis on technical aspects which was remarked in Chapter 3. But there was clear resentment amongst many residents that an official who claims the right to spend maybe an hour making a detailed inventory of housing conditions in their homes should give so little information in return.

Although most residents could expect to receive an official visit from a PHI at the beginning of the clearance process only the minority of residents who were also owner occupiers received statutory notices. In the survey areas only 28 per cent fell into this category (see Table A8, Appendix A).

The most important of the notices sent to owner occupiers is Form 26, the notice of making a CPO and its submission to the Secretary of State. At the time of survey, for an owner occupier making no objection

Residents' Knowledge of the Slum Clearance Process

to the CPO, Form 26 could be the only written information he received from an official source before receiving a copy of the order after it had been confirmed. Form 26 informs the owner that his house is included in a CPO and whether the local authority have classified it as fit or unfit; it also includes notes about objections and compensation.[15]

The great majority of owner occupiers, 86 per cent, remembered receiving Form 26 and the notes but the majority of those who remembered it had a low opinion of its value. As many as 64 per cent said that it had not told them anything about clearance which they did not know before and only 18 per cent said they had definitely found it useful. Many of those who had found Form 26 useful said that this was because it had told them officially that their house was included in a clearance scheme, though most had already heard unofficially. Very few said that they had learned anything about compensation or other matters dealt with in Form 26 which they did not already know. However, from the replies given to other questions it is difficult to accept that many of these respondents really were well-informed. Rather, it seems likely that most realised that Form 26 stated that their house was included in a clearance scheme, which they already knew, but failed to appreciate that it also contained a good deal more information about compensation, objections and so on. Indeed, some of those who had learned nothing admitted that this was because Form 26 was too difficult to understand.

Even the explanatory notes about objections and compensation which are attached to Form 26 were found difficult to understand by most respondents. (Table 11). A fifth thought that the notes were very difficult to understand and 12 per cent found them fairly difficult. A third said that they did not even try to understand them, but sent Form 26 straight to their solicitor or other professional adviser. Over half the owner occupiers who remembered receiving Form 26 had, therefore, found the explanatory notes very difficult to understand or had not tried to understand them. These answers may account for some of the confusion about compensation among owner occupiers, a matter with which the notes deal in some detail. Confusion was compounded because the notes in use at the time of survey were out of date and dealt with the situation before the Housing Act 1969 altered the basis of compensation for most owner occupiers.

Apart from the obvious point that Form 26 needed bringing up to date, these findings suggest that it should also be made more intelligible to the ordinary owner occupier without specialist knowledge. As an important stage in the process of compulsory purchase Form 26 must set out legal rights precisely, but additional explanations in simple language are required. Statutory notices may adequately meet the needs of landlords to whom property management is a business but they seem to be inadequate for the growing proportion of owner occupiers in areas affected by slum clearance.

Table 11. Assessment of difficulty of understanding Form 26 notes

Degree of Difficulty	Per cent stating each degree of difficulty %
Very difficult	19
Fairly difficult	12
Not difficult at all	27
Didn't try — sent to solicitor, etc.	34
Don't know	8
Base	365

The Public Local Inquiry and After

Apart from giving property owners an opportunity to argue their case the PLI can also act as a general source of information for all residents, whether or not they object. But there was substantial variation in the proportions who were aware of the PLI depending on whether or not they were owner occupiers and whether or not they had objected to the CPO. Whilst all objecting owner occupiers remembered the inquiry only three-quarters of the remaining owner occupiers and half of the tenants did so. Further, whilst virtually all objectors heard of the inquiry in advance of it taking place, 17 per cent of non-objectors and 23 per cent of tenants only heard about it afterwards. These differences can be related to the sources of information available to different categories of resident. Objectors receive a personal notice of the time and place of the PLI from the Department but other residents have to rely on public notices. Notices are put up in the street in areas covered by a CPO and local authorities have been asked to inform the press about inquiries[16] but they are not actually advertised in local newspapers.

Residents were asked how they had first heard of the PLI (Table 12). The main source of information for objectors, mentioned by 65 per cent, was a letter from the council or Ministry, in most cases the personal notice from the Ministry. As all objectors should have received

Residents' Knowledge of the Slum Clearance Process 131

this notice it is perhaps surprising that the proportion was not even higher. Substantial numbers of other respondents also mentioned letters: most non-objecting owner occupiers were probably referring to Form 26, which mentioned the PLI in general terms. Tenants were probably thinking of the special letters about well-maintained payments which often referred to the inquiry in connection with the need for the house to be viewed by the inspector. For non-objectors and for tenants the most important source of information was friends, neighbours and relatives, mentioned by 22 per cent of non-objectors and 34 per cent of tenants. Newspapers were also an important source of information. In general, the crucial distinction was between objectors, who were directly informed of the PLI, and others who relied much more on informal channels of information.

Table 12. Source of first information about the Public Local Inquiry by tenure and whether objected

Source of first information about PLI	Objecting owner occupiers %	Other owner occupiers %	Tenants %	All residents %
Newspapers	14	18	24	21
Friends, neighbours or relatives	–	22	34	28
Landlord or agent	10	7	2	4
Letter from council or MHLG	65	28	18	25
Notice in street	10	12	14	13
Other	1	8	7	7
Don't know	–	6	2	3
Base	72	261	571	904

Very few of the people who had heard about the PLI actually attended; only 15 per cent of the total and less than half of the objectors themselves. Whilst the absence of many objectors can be related to the fact that 63 per cent were represented at the inquiry by a solicitor or agent the generally low level of interest of other groups seems to have stemmed from a fatalistic or cynical view of the PLI.[17] Only a quarter of all residents thought the PLI gave people a chance to influence events (Table 13). Owner occupiers who did not lodge an objection were the most dismissive of the PLI; 64 per cent thought that inquiries could not influence events compared with 57 per cent of tenants and 46 per cent of objecting owner occupiers.

Table 13. Opinion of whether Public Local Inquiries give people a chance of influencing what happens by tenure and whether objected

Opinion of PLI	Objecting owner occupiers %	Other owner occupiers %	Tenants %	All residents %
Can influence what happens	33	22	24	24
Cannot influence what happens	46	64	57	58
Don't know	21	13	20	18
Base	72	255	553	880

These views are perhaps understandable when the great majority of CPOs are confirmed without substantial modification. However, the tone of replies suggests that many people did not realise that the proposals of the local authority were open to challenge at the inquiry. Over three-quarters of those who said that inquiries did not give them an opportunity of influencing events thought that this was because the authorities — council or government — always get their own way regardless of the opposition of citizens. Neither did residents who attended the PLI find it useful as a source of information; only a fifth said that they had learned anything new about clearance.

Objections were made in respect of 31 per cent of owner occupied houses though not all these were recalled by the respondents; some were made by other interested parties such as mortgagees.[18] By far the most important way in which objecting owner occupiers found out that they could object was from Form 26, which was mentioned by over half; professional advisors were also important.

Objectors can seek to have a house excluded from the CPO altogether or, if it is unfit, merely reclassified. The second is usually a more realistic objective in that it is rarely practical not to demolish an individual fit house in a generally unfit area. Most of the houses on which objections were made had been classified as unfit and in most cases the aim was only to have them reclassified. The practical significance of reclassification is mainly its effect on compensation — full market value for a fit house instead of site value for an unfit one. But, except in Manchester and Liverpool where the pre-1969 Act rules applied, owner occupiers did not stand to gain financially because almost all of them would receive full market value in any case. Nevertheless, in all the survey areas except Leeds and Tower Hamlets, objections were made in respect of owner occupied houses. The proportions varied from 16 per cent in Manchester to 46 per cent in Liverpool. Whilst the high proportion in Liverpool is not surprising it is paradoxical that the proportion in Newcastle and the pool areas, where few owner occupiers could benefit financially, should have been almost as large and that the proportion in Manchester was relatively low.

There are two possible explanations. The first is faulty professional advice. Some solicitors and property agents seemed to be unaware of the changes recently introduced by the 1969 Act. Second, there is no doubt that some owner occupiers resented the classification of their home as unfit for human habitation and wished to remove this stigma. But objections had only very limited success; only 4 per cent of owner occupied houses were reclassified as fit after an objection and none was excluded from a CPO.

Immediately after the PLI the Department of the Environment inspector visits the properties included in a CPO to assess their condition and to decide whether the acquisition of any added lands is reasonably necessary for satisfactory redevelopment of the area. He visits each house in respect of which an objection has been made or, until 1974, for which a WMP had been claimed. He usually also visits other houses, including any that are reclassified and some in respect of which no claim for a WMP or objection has been made. On this basis a minimum of 60 per cent of the houses covered by the survey were visited. Taking these houses alone, 59 per cent of respondents who were visited by the government inspector remembered the occasion. But as in the case of the PHI, residents were not well informed about the purpose of his inspection (Table 14).

Whilst 9 per cent and 8 per cent respectively said that the purpose of the visit was to decide a WMP claim or objection, most respondents thought that it was 'just another inspection'. Fifteen per cent said that the Ministry inspector came merely to check on the work of the PHI which was in a sense correct though many seem to have thought of him as the latter's superior rather than the representative of another body. Almost a quarter of respondents said that they did not know why he came. Therefore only 17 per cent were really well informed about the purpose of the visit and many had little or no idea. This is hardly surprising. Inspectors seem often not to have spoken at all and certainly not to have explained the reason for their visit. Respondents were able to distinguish them from other official callers as higher status individuals who swept in and out accompanied by a retinue of local authority officials. Objectors and WMP claimants had been warned to expect the inspector but there is no reason why other people, unless they were unusually well informed about slum clearance procedure, should have known the purpose of the visit. Although this ignorance of the government inspector's role does not prejudice residents' rights directly it is typical of the lack of real understanding of the clearance process that residents should have opened their houses to another official visitor without a clear understanding of why he was there.

Table 14. Understood purpose of the Government Inspector's visit

Understood purpose of the visit	Per cent stating each purpose %
To decide WMP claim	9
To decide objection	8
To check on PHI	15
Other reasons	45
Don't know	24
Base	620

Sources of Information in General

It would be surprising if, at the final stage of the clearance process when residents were being rehoused and their houses boarded up, those remaining had not realised that their house was to be demolished. In fact all respondents were aware that their houses were to be cleared. But there were substantial variations in their sources of information. Realising that your house is going to be cleared is unlikely to be a once-for-all event, particularly in large cities where common observation tells people that old and ill equipped houses like their own have a limited life. To avoid ambiguity respondents were asked when they first heard definitely that their house would be included in a clearance scheme and how they first heard.

Taking the sample as a whole the most striking feature (Table 15) is the substantial proportion of residents who identified an official or quasi-official source of definite information. Overall 31 per cent of residents cited a letter from the council as their first source of information. A further 15 per cent identified the PHI whilst street notices or newspapers were mentioned by 24 per cent. Friends, neighbours and relatives accounted for only 9 per cent of cases. Landlords and property agents, mentioned by only 5 per cent of tenants (3 per cent of all respondents), were insignificant as sources of information despite the request in Form 26 for them to pass on information about WMPs.

The advantage enjoyed by owners because of their receipt of statutory notices is shown clearly by the far higher proportion of owners than of tenants who first received definite information from an official letter; 43 per cent identified this source compared with only 26 per cent of tenants. This marked contrast between the two groups held true for all main areas except Liverpool where slightly over half of both owners and tenants had first heard from an official letter. In no other area did more than 28 per cent of tenants mention this source. The prominence of Liverpool in this respect is due to the council's policy, not followed elsewhere in the survey authorities, of sending out an explanatory letter to all occupiers of houses in a clearance area as soon as it has been declared.

Table 15. Source of first definite information about clearance by tenure

Source of first definite information about clearance	Owner occupiers %	Tenants %	All residents %
Newspapers	24	15	17
Friends, neighbours or relatives	5	11	9
Landlord or agent	–	5	3
Letter from council (including Form 26)	43	26	31
Notice in street	3	8	7
Public Health Inspector	15	15	15
Other	7	16	14
Don't know	2	4	4
Base	420	1101	1521

Owner occupiers were also much better off than tenants in having the support of professional advice. The notes to Form 26 point out that the council pay professional fees incurred in negotiating compensation and as many as 90 per cent of owner occupiers had had professional assistance, usually from a solicitor. Since only about 30 per cent of owner occupiers in the survey objected formally to the CPO it seems that professional help was mainly required to deal with the routine of compulsory purchase and compensation. The property rights of owner occupiers should have been well enough protected.

Compensation and Well Maintained Payments

Compensation

Compensation was of direct concern only to the 28 per cent of households who were owner occupiers. About 22 per cent of the owner occupied houses were classified as fit for human habitation when the CPOs had been confirmed and the general law of compensation for compulsory acquisition applied to them. The owners were entitled to full compulsory purchase value compensation.

For owner occupiers living in houses which were confirmed in the CPO as unfit the site value rule applied but with various additional payments. In particular the amendments introduced in the Housing Act 1969 had fundamentally altered the position of most owner occupiers in the sample. All the clearance areas covered by the survey, except those in Manchester and Liverpool, had been declared after April 1968. Whereas in Manchester and Liverpool only about 17 per cent of owner occupiers were entitled to full market value, in the other areas at least 94 per cent were entitled to it. Clearly, therefore, the 1969 Act has transformed the position of owner occupiers. In the clearance areas which came under the new legislation only a small minority of owner occupiers who had bought their houses very recently would not receive full market value, and even some of these might get it if the last owner had been an owner occupier. In these areas the special code of compensation for slum clearance had virtually ceased to be of any importance for owner occupiers. The change was, however, fairly recent at the time of the survey and it is clear that many owner occupiers were confused about compensation.

Overall 80 per cent of the owner occupiers were entitled to receive full market value compensation, either because their houses had been classified as fit or, more usually, because they benefited from the provisions of the 1969 Act. But how well informed were owner occupiers about the amount of compensation they would receive? This is an important matter if for no other reason than that accurate knowledge about compensation is necessary before owners can make informed choices about their housing options. In particular, some owner occupiers want to know whether it is realistic to plan to buy another house

Residents' Knowledge of the Slum Clearance Process

or whether they should accept a council tenancy.

About two thirds of owner occupiers had a realistic expectation of whether or not they would receive full market value, a fifth did not know, and only a seventh had an incorrect expectation. The difference in level of knowledge between those who were entitled to full market value and the remainder was small (Table 16). The only substantial difference was that more than double the proportion wrongly thought that they would not get full market value than wrongly expected to receive it. This difference is unsurprising in view of the relative newness at the time of survey of the more liberal treatment of owner occupiers under the 1969 Act.

Table 16. Owner occupiers: whether full market value (FMV) expected by whether entitled to FMV.

Whether FMV expected	Entitled to FMV %	Not entitled to FMV %	All owner occupiers %
FMV expected	63	7	52
FMV not expected	16	72	27
Don't know	22	21	22
Base	337	85	422

The survey was undertaken quite soon after confirmation of the relevant CPOs so as to minimise the proportion of residents who had been rehoused. At the time they were interviewed only 14 per cent of owner occupiers had received an offer of compensation from the local authority. There were considerable differences between areas, from 26 per cent in Liverpool to none in Newcastle, which mainly reflected the varying length of time since the confirmation of CPOs. As might be expected, there was a striking difference between the amounts of compensation offered to owner occupiers who were entitled to full market value and those who were entitled only to site value. The former had been offered between £800 and £2,200, with a median of £1,300. Offers in respect of site value ranged from £1 to £215, with a median of £48. In 82 per cent of the cases the offer of site value was £55 or less, and in 24 per cent, £10 or less. In most cases, therefore, even full market value compensation was insufficient to finance the purchase of another house, particularly in the case of older owner occupiers. But site value compensation could do little more than meet the incidental expenses of moving and in some cases not even that.

Over 85 per cent of owner occupiers had not received an offer of compensation at the time that they were interviewed and of these 47 per cent did not feel able even to estimate how much compensation they would get. But for those who did make an estimate it is possible to make some judgement of how realistic their expectations were.

Owner occupiers who were entitled to full market value expected to get from nothing to £5,000, with a median of £1,000. Only 7 per cent expected to get £100 or less, and 29 per cent expected £500 or less. Twenty-one per cent expected over £2,000. The estimates of a quarter to a third were clearly unrealistically low and were often, no doubt, related to expectations based on typical site value compensation. Otherwise, expectations seem to have been broadly realistic, bearing in mind the sums that had already been offered to other owner occupiers. Owner occupiers getting full market value were also able to relate their expectations to the value of their property on the open market, which provided a reasonable if perhaps a rather optimistic guide. The small number of owner occupiers who expected from £2,500 to £5,000 were not necessarily seriously over-optimistic because their properties were either unusually large, were situated in high value areas such as London, or had shops attached to them.

The expectations of owner occupiers who were entitled only to site value compensation ranged from nothing to £400, with a median of £85. As many as 70 per cent expected to get £100 or less. Only in one or two cases did it seem likely that the estimate was unrealistically high. The average estimate was somewhat higher than the sums that had been offered to other owner occupiers but expectations seem generally to have been very realistic.

Therefore, the slightly curious situation existed where nearly half the owner occupiers were not willing even to estimate how much compensation they would receive but the remainder appeared to be reasonably well informed. It has been pointed out that two thirds of owner occupiers knew correctly whether they were entitled to full market value compensation and given this knowledge it was not difficult for them to make a reasonable guess. Those getting full market value had general property values as a guide, whilst the remainder generally knew something of the experience of other owner occupiers whose houses had been affected by slum clearance in the past. Nevertheless, there was no indication that owner occupiers had received systematic guidance about the amount of compensation they could expect.

One consideration which might affect owner occupiers making housing choices is whether their compensation would be reduced if they accepted a council house. As far as is known none of the survey authorities did reduce compensation in these circumstances, but the practice was known to exist in some areas of the country:

> Some councils consider that owner occupiers of houses being acquired at full market value can in many cases fend for themselves and provide their own accommodation . . . Some councils take the view that, if they give an owner occupier a tenancy and the benefit of a subsidised rent, this has a value and they ought not to have to pay him as much for his existing house as its full value in the market with vacant possession. . . Our inquiry among a sample of local authorities revealed that 15 per cent made a reduction in compensation if they rehoused an owner occupier.[19]

This practice was officially discouraged in Circular 68/69 which emphasised that 'there should be no question of an offer of a tenancy to a displaced owner occupier in housing need carrying with it an abatement in the compensation that is statutorily due to him', and reduction of compensation on account of rehousing by a local authority has since been made illegal by the Land Compensation Act 1973.

In the event only a small minority of owner occupiers thought that their compensation would be reduced if they accepted a council house. Sixteen per cent of those entitled to full market value thought that their compensation would be reduced, rather more than half thought that it would not be affected, and a third were not sure. However, though few owner occupiers were misinformed, almost all were more or less uninformed and expressed a view on the basis of assumption only.

The picture which emerges is of owner occupiers trying to understand the complications of compensation, despite generally rather inadequate information from official sources. Of those who felt able to make estimates of their compensation most had modest and usually realistic expectations of what they were likely to receive. Indeed, the major miscalculation was made by those owner occupiers who did not realise that they were entitled to full market value compensation and consequently made serious underestimates. But nearly half the owner occupiers were not able even to estimate how much compensation they were likely to get and a substantial minority were not certain that it would not be reduced if they accepted a council house. If owner occupiers are to make a rational choice about their futures, particularly whether to become council tenants or to buy another house, they obviously require sound information on the compensation they can expect. Many owner occupiers were clearly not in a position to make an informed decision even at the final stages of the clearance process.

Well-Maintained Payments

Until the introduction of home loss payments and disturbance payments under the Land Compensation Act 1973 a well-maintained payment was the only sum of money which a tenant was able to claim under slum clearance legislation. Before 1974 local authorities were not required to inform tenants directly of their right to a WMP and not all local authorities did so. Six of the fifteen survey authorities did not send a letter about WMPs to tenants. Of the other nine, eight sent informal letters and one sent Form 26 and notes to all occupiers, tenants as well as owner occupiers.

Of all tenants no more than 54 per cent had heard of WMPs, but 56 per cent had heard in letter areas compared with 48 per cent in non-letter areas, a modest but significant difference (Table 17). There was, however, considerable difference in their sources of information. Whereas 66 per cent of tenants in letter areas had heard about WMPs from the council, only 46 per cent in non-letter areas had done so. Even so, the proportion in non-letter areas is quite large and may have been partly the result of PHIs telling people about WMPs during their inspections. In all areas a substantial proportion had heard in other ways, mainly from friends and neighbours but it is striking how few people had found out about WMPs from their landlord or agent. Only 1 per cent had learnt from their landlord or agent in letter areas and 9 per cent in non-letter areas. This points to the ineffectiveness of the request to landlords in Form 26 to inform tenants about their right to claim them.

Only 36 per cent of tenants who had heard of WMPs in fact made a claim, and only a quarter of these had heard whether or not their claim had been successful. As the inspectors' decisions on good maintenance had become available when the CPOs were confirmed local authorities do not seem to have been very effective in communicating them to tenants.

A mere 3 per cent of tenants who had heard of WMPs but not applied had tried to find out any more about them. However, as many as 79 per cent said they did not know how much could be claimed on houses like their own. Those who had claimed WMPs but did not know how much they would be getting were hardly better informed; 65 per cent said they did not know how much could be claimed.

Table 17. Tenants: whether heard of well-maintained payments (WMPs) by whether official letters were sent

Whether heard of WMPs	Letters sent %	Letters NOT sent %	All tenants %
Heard of WMPs	56	48	54
Not heard of WMPs	43	53	46
Don't know	1	–	1
Base	790	324	1114

Most tenants who had heard of WMPs but had not applied said that they had a particular reason for not claiming (Table 18). The most important reason, mentioned by 40 per cent, was that they had not spent enough on the house to warrant claiming or, as a few put it, the house was not in sufficiently good condition. This was in some cases a perfectly realistic assumption that a claim would have been hopeless in view of the bad state of the house. On the other hand, many tenants appeared to be under the misapprehension that the amount that could be claimed was directly related to what had been spent. A further 5 per cent specifically said their reason for not claiming was lack of bills. The special letters from local authorities generally gave the impression that it was necessary to produce bills to prove expenditure but, whilst bills would be useful if the apportionment of a payment was contested by the landlord, they were not a necessary precondition for making a claim. Whether an unfit house is accepted as having been well maintained depends on its condition.

The other main reason given for not claiming, mentioned by 21 per cent, was a belief that tenants could not claim any money. People who clearly knew of the existence of WMPs and had received letters about them stated categorically that only landlords could claim. In addition some of those who gave other reasons, such as general statements that they were not entitled to claim, thought that WMPs did not extend to tenants. This assumption is not difficult to understand and local authority letters needed to emphasise that WMPs are a right that tenants, despite their general lack of entitlement to compensation, can claim.

Like Form 26, special letters to tenants seemed invariably to state that a claim for a WMP must be submitted before the end of the objection period. While it was obviously desirable that claims should be submitted before the PLI so that the houses concerned could be examined by the inspector, the Department would, in fact, consider claims submitted at any time before a house was demolished. In these cases it was inspected by a district valuer. Although the PLI had long since passed at the time residents were interviewed it was still possible for anyone who had not done so to claim a WMP. But a mere 7 per cent of tenants who had not applied thought that they could still make a claim.

Table 18. Tenants: stated reasons for not applying for well-maintained payments (WMPs)

Stated reasons for not applying for WMPs	Per cent of tenants stating each reason
Tenants cannot claim	21
Not spent enough to warrant claiming/bad state of house	40
No bills	5
Official advice	3
Other reasons	31
Base	335

It has been pointed out that before 1956 all unfit houses were visited by the Ministry inspector with a view to the award of WMPs, so that the problem of claims did not arise. Presumably the practice was altered on grounds of economy and practicability in view of the build up of the slum clearance programme. But in the survey areas inspectors visited at least two-thirds of the houses to consider WMP claims and objections so that the change could not have introduced a very substantial economy. Since the survey, however, the procedure for deciding whether houses are well maintained has been altered and local authorities make an initial decision on every unfit house. The new system is likely to be much more satisfactory than one in which little more than half of tenants interviewed had even heard of WMPs and less than one fifth had actually applied. But the survey findings demonstrate the dangers of the easy assumption that people in clearance areas are in general well aware of their rights.

Effectiveness of the Housing Visitor

For residents the most significant event of the rehousing stage is a visit from a housing visitor. For many people it is the only occasion on which they can discuss their move with an official. The survey of clearance areas was therefore timed to take place in areas where the majority of residents had already been visited by housing department staff. At the lowest, 88 per cent in Tower Hamlets said that they had been visited by a housing visitor and the highest proportion, in Leeds, was 97 per cent. Hence, for most respondents questions about their opinions of visiting staff and their knowledge of rehousing arrangements could be meaningfully pursued.

The most direct question on residents' understanding of the home visit asked what was the main purpose of the visit. Most people identified two or more principal reasons for the visit but by far the largest proportion replied that the main purpose was 'to find out what we wanted'. Checking the house keeping standards, household requirements and eligibility were the next most common reasons given (Table 19). Although in all areas the largest proportion identified the main reason as establishing residents' preferences this was least often mentioned in Manchester and Tower Hamlets where only 52 per cent and 42 per cent of residents respectively identified the housing visit in this way; in the remaining areas at least 60 per cent of replies included this category. Checking eligibility was identified by around one quarter of respondents in most areas but in Manchester by 48 per cent — a clear awareness of the Manchester inspectors' stress on eligibility. Assessment of housekeeping standards was mentioned most frequently by respondents in Leeds, 38 per cent, but overall by only one fifth of respondents. In view of the universal practice of grading in one form or another, even if it did not count in subsequent allocation, it seems that visitors were often highly successful in their common tactic of disguising their real motive for 'looking at the rooms'. Taken overall, residents' perceptions of the housing visit over-emphasised the visitors' interest in their preferences and understated the investigatory aspects.

A vital piece of information for residents who have been visited and who can expect to receive offers of council housing is the number of offers that are likely to be made to them before the council considers eviction proceedings. The applicant for council housing is in a peculiar situation compared with either the owner occupier or the private tenant in that he is never in the situation of making a choice between two or more alternative houses which are available to him simultaneously. With the rare exception of emergency circumstances residents are never offered more than one house at a time. The choice is accept or reject *this* particular house.

Table 19. Main stated reason for the visit of the housing visitor by area*

Area	Main stated reasons for visit				Base
	To ask residents what they wanted %	To check household eligibility %	To ascertain accommodation needs %	To assess housekeeping standards %	
Newcastle	69	24	26	20	159
Leeds	62	15	22	38	144
Manchester	52	48	36	28	134
Liverpool	65	24	36	18	191
Tower Hamlets	42	26	39	18	124

*Figures add to more than 100 per cent because more than one reason was stated in many cases.

The position of the council house applicant is made more difficult if he cannot make an accurate appraisal of the consequences of refusal in terms of its effect on future offers. Viewed in this way knowledge of the housing department's policy on making offers is crucial. Table 20 shows that in all areas a substantial proportion of residents either did not know how many offers would be made to them or were misinformed. In Newcastle, for example, 55 per cent of residents thought that they would get only three offers and a further 27 per cent said they did not know how many offers the council were prepared to make. In fact, policy was to make unlimited offers to a family. By comparison, in Liverpool, which also had a policy of unlimited offers, almost half of respondents knew this. In Leeds, where offers were formally restricted to one or two offers 44 per cent knew this. Manchester's strict policy of three offers before review was appreciated by 57 per cent of respondents and a similar policy in Tower Hamlets by 44 per cent. However, it is not legitimate to argue that there was only one right answer to the number of offers made by the local authority. Although the system in Leeds was geared to making only one offer if possible, two or three offers would often be made depending on the discretion of the district housing managers. Allowing for some confusion in the replies between what is the *policy* and what is the *norm* we might accept that replies of three offers in Newcastle were not unrealistic. Similar generous assumptions can be made for other areas. A booklet available in Manchester for slum clearance residents stated explicitly that 'each tenant is given at least two offers of suitable accommodation' so 'two offers' can be accepted

Residents' Knowledge of the Slum Clearance Process 145

as a realistic reply there. In Liverpool only 'one offer' and 'don't know' are excluded from the 'realistic' category and in Tower Hamlets only the 'unlimited' and 'don't know' categories of Table 20. Despite the generous assumptions of this subdivision over one quarter of residents in Newcastle, Manchester and Tower Hamlets showed no realistic knowledge of numbers of offers. In Tower Hamlets the proportion was 41 per cent.

Table 20. Number of offers of housing expected by area

Area	Number of offers expected						Base
	1 offer %	2 offers %	3 offers %	4 or more offers %	Unlimited offers %	Don't know %	
Newcastle	—	3	55	8	8	27	150
Leeds	39	15	28	1	3	13	138
Manchester	1	6	57	9	7	20	123
Liverpool	—	1	30	6	48	15	181
Tower Hamlets	4	4	44	7	21	19	99

The source of residents' information on numbers of offers clearly shows the effect of the different practices adopted by housing departments in our five areas. In the sample as a whole 17 per cent of respondents cited the housing visitor as their source of information and 11 per cent cited other official council sources. The vast majority, 67 per cent, had picked up their information from rumour or the observed behaviour of other people. But some of the differences between the five areas in these respects are striking (Table 21).

In Leeds the stress on lengthy discussion at the housing visit had a very obvious impact and 56 per cent specified the housing visitor as their source of knowledge. Liverpool, where 48 per cent knew that they would get unlimited offers, showed a particularly marked dependence on council sources other than the housing visitor. This reflects the practice of the Liverpool clerk's and housing departments in sending out numerous letters and notices to tenants one of which stated clearly in its first section 'There is no limit to the number of offers of dwellings which can be made . . . ' Elsewhere than Leeds or Liverpool less than one third of respondents mentioned official sources for their knowledge of offers policy.

The variation between authorities in practice and effectiveness which is shown in the tables was reflected also in residents' own appraisal of

Table 21. Stated source of information about numbers of offers by area

Area	Stated source of information					
	Housing visitor %	Other Council %	Rumour %	Observed Others %	Other and Don't know %	Base
Newcastle	6	1	67	23	3	109
Leeds	56	3	29	6	6	117
Manchester	8	13	62	14	2	97
Liverpool	10	37	39	13	1	153
Tower Hamlets	20	11	50	13	7	76

the home visit. They were asked directly whether the housing visitor had offered any advice at the time of visit, whether he or she had spent enough time and whether the visit gave a fair chance for the resident to make up his/her mind about rehousing. The vast majority said that they had been offered no advice or guidance; around one third criticised the time allowed for the visit but only twelve per cent of the complete sample felt that they had not been allowed to make up their own minds about their preferences. The differences between areas are revealing.

Table 22. Criticisms of the housing visitor (HV) by area

Area	Per cent stating each criticism			
	HV gave no advice %	HV gave too little time %	HV gave no chance of personal choice %	Base
Newcastle	70	26	12	138
Leeds	70	32	13	136
Manchester	87	37	18	110
Liverpool	66	24	10	168
Tower Hamlets	90	35	21	91

In each case respondents in Manchester and Tower Hamlets were more critical than in the three other cities. Eighty-seven per cent in Manchester and 90 per cent in Tower Hamlets said they were given no advice compared with 70 per cent or less elsewhere. In respect of critical comments on other aspects of the home visits, residents in Manchester and Tower Hamlets again showed the highest levels of criticism. Taken together with the material in previous tables the reactions of residents in this respect accords with the conclusions of Chapter 5 which highlighted the fragmentation of the interviewer role in Manchester and the very limited interpretation of job requirements in Tower Hamlets.

NOTES

1. Central Housing Advisory Committee, *op. cit.* (1956).
2. Central Housing Advisory Committee, *op. cit.* (1969), p. 26.
3. R. Wilkinson and E. Sigsworth, 'A Survey of Slum Clearance Areas in Leeds', *Yorkshire Bulletin of Social and Economic Research,* Vol. 15, No. 1, May 1963.
4. D.G. Bull, *op. cit.* (1967), p. 177.
5. Shelter, *op. cit.* (1974), p. 23.
6. Sidney Jacobs, *op. cit.,* p. 27.
7. See for example Nick Bond, 'The Hillfields Information Centre: A Case Study', in Ray Lees and George Smith (eds.), *Action-Research in Community Development,* Routledge and Kegan Paul, 1975.
8. For example *Community Action,* issues 9 to 11, July to December 1973.
9. June Norris, *op. cit.,* p. 76.
10. Hilda Jennings, *op. cit.,* p. 235.
11. These aspects are considered in detail in June Norris, *op. cit.,* especially p. 81 and in D.G. Bull, *op. cit.* (1968).
12. D.G. Bull, *op. cit.* (1969 and 1970).
13. Central Housing Advisory Committee, *op. cit.* (1969), p. 28.
14. Jacobs, however, doubts whether improvements in information, amongst other things, would substantially alter the situation ' . . . the system cannot be improved. A more enlightened and efficient bureaucracy is not the answer, but power to the people.' Sidney Jacobs, *op. cit.,* p. 153.
15. Since there was some variation between authorities in the printed format of Form 26 handed out, interviewers were each equipped with a copy of the locally produced version and instructed to show it to respondents.
16. Ministry of Housing and Local Government Circular 68/69, *Housing Act 1969: Slum Clearance,* HMSO, 1969.
17. This view of public local inquiries is probably well founded see 'Benwell's Real Public Inquiry', *Community Action,* No. 13, April-May 1974.
18. Part of the research programme involved an analysis of the reports of the government inspector to give independent figures of objectors' claims for WMPs etc.
19. Central Housing Advisory Committee, *op. cit.* (1969), p. 88.

7 SOME DETERMINANTS OF ATTITUDES TOWARDS MOVING

The approach of previous chapters assumes that large-scale slum clearance is an acceptable objective of government policy and that the main requirement is an improvement of the administrative system through which clearance is achieved. But arguments supporting the recent switch of policy from slum clearance to rehabilitation and gradual renewal make much of the unacceptable social costs of wholesale redevelopment however well it might be administered.[1] Although this view can find much support in post-war academic studies of slum areas[2] it is misleading to represent clearance as a universally unwelcome onslaught on the lives of existing communities. For many people, deplorable living conditions over-ride all other considerations and redevelopment has provided their one real chance of getting a decent home. While opposition to clearance has received most attention and publicity many thousands of residents in inner city areas have gratefully accepted slum clearance as a change for the better.

Any area affected by clearance will obviously have its own unique characteristics which play their part in determining the strength of opposition or support for clearance proposals. The virtue of locality-based studies is that they can bring these features into any analysis of attitudes; their limitation lies in the very uniqueness which undermines their value as a basis for generalisation to other areas. A national sample such as was used in the present study suffers from a lack of depth but does provide a firm basis for generalisations about the strength of support or opposition across the country as a whole. This chapter draws on material from the sample survey to investigate households' attitudes for or against moving from their accommodation in the course of clearance, relating them to major factors of housing conditions, tenure and life cycle stage. Where possible the tables provide comparative data from the General Household Survey 1971.

Household Characteristics and Housing Conditions

Slum clearance mainly affects stable working class areas. Almost half of sample households were in skilled manual occupations, a further quarter in semi-skilled jobs and 14 per cent were unskilled (Table 23). This leaves only 14 per cent altogether in non-manual categories compared

Some Determinants of Attitudes Towards Moving 149

with 38 per cent nationally.

Table 23. Households by socioeconomic group (SEG)

SEGs	Survey %	GHS 1971 %
Professional and Managerial	4	18
Other Non-Manual	10	20
Skilled Manual	46	33
Semi-skilled Manual	27	19
Unskilled Manual	14	6
Miscellaneous	–	3
Base	1,333	11,664

Variation between areas was substantial although in no instance did the survey population approach the national proportions of non-manual occupations (See Appendix Table A1). Newcastle and Leeds represented one extreme with less than 10 per cent in non-manual occupations and very heavy concentration in skilled manual work. In Liverpool and Tower Hamlets the proportion of skilled workers was substantially lower than elsewhere due to a particularly large group of unskilled workers in Liverpool and of semi-skilled workers in Tower Hamlets; the latter were mainly personal service workers concentrated amongst immigrant households there.

The basic stability of the population is indicated both by households' length of residence in their present accommodation or elsewhere in the town (Table 24) and by household characteristics. Altogether a quarter of households had occupied their dwellings for at least thirty years or either husband or wife had been born there. A further 30 per cent had occupied their present dwelling between ten and thirty years and only 15 per cent for less than two years. As comparative figures from the General Household Survey 1971 show, this represented a far more stable population than in the country as a whole where only 41 per cent of households had occupied their houses for ten years or more. On the other hand, these figures resemble closely some of the findings of previous surveys: Dennis found that 39 per cent of households had lived in their present dwellings for twenty years or more compared with 37 per cent in the present survey.[4] Wilkinson and Sigsworth found only 17 per cent of households who had occupied their accommodation for more than twenty years in a slum area of Batley where immigrant influx had been heavy but in slum areas of Leeds and York one third of households had occupied their accommodation for this length of time.[5]

Table 24. Households by length of residence in present house and length of residence in town where interviewed

	Length of residence in present house		Length of residence in town
Period	Survey %	GHS 1971 %	Survey %
⟨ 2 years	15	15	3
2 ⟨ 5 years	17	21	3
5 ⟨ 10 years	13	23	4
10 ⟨ 20 years	18	20	6
20 ⟨ 30 years	12	8	4
30 + years	21	13	8
Born here	4	–	71
Base	1,547	11,981	1,547

Amongst the main survey areas of the present sample there were some interesting variations (see Appendix A, Table A2). In Leeds the population was polarised between a very substantial group of long-term residents, 28 per cent, and the 48 per cent of households who had lived in their present house for less than five years. The recent arrivals in Leeds were not immigrants from abroad or elsewhere in the country as can be seen from the length of residence of the population in Leeds (Table A3). Further analysis suggests that many of the newcomers had moved into the area in the hope of soon being rehoused in a council house; of the seventy households in this short-term category, forty-nine were young married couples, most of them having children. Although a few had bought their houses most were renters. But perhaps most significant is the fact that forty-seven of the seventy households said that they knew before coming to live in the area that the houses would be knocked down.

In four of the main area samples at least three quarters of household heads or their wives had been born in the town (Table A3) and the proportion was 95 per cent in Liverpool. In Tower Hamlets, where only one third of household heads or their wives were born locally most households had nevertheless been established in the area for at least five years.

Data on age, marital status and presence of children summarised in terms of life cycle stage of the 'housewife',[6] shows that the great maj-

Some Determinants of Attitudes Towards Moving   151

ority of households consisted either of old people or of stable family units (Table 25). Almost 90 per cent of the 'housewives' in the survey population were either currently married or were aged over 60. There were very few households in which the 'housewife' was aged less than 60 but not currently married — only twelve per cent. This meant that most households also contained children or old people. Only 20 per cent of households altogether contained a housewife aged less than 60 but not children under 16 living at home.

Table 25. Households by life cycle stage

Life cycle stage,* first alternative	%	Life cycle stage,* second alternative	%
Young non-married	5	Non-married childless	8
Middle aged non-married	7	Married childless	12
Young married	36	Non-married with children	4
Middle aged married	17	Married with children	41
Old people 60+	36	Old non-married 60+	23
		Old married 60+	13
Base	1,532		1,532

*For definition of life cycle stage see Appendix B

In summary, the large majority of clearance area residents lived in conventional households. Not unnaturally such areas tend to house particularly the old whose families grew up before council housing was a major alternative form of accommodation and the young couples who have not yet qualified for a council house. Despite the tendency of such areas during the later stages of clearance to become a temporary refuge for a floating population there is, on the evidence of this survey, no reason to regard slum clearance areas as a whole as 'social problem' areas.

Although, in all areas, housing conditions were mostly extremely poor there was considerable variety of physical structures which produced these poor conditions. The houses in every area, with only minor exceptions, were purpose-built in the nineteenth century for a working class population; but the variation in detail of design and structure was considerable. In Table 26 the accommodation occupied by sample households is divided up by physical type. The total figures show clearly the dominance of terrace through houses in clearance areas making 56 per cent of the total. A further 28 per cent of the total could also be classified as terrace housing but the peculiarities of back-to-back housing and Tyneside flats warrants their separate treatment. The latter are a type of accommodation peculiar to the North East of England consisting of pairs of dwellings, one a ground floor flat and the other a first floor flat both with separate front and rear access. In the Byker area of Newcastle this type of accommodation housed 84 per cent of sample households (Table A5). In Leeds, back-to-back houses were the characteristic form of housing comprising 93 per cent of accommodation whereas in the Spitalfields area in Tower Hamlets 95 per cent lived in purpose-built tenement blocks provided by charitable trusts in the late nineteenth century.[7] Only in Manchester and Liverpool did the 'normal' type of terrace through house predominate.

Table 26. Households by type of dwelling

Type of dwelling	%
Terrace house	56
Back-to-back house	14
Tyneside flat	14
Purpose-built flat	9
Other (including converted houses)	8
Base	1,540

The marked difference in house type is also clearly seen in Table 27 giving the number of rooms available to each household. It is important to note that the data from this table are not strictly comparable with census or other sources. Respondents were specifically asked how many rooms they had for living, sleeping or eating in; bathrooms were excluded as were kitchens and sculleries used only for food preparation. In addition rooms which were not useable because of damage or severe damp were excluded from the count. The figures therefore refer to the households' actual living pattern and not to the physical characteristics of the dwellings alone. By these criteria roughly one third of sample households lived in three rooms or less, one third in four rooms and one third in five rooms or more.

From this overall pattern both the Newcastle and Tower Hamlets areas were distinguished by a much higher proportion of small units of two rooms, 20 per cent and 60 per cent respectively (Table A6). Overcrowding above the 'official' level of 1.5 persons per room was particularly prevalent in Tower Hamlets with 21 per cent of households living at this density compared with 8 per cent overall.

Table 27. Households by number of useable rooms

No. of rooms	%
1	1
2	12
3	22
4	34
5	20
6 or more	12
Base	1,531

It is important to keep differences of house type in mind when interpreting information about other aspects of housing conditions in each area. As Table 28 shows, most households, although having sole use of a water closet, were obliged to go outside their house to use it. In Manchester, Newcastle and Liverpool this was the standard arrangement (Table A7), but every other household in Newcastle had to go down the back stairs from an upstairs flat to the WC in the back yard. In Leeds, where back-to-back construction made back yards impossible, the WC was located either in the cellar accessible only from outside the front door or, in houses opening directly off the street, in common yards located at intervals along the terrace. This last arrangement explains the very high proportion of households in Leeds who shared a WC outside their house. The situation in Tower Hamlets appears, on face value, to have been substantially better in this respect than elsewhere with 86 per cent of households having sole use of a WC inside the house. However, this could be a mixed blessing; in some cases the toilet pan was located not in its own cubicle inside the house but in the kitchen amongst the cooker and other kitchen equipment. As one respondent commented, 'how would you like to be able to sit on the lavatory and cook your breakfast?'!

The availability of fixed baths shows less variation between areas from the overall proportion of only 27 per cent of households (Table A7). Even where fixed baths were available they were often located in the kitchen and many were plumbed in with a fixed waste outlet but no independent water supply. In these cases baths had to be filled from the sink or from a kettle. But the most surprising feature of housing conditions was the substantial proportion of the sample — over half — who did not have a constant supply of hot water (Table 29). Households were counted as having a 'constant' supply if they had a geyser or

Table 28. Households by availability of WC

Availability of WC	%
Sole use inside house	21
Sole use outside house	66
Shared use inside house	1
Shared use outside house	12
None	1
Base	1,544

electric instant hot water heater but not if the supply depended on a fixed capacity water heater with the same limitations as a kettle. Only 46 per cent of households could be counted as having such a supply of hot water. Residents frequently mentioned low water pressure as one difficulty that prevented even a gas geyser being installed.

These housing conditions are fairly closely comparable with the findings of the government's survey of house conditions undertaken in 1971.[8] Comparison with figures from the previous survey of 1967[9] shows a marked improvement in the availability of basic amenities in houses in potential clearance areas, particularly in the provision of baths, but the vast majority of 'slum' houses still lacked both bath and inside lavatory.

Table 29. Comparison of findings of National House Condition Survey and 1970 Slum Clearance Survey

	Dwellings (or households) lacking fixed bath %	Dwellings (or households) lacking internal W.C. %
1967 Survey	86	85
1971 Survey	65	75
1970 Clearance Area Survey	73	78

Source: 1967 Survey figures from: White Paper, *Old Houses into new Homes*, Cmnd. 3602, Table 8; 1971 Survey figures from: Department of the Environment, *House Condition Survey, 1971, England and Wales, Housing Survey Reports, No. 9*, DOE, Table 9.

In both respects the present survey shows a slightly worse situation than the National House Condition survey undertaken one year later. But the comparable data from the 1971 survey covers only dwellings in or adjoining potential clearance areas whereas the clearance areas of this study had been declared several years before in the prevailing conditions of the late sixties and might be expected to be worse.

For the most part the houses were rented from private landlords, 70 per cent altogether; a further 2 per cent were houses acquired in advance of demolition and rented from the council. The remainder were owner occupied, most of them bought outright (Table 30).

Table 30. Households by tenure of accommodation

	Tenure	%	
Tenants	Unfurnished	67	
	Furnished	2	
	Council	2	72%
	Other (incl. tied houses)	1	
Owner Occupiers	Finished paying	23	
	Still paying:		28%
	Mortgage/loan	3	
	Rental purchase	2	
	Base	1,547	

Table A8 (Appendix A) shows that owner occupation was most common in Manchester and the 'pool' areas with one third or more households owning and in Liverpool where 20 per cent owned their homes.
In Tower Hamlets all the houses were still owned by large charitable trusts. The overall proportion of 28 per cent owner occupiers is very close to the proportions found in potential slum clearance areas in the two national house condition surveys which counted 27 per cent owner occupiers in both 1967 and 1971.[10] For the majority renting their houses weekly outgoings were mostly very small. Over three-quarters of tenants paid less than £2 per week rent and rates. The majority of owner occupiers had finished paying for their houses and had to meet only the low rates of such property. But purchase prices themselves had in most cases been remarkably low. Sixty per cent of households who owned their houses outright had paid less than £600 for them and only 9 per cent had paid £1,000 or more.

Attitudes Towards Moving

In contrast to the earlier community studies which portrayed the entire community as hostile to redevelopment, previous sample surveys have generally shown that residents are fairly evenly divided between supporting and opposing a move. An early study of the Crown Street district of Liverpool by Vereker and Mays set out to investigate the range and variety of household requirements that planning schemes should satisfy during redevelopment; the motivations of those who might want to leave were recognised to be just as important as the motivations of people who wanted to remain.[11] Taking the district as a whole the findings were consistent with the view that the majority of people did not wish to leave their home area because of redevelopment; only 39 per cent positively wished to move away altogether and the remaining 61 per cent preferred either to stay put or at least to be rehoused within their own locality.[12] But taking only the houses scheduled for demolition under slum clearance 43 per cent preferred to move away entirely.[13] The authors emphasised the diversity of views: 'Variety, confusion and conflict prevailed both in the district as a whole and its sub-areas.'[14]

Further studies of slum clearance areas generally support the evidence from Liverpool. Wilkinson and Sigsworth's survey of housing attitudes in three towns,[15] like the Liverpool survey, distinguished between moving from the present accommodation alone and total removal from the area. Although these aspects were separately treated in the analysis it is possible to combine information on the two topics to arrive at figures closely comparable with the Crown Street survey (Table 31). Taken together these figures suggest that a typical pattern of response in a poor condition inner city area would be between one quarter and one third of households in favour of staying put, one quarter to one third in favour of a change of accommodation within the same locality and between one third and one half of households in favour of a complete change of both houses and locality. Only in the 'slum' areas of Leeds did a clear majority appear to be in favour of a complete change.

This interpretation is consistent with evidence from other studies which have been undertaken along similar lines. Coates and Silburn found that two thirds of residents in the St Anne's area of Nottingham welcomed the prospect of redevelopment and nearly one half said they would like to leave the area altogether.[16] They also cite a Nottingham Corporation survey which found some 38 per cent of households happy to move right away from the area.[17] Liverpool Corporation's Social Survey, undertaken in 1966, found that, given a choice, 50 per cent of people living in unfit dwellings in the Inner Area would prefer to be rehoused within that area while the other half would prefer to move right

Table 31. Attitudes towards being rehoused and towards moving from the district in 'slum' areas of York, Batley and Leeds

| Attitude | Attitude towards: | | | | | |
| | Being rehoused | | | Moving from the district | | |
	Batley %	Leeds %	York %	Batley %	Leeds %	York %
In favour	67	72	64	42	53	20
Against	30	27	33	52	46	67
Don't know	2	–	2	5	–	2
Base	140	261	103	138	262	103

Source: R.K. Wilkinson, 'Attitudes to the Housing Environment', *Urban Studies,* Vol. 9, No. 2, June 1972, pp. 197, 206.

Note: 'Slum' areas were defined by rateable value and age of houses in consultation with local officials; they are not confined to areas formally represented for slum clearance.

Table 32. Comparison of York, Batley, Leeds findings with Liverpool study

Expressed desire	Batley %	Leeds %	York %	Liverpool (Crown St Area) %
Not to move	31	27	33	36
To change accommodation but remain locally	26*	20*	37*	25
To move elsewhere	43	53	30	39
Base	140	262	103	574

*The figures for York, Batley and Leeds are derived from the previous text table. The intermediate category wishing to change accommodation but not leave the district is the residual of the other two groups including a small proportion of don't knows in each case.

away.[18] Finally, Dennis's study of Sunderland, although not concerned with respondents' direct willingness to change their accommodation or their district of residence, did examine their feelings about the demolition of their present house. In a sub-sample of households included in the 1960 to 1965 clearance programme 57 per cent were in favour of demolition and 42 per cent very much so compared with 19 per cent who were strongly opposed; a second sub-sample of households affected by the 1965-70 programme produced 53 per cent in favour of demolition and 47 per cent against.[19]

In none of these studies is there any evidence of a clear cut and overwhelming majority favouring one simple course of action. Dennis wisely concludes:

> the problem is not one of large majorities pitted against a negligible few who are comfortably and well housed or who are simply obstructive, selfish and misguided . . . Overall, those wanting to be rehoused outnumber those who want to retain their present homes; but the latter are not overwhelmingly outnumbered and in some areas and parts of areas the position is reversed. Under these conditions policies which have been formulated prior to surveys of the circumstances and preferences of the consumer, and which recommend clearance without discrimination between sub areas and different dwellings cannot, *prima facie,* be justified by using the concept of 'minority' and 'majority'.[20]

In each survey area of the present study it was already a foregone conclusion that the houses would be demolished and the population rehoused. In some cases rehousing from the area had already started and often the demolition gangs were at work nearby. In these circumstances no-one had a realistic option of remaining where they were. Nevertheless a substantial proportion of households still showed a basic satisfaction with their houses. Forty two per cent overall said that they would be happy to carry on living in their houses even in their present condition and a further 14 per cent would have been happy to stay if the houses could be improved. Considering the generally poor condition of the property and lack of repair these are surprisingly high figures. But there still remained 41 per cent who were not interested in staying where they were even if the houses could be improved (see Table 33). The distinction between moving from their house and moving from their area of residence was not made in the present survey. Most people knew quite well that the phasing of redevelopment and the sifting pro-

Some Determinants of Attitudes Towards Moving 159

cess of housing allocation ruled out their remaining in the area and amongst their present neighbours. Hence 'living in a different place' meant both a different house and a different area.

At so late a stage in the clearance process when all steps had been completed except rehousing, it is hardly surprising if most people had become anxious for the whole business to be finished. Compared with the minority of 41 per cent who were unequivocally dissatisfied with their present housing 71 per cent of respondents said they were looking forward to living in a different place. Again, it is perhaps surprising that this figure was not higher. The process of decay and dereliction which sets in when houses are vacated and the population of an area begins to leave can wear down even the most rooted of residents. But there were still 25 per cent of respondents who said they did not look forward to living in a different place.

The present survey also investigated residents' opinion of the demolition and clearance of old houses as a general policy. The proportion of respondents who definitely disagreed with their council's plans was smaller, at 20 per cent, than the proportion who said they were happy to go on living in their houses but still comprised an important minority group. A further 17 per cent had either no opinion or some reservations tempering their agreement with the policy, leaving 64 per cent in outright agreement.

From comparison of the pattern of replies on these three topics it appears that attitudes towards moving from a slum clearance area are not easily investigated by means of one simple measure. Appraisal of personal housing requirements, anticipation of the move itself and opinion of council policy each show a different distribution of opinion and concentration on any one aspect is bound to be arbitrary. Juxtaposition of the figures for each topic in Table 33 suggests that some residents at least discounted their evaluation of their personal housing situation in adjusting their expectations of a move and some were also prepared to overlook conflict with their personal interests in supporting the general policy of slum clearance. But for a more complex analysis of attitudes to moving it is too cumbersome to pursue three distinct approaches.

To simplify the analysis, data on residents' satisfaction with their present house and on their anticipation of a move were brought together in a summary measure of 'attitude to moving'. In Table 33d the material of Tables 33a and 33b is combined. The 51 per cent of households 'in favour' of moving were both against remaining in their present house and looking forward to moving. Twenty-one per cent of households unequivocally against moving combined satisfaction with their present house and apprehension at the prospect of moving. Finally, ambivalent combinations of replies to questions on these two topics were classified as having reservations about moving; this group made up 28 per cent of all households. In summary we can say that, whereas 42 per cent of households would have been happy to stay put in their present house if they had had the option, the hard core of households who still disliked the prospect of moving and were opposed to the policy of clearance made up only one quarter of residents. The summary measure of 'attitude to moving' which is used in all subsequent analysis maintains these proportions quite closely.

Table 33. Households by attitude to moving

a) Satisfaction with present house

	%
Happy to stay anyway	42
Happy to stay if improved	14
Prefer to leave anyway	42
Don't know	2
Base	1,547

b) Anticipation of moving

	%
Looking forward to living in a different place	70
Not looking forward to living in a different place	25
Don't know	5
Base	1,547

c) Opinion of council's plans

	%
Agree with plans	63
Agree but with reservations	12
Disagree with plans	20
Don't know	5
Base	1,547

d) Summary attitude to moving

	%
In favour	51
With reservations	28
Against	21
Base	1,544

Some Determinants of Attitudes Towards Moving

Figures for the sample as a whole show barely half of households in favour of moving; however, a comparison of data for each of the separate survey areas (Tables A9 to A12, Appendix A) shows that opinion in the pool areas was substantially less favourable to moving than in any other areas. Only in pool areas were a majority of households happy to remain in their present house — over 10 per cent more than in any main area. To some extent this distinct pattern of response is explained by the differences of tenure, age structure and housing conditions. But there appears also to have been a residual influence of local conditions which in these smaller areas increased resistance to the changes wrought by slum clearance.

If residents' appraisal of their housing options was based on the same physical criteria as those which officially define a slum we would expect to find that physical conditions alone would dictate attitudes. Certainly living conditions do have an important influence; only 38 per cent of households with sole use of an internal WC favoured moving compared with 54 per cent whose WC was outside and 58 per cent who shared a WC. Similar differences applied in respect of the availability of baths and a hot water supply (Table 34a). But, as Dennis has pointed out,[21] the same conditions can be differently perceived depending on the needs and aspirations of the individual. People judge their living conditions more harshly when they are for other reasons predisposed to move and overlook faults when they are keen to stay. For instance, although 78 per cent of households had outside WCs only 59 per cent thought that their toilet facilities were inadequate. While some did defend outside WCs as more hygienic it was clear that others, although not finding such an arrangement preferable, were willing to tolerate it given their perception of the disadvantages of moving.

Residents' subjective appraisal of the suitability of their accommodation therefore shows a closer relationship with attitude to moving than the 'objective' criteria of household amenities (Table 34b). Whereas respondents making a favourable appraisal of their accommodation divided fairly consistently one third in favour and one third against moving, around three-quarters of households who judged their accommodation to be unsound, damp or too small favoured the move and less than 10 per cent were against it.

The importance of subjective judgement in determining attitudes to moving means that we can only hope to understand such attitudes in relation to the wider social context within which residents find themselves and in which they evaluate the costs and benefits of moving to themselves and to their households.

Table 34. Households' attitude to moving by 'objective' and 'subjective' housing conditions

Conditions	Attitude towards moving			
	In favour %	With reservations %	Against %	Base
(a) OBJECTIVE CONDITIONS:				
WC				
Sole use inside house	38	30	32	319
Sole use outside house	54	28	18	1,014
Shared or none	58	25	17	211
Bath/shower				
Sole use	36	33	31	423
None or shared	57	26	17	1,119
Constant hot water				
Sole use	43	31	26	701
None or shared	57	27	16	835
(b) SUBJECTIVE CONDITIONS:				
House basically sound	33	34	33	746
House not basically sound	70	21	9	763
No damp	32	33	35	637
Some damp	55	32	13	432
Much damp	75	17	8	467
Enough space	40	33	27	1,117
Not enough space	81	15	4	416
All households	51	28	21	1,544

Previous work has shown that age and tenure of accommodation have particularly important influence on attitudes to moving but the relationship is not a simple one nor are age and tenure alone sufficient to explain differences in attitude. The Crown Street study sounded an early warning against simplistic analysis. The salient finding was an apparently inverse relationship between the stability of an area and residents' willingness to move away from it. Measured by a range of indices of social stability including birthplace, nearness to relatives and geographical mobility since the Second World War, the Low Hill and Smithsdown areas of the study were far more stable than the Abercromby area.[22] Yet the more stable area contained a substantially higher proportion of households who wished to move than the more mobile areas; whereas only 36 per cent of residents in Abercromby wished to move from the locality and 34 per cent even wanted to stay in their present accommodation, in Low Hill and Smithsdown 44 per cent favoured a move and only 32 per cent preferred to be left entirely alone. In contrast to Willmott and Young's emphasis on the significance of mere passage of time in rooting people to an area[23] the authors concluded:

> doubt must now be cast on all historical estimates which assess an area in terms of the firmness of its roots in the past, without at the same time bringing into account the possibly quite different aspirations which the inhabitants may have for the future.[24]

The ecological association between higher stability and greater willingness to move is not explained by elaboration by age of household head, type and condition of accommodation, rent levels or tenure. Put crudely, regardless of age, housing conditions and tenure, people in Low Hill and Smithsdown were more inclined to move away than people in Abercromby. Nevertheless these factors and others were shown to have an important influence on willingness to move and the authors made a number of suggestions as to why the area difference was so marked. In particular an awareness of declining standards in the stable area and the presence of many family houses containing households with high aspirations for their children may have been responsible. From the point of view of residents of the more transient Abercromby area the style of life of a twilight zone may have suited their purposes far better than any alternative, particularly if a move would involve changing to a tenancy under a local authority rather than a private landlord.

The sample size of an official study in Oldham permitted only limited elaboration of the data but confirmed the importance of youth and the presence of children in encouraging a move.[25] Wilkinson and Sigsworth's study of clearance areas in Leeds sought evidence on a set of hypotheses relating attitude towards moving to: a) the district or street in which the household lived; b) condition of the houses and standard of amenities; and c) the structure of the household.[26] Crudely stated, their analysis found support for the two latter hypotheses but little support for the former. Concentrating on the 16 per cent of the sample who were *against* moving they found a particularly large proportion of old, long-established and childless households living on small incomes but in comparatively better housing conditions. Seventy-six per cent of household heads who were against moving were aged over 50 and 82 per cent had no children. Owner occupiers were more prominent amongst 'stayers' than amongst 'movers', comprising 18 per cent compared with only 6 per cent of movers.[27]

It was apparent from direct experience interviewing in the survey areas of the present study that age was a major factor predisposing residents to favour or oppose moving. A broad grouping of households by age of housewife shows that a substantial majority, 67 per cent, of younger households with housewives aged under 45 favoured moving. For middle-aged households with housewife aged 45-59 only 44 per cent favoured a move and for old people aged 60 or more the proportion was 37 per cent. But these differences are more pronounced when marital condition as well as age is taken into account (Table 35).

Whereas 71 per cent of younger married households were in favour of moving and only 8 per cent against, only 39 per cent of younger non-married households were in favour of moving and 30 per cent were opposed. This profile of opinion exactly mirrors the distribution for old people aged 60 or over. For the old people reluctance to move is partly explicable in terms of their very long attachment to the area: 47 per cent of old households had been living in their present house for 30 years or more! For young non-married households, however, length of residence was not an important factor as 77 per cent of such households had been in their present house for less than five years. Opposition to or support for moving is therefore not explicable simply in terms of age or length of residence. Rather, life cycle stage is a summary measure of the demands on housing expressed by individual households.

The second major factor affecting attitudes is tenure of accommodation. As Table 36 shows very few tenants, only 15 per cent, were against moving and well over half, 57 per cent, were unequivocally in favour. But owner occupiers were divided roughly one third in favour and one third against moving.

The interplay of 'net gains and losses' for a family which would result from a move is elegantly articulated in Dennis's formulation of the consumer's preference-array. 'A family's judgement upon its total housing experience is a matter of weighing up gains and losses in the light of the family's total circumstances.'[28] Expenditure on housing has to be weighed against the other claims on the family budget; the advantages and disadvantages of the present house have to be weighed against

Table 35. Households' attitude to moving by stage in life cycle

Life cycle stage	Attitude to moving			
	In favour %	With reservations %	Against %	Base
Young non-married	39	31	30	74
Young married	71	21	8	546
Middle-aged non-married	49	32	19	109
Middle-aged married	42	31	26	258
Old people 60+	37	33	30	542
All households	51	28	21	1,529

Table 36. Households' attitude to moving by tenure

Tenure	Attitude to moving			
	In favour %	With reservations %	Against %	Base
Owner occupiers	34	31	35	426
Tenants	57	27	15	1,118
All households	51	28	21	1,544

the merits and drawbacks of the particular local authority housing that the family is likely to be allocated.[29] Economic imperatives may reinforce the claims of sentiment or may work against them. For each household their attitude towards the prospect of another house depends on the balance of loss and advantage which only they can appraise. The same *physical* condition of a particular dwelling will be differently perceived by its occupants depending on their view of their own requirements and the place occupied by good housing in their hierarchy of values. Hence no simple approach to the physical definition of 'slum' areas suitable for demolition can expect to meet the approval of all households. In fact Dennis found the same regularities of association between age, length of residence, owner occupation, family structure and housing preferences as previous studies. But none of these factors alone explained resistance to or approval of change. Although 64 per cent of owner occupiers were against demolition, over 30 per cent favoured it;[30] although most young families favoured demolition a substantial minority were against it.[31] The influence of house condition, tenure and life cycle stage is therefore only a very limited representation of the complex of interacting forces determining attitude to moving. Nevertheless Table 37 draws together all three factors to explore their relative importance in affecting a household's inclination to move. Such a multivariate table requires a summary measure of house conditions whereby housing can be simply divided into 'good' and 'poor'. Table 37 divides households into those with sole use of an inside WC which are classified as living in good conditions and the remainder which are classified as having poor housing conditions. The analysis is confined to households where the housewife was currently married or was an old person aged 60 or over.

The figures of Table 37 show that there was a major division of opinion between couples below the age of 45 and those above that age. A higher proportion of young couples favoured moving regardless of housing situation than amongst households even in the worst housing situation in older age groups. The only exception to this rule is the 32 per cent of young couples owning good houses who nevertheless favoured moving. This is a smaller proportion than the 60 per cent of middle aged couples and 46 per cent of old people who rented poor houses. The argument also holds for the opposite extreme of opinion — those unequivocally against moving. Again, excepting young owner occupiers, smaller proportions of young couples opposed moving regardless of conditions than any group of older couples. A further distinctive feature of young couples compared with the rest is the relative importance of tenure and house conditions in determining attitudes. For young couples house conditions were a more important determinant than tenure so that owners of poor houses were slightly more favourable to moving than renters of good houses. For older households owner occupation, regardless of house conditions, was more attractive than renting even a good condition house.

The commonest household situation was to be a tenant of a poor condition house, regardless of age and the criterion by which poor condition is defined. For this majority group of the population there was very little resistance to moving and, except for old people, a clear majority in favour; almost 80 per cent of young couples and 60 per cent of middle-aged couples favoured moving and for old people the proportion was almost one half. This dominant distribution of opinion also holds for young couples in intermediate housing situations whereas

Table 37. Households' attitude to moving by life cycle stage, tenure and housing conditions (use of WC)

Life cycle stage	Tenure	Housing conditions	Attitude to Moving			Base
			In favour %	With reservations %	Against %	
Young married <45	Rent	poor	79	17	4	316
	Rent	good	61	26	13	90
	Own	poor	64	23	13	118
	Own	good	32	37	32	19
Middle-aged married 45 – 59	Rent	poor	60	24	16	138
	Rent	good	35	38	27	26
	Own	poor	24	39	37	71
	Own	good	4	39	57	23
Old people 60 and over	Rent	poor	46	37	17	324
	Rent	good	39	28	33	67
	Own	poor	22	31	47	110
	Own	good	7	17	76	41
All households			51	28	21	1,544

older households in intermediate situations were divided fairly evenly between favouring and opposing a move. The only groups with a clear balance of opinion against moving were older owner occupiers living in good condition houses; three quarters of the old people in this situation were against moving. But we should not assume that this trend in opinion is the result only of a natural psychological inclination to conservatism among the old. The evidence of Table 37 in particular points to the division of opinion being firmly based in a rational appraisal of the effects of slum clearance on household circumstances and requirements. Old people were more resistant to the change largely because they had much less to gain from it given their household circumstances.

For the extreme groups — young couples renting poor houses and old people owning good houses — the three factors of life cycle stage, tenure and housing conditions do largely explain their attitude to moving but there are clearly other important influences particularly for intermediate groups. The next chapter considers the housing market situation and aspirations of these sub-groups in the light of further survey data.

NOTES

1. '... It is monstrous, if it can be avoided to break up existing communities and force people against their will to move and to live miles away from the area which they have come to regard as their home ... ' Paul Channon during the second reading of the Conservative government's Housing and Planning Bill, February 1974; House of Commons, *Official Report,* Vol. 868, Col. 1058.
2. Young and Willmott foreshadowed the policy of house improvement by almost twenty years when they argued that the right policy for Bethnal Green 'would certainly mean saving as many as possible of the existing houses where they are structurally sound by installing within the fabric new bathrooms, lavatories and kitchens'; Michael Young and Peter Willmott, *op. cit.,* p. 198.
3. Office of Population Censuses and Surveys, Social Survey Division, *The General Household Survey; Introductory Report,* HMSO, 1973.
4. Norman Dennis, *op. cit.* (1970), p. 313.
5. R. Wilkinson, 'Attitudes to the Housing Environment: An Analysis of Private and Local Authority Households in Batley, Leeds and York', *Urban Studies,* Vol. 9 No. 2, June 1972.
6. The definition of 'housewife' used in this survey could include a male as the housewife. This occurred in all-male households or households with only a male adult.
7. For a description of the building of this particular area see J.N. Tarn, *Five Per Cent Philanthropy: An Account of Housing in Urban Areas between 1860 and 1914,* Cambridge University Press, 1973, pp. 87-89.
8. Department of the Environment, Cmnd. 5339, *op. cit.*
9. Ministry of Housing and Local Government, Cmnd. 3602, *op. cit.;* also

Housing Statistics, Great Britain, op. cit., Nos. 9, 10 and 14.
10. Cmnd. 3602, *op. cit.,* Table 3; Department of the Environment, Cmnd. 5339, *op. cit.,* Table 4.
11. Charles Vereker and J.B. Mays, *Urban Redevelopment and Social Change: A study of Social Conditions in Central Liverpool 1955-56,* Liverpool University Press, 1961, pp. 7-8.
12. *Ibid.,* p. 94.
13. *Ibid.,* derived from Table XXX, p. 98.
14. *Ibid.,* p. 110.
15. R. Wilkinson, *op. cit.*
16. Ken Coates and Richard Silburn, *Poverty: the Forgotten Englishmen,* Penguin Books, 1970, p. 88.
17. *Ibid.,* p. 88.
18. F.J.C. Amos, *Social Survey: A Study of the Inner Areas of Liverpool,* Liverpool Corporation, mimeo, p. 11.
19. Norman Dennis, *op. cit.* (1970), p. 180 and p. 206.
20. *Ibid.,* p. 336. However some surveys have produced evidence of large majorities for or against clearance. Wilkinson and Sigsworths' earlier study of clearance areas in Leeds found 81 per cent of sample households in favour of moving; see R. Wilkinson and E. Sigsworth, 'A study of slum clearance areas in Leeds', *Yorkshire Bulletin of Social and Economic Research,* Vol. 15, No. 1, May 1963; also R. Wilkinson and D.M. Merry, 'A Statistical Analysis of Attitudes to Moving', *Urban Studies.,* Vol. 2, No. 1, May 1965. By contrast a Ministry of Housing survey of St. Mary's Ward, Oldham found 75 per cent of the population wanting to stay in the area: see Ministry of Housing and Local Government, *Living in a Slum: A Study of St. Mary's Oldham, op. cit.* (1970).
21. Norman Dennis, *op. cit.* (1970), p. 248.
22. Charles Vereker and J.B. Mays, *op. cit.,* pp. 82-83.
23. Michael Young and Peter Willmott, *op. cit.*
24. Charles Vereker and J.B. Mays, *op. cit.,* p. 94.
25. Ministry of Housing and Local Government, *op. cit.* (1970), p. 28.
26. R. Wilkinson and D.M. Merry, *op. cit.,* p. 4.
27. *Ibid.,* p. 13.
28. Norman Dennis, *op. cit.* (1970), p. 291.
29. *Ibid.,* p. 292.
30. *Ibid.,* p. 311.
31. *Ibid.,* p. 311.

8 HOUSING MARKET SITUATION AND ATTITUDES TOWARDS MOVING

The range of characteristics incorporated in the analysis of the previous chapter cannot encompass the full variety of conditions which individual households will take into account when deciding for or against a move. In particular, the analysis so far has taken no account of the difference between households in their likely access to alternative housing. The present chapter therefore analyses separately the situation of some important subsections of the population in relation to their prospects for future housing. The groups considered are young households, the middle-aged and old, owner occupiers and immigrants. Except for the first two these are not discrete groups but taking up the perspective of each group in turn brings out clearly the different needs, priorities and advantages of different types of household.

Younger Households

It is apparent from Table 38 that within the group of households with a housewife aged under 45 there was a very sharp distinction between the households of married couples and households where the housewife was single, separated, widowed or divorced — the non-married. Whereas young married couples were the most favourable towards moving, young non-married households were as reluctant to move as old people aged 60 or over.

This division of opinion reflects the very different housing requirements of the two groups. About half of the young non-married households in the sample were genuinely 'unattached' adults living in households without children, some of them young single people living alone or with friends (Table 38). They included a number of students or young professional people taking advantage of small, cheap, central accommodation. They had little to gain from demolition because their claim on a council house was at best doubtful. By and large they had made a positive choice to live in the area and regretted the loss of a 'human' and non-bureaucratic housing environment. Most had not previously considered the alternative of a council house and only two thirds expected to be rehoused by the council now that their houses were being demolished.

The remaining group of non-married households were those con-

Housing Market Situation and Attitudes Towards Moving   171

taining children under 16, that is, households of single parent families. Although proportionately fewer of these households opposed moving than amongst childless households there was a far smaller proportion in favour of moving than amongst married couples with children, only 40 per cent compared with 73 per cent. It may well be that these 'irregular' households which are often disadvantaged by very low household income viewed council housing as a particularly expensive alternative compared with their present accommodation.

Table 38. Young households, detailed life cycle stage by attitude to moving

	Attitude to moving		
Life cycle stage	In favour %	Against %	Base
Single, aged 15-34	38	50	26
Widowed, etc. aged 15-34 without children at home	33	22	9
Widowed, etc. aged 15-44 with children at home	42	18	39
All young non-married	39	30	74
Married aged 15-44 without children at home	61	9	81
Married aged 15-44 with children at home	73	8	465
All young married	71	8	546

Numerically far more important were the young married couples, particularly those with children. Although childless households were slightly less predisposed to move than established families the overwhelming opinion of both categories positively favoured moving. 46 per cent could think of nothing they disliked about the idea of moving and only 3 per cent said there was nothing they looked forward to (Table A13). The benefits of a modern house with up-to-date amenities and a better environment for children were the main attractions of the move; 55 per cent of young married households specifically mentioned the advantages of a bathroom, hot and cold water or inside WC and two thirds mentioned other advantages of modernity — more space, a kitchen suitable for modern appliances, rooms and materials easier to clean. Mrs V. In Liverpool summed it up. She looked forward to 'a bathroom, grass outside the door, no broken glass or bad smells. Everything a new house can offer.' Altogether 42 per cent of young married households had been on the waiting list for a council house before slum clearance began compared with less than a quarter of any other group.

Respondents' aspirations were often expressed in terms of opportunities for the children. The cramped old fashioned surroundings of their present homes were particularly inadequate for younger, larger, households. Comparing the number of usable rooms in their accommodation with the number of bedrooms required by the bedroom standard for that size of household over one quarter of young married households would require to have had someone sleeping in every room, including the kitchen to meet the standard. A further 26 per cent would have had to keep no more than one room free for eating in and as a general living room. However, most families with four rooms, for instance with two up and two down, defined the upstairs rooms as bedrooms, leaving the downstairs rooms as kitchen and living room unless they were really hard pressed. Thus Mrs A., 33 years old and living with her husband and two children, a boy of 11 years and a girl of 9 years, used only two rooms as bedrooms so the boy and girl were still sharing. She wanted to move 'for the kids, to give them a room each of their own'. They had been on the waiting list for fourteen years and saw no alternative to council housing:

> It's about time I got something. These houses are finished. If they don't knock 'em down they'll fall down. We're just waiting and waiting. Can't do any decorating. Just hanging on all the time waiting.

The lower densities of new estates implied some adaptation of life style but many younger couples gave the impression that they were prepared consciously to sacrifice their own interests 'for the sake of the kiddies'. Although many shared the view of their older neighbours that 'streets are friendlier than the estates' they still felt that the estates were better for the children.

But whilst the young married couples were most committed to moving they were not all reconciled to accepting a council house. Indeed, apart from young, unmarried households, young couples included the largest proportion of households expecting to rehouse themselves, 14 per cent. The great majority of these intended to buy another house.

In making their appraisal of a council house alternative younger households were far better equipped by personal experience than older households. Younger households are distinguished from the old not only by their stage in the life cycle and the attendant household size and structure but also by a different historical experience. Council housing as a major element of working class housing is even now relatively new and only younger households have grown up to take it for granted. Thus Table 39 shows a very marked difference between younger and older households in their experience of council housing.

Table 39. Life cycle stage by experience of council housing

Life cycle stage	Never lived in a council house %	Lived in a council house:		Base
		as tenant %	as child %	
Young married	51	9	40	455
Middle-aged married	80	11	9	230
Old people 60+	83	13	4	505
All households	71	11	17	1361

This table excludes households who were definitely planning to rehouse themselves and we do not know whether their experience of council housing was comparable. But among the majority expecting to be rehoused by the council 49 per cent of young households had experienced life in a council house compared with only 20 per cent of middle-aged and 17 per cent of old households. Most of the young households expecting council housing had lived there as children and were following a cyclical pattern. At marriage they had moved from a house on a council estate to the cheap accommodation of the inner city often hoping that through slum clearance, or, following the establishment of a family, through the waiting list, they would move back again to a council estate. A typical example is the case of Mrs A. and her husband, aged 20 and 21 without children. They had moved into their house less than two years previously when first married, explicitly to get a council house:

The new houses are much better, that's why we took this house. We put our names on the waiting list as soon as we got married. I don't like it down here. Used to live in a council house with Mum. I want to move back there to the same estate. I wouldn't rehouse myself because it would be an old house and I want a new one. I wouldn't like my own bought house — too much responsibility. I wouldn't rent because I don't want another place like this.

Many younger households explicitly regarded their present accommodation in this way as only a temporary home. Fifty-two per cent of respondents in young couples' households claimed to have known when they moved to their present house that the area was likely to be knocked down. This does not mean that they all moved in with the express intention of being rehoused, particularly as their knowledge was often only speculation based on what they saw happening in similar areas elsewhere. But it does mean that many young households had never settled, knowing that their present accommodation was not going to be their final house.

Reflecting this instrumental view of their present housing and their expectations of future change, young couples on the whole were far more critical of the performance of council officials, particularly housing officials, than were older people. While agreeing with the general policy of slum clearance a substantial proportion of young respondents were highly critical of its implementation. As one woman commented 'they mess things up the way they do it but it's marvellous'. Older respondents who were more likely to oppose the policy outright were far less critical of the manner of its execution. In Table 40 criticism of the council's activities is operationalised in terms of answers to three questions concerning respondents' opinions of their treatment by council staff. In each case a far higher proportion of young couples made critical comments than amongst older households.

Table 40. Life cycle stage by criticisms of the council

Life cycle stage	Opinion of council			Base
	Staff are not helpful %	Staff do not treat people equally %	Council have not kept people informed %	
Young married	38	45	68	546
Middle-aged married	34	35	59	259
Old people 60+	21	27	48	542

Young couples, with a wider experience of the council housing alternative and a clear articulation of their material expectations of rehousing may well alienate local authority officials by making the best of their bargaining position to get the house they want. Mrs A. in Liverpool who was 'just waiting for the day' she could move had nevertheless turned down two offers of accommodation because they were 'relets' and in poor condition. With only two children and no chance of an offer from the waiting list, slum clearance represented her one real chance of getting what she wanted from the council. Council staff expecting gratitude and constrained by deadlines may well be resentful of people who 'stick out for what they want' and to this extent the antipathy expressed by many young couples may reflect a real difference of treatment.

For young couples, the largest single group of households in clearance areas, there was a strong emphasis on the material benefits of a move to another house and few regrets over the passing of the old order. For many, their period of residence in a slum area was only a temporary expedient in any case before they could return to the council house environment they knew as children. For others, any advantages of the old area were outweighed by the benefits of a new environment for the children. For either group the inadequacies of the local authority's performance frustrated the fulfillment of their aspiration towards a decent house.

The Middle Aged and Old

Amongst households in which the housewife was aged 45 or over there was comparatively little difference between the middle aged and the old. Table 41 shows some anomalies amongst the middle aged non-married households; in sharp contrast to the young non-married households there was a larger proportion in favour of moving than amongst married households of the same age. In addition, non-married households with children were less favourable to the move than unattached households of the same age. But amongst the main categories of older life cycle stage there was generally very little difference in the proportions unequivocally favouring or opposing a move; the proportion favouring the move ranged only between 36 and 44 per cent and the proportion opposing it varied only from 26 to 30 per cent.

For both middle aged and old households there is often less chance than amongst younger households of being allocated a house rather than a flat or maisonette. Since 83 per cent of old households consisted of only one or two persons they were very likely to be rehoused in less conventional small units, often multi-storey flats. Middle aged households, though typically larger than households of old people, often with adult children still at home, were still unlikely to be allocated a house rather than a flat. Liverpool, for instance, allocated houses only to households with a child still aged under 9 at the time of allocation. For many a move to a flat would therefore mean a real loss of amenity, particularly a spare bedroom for visiting relatives and the storage or work space of a shed or yard.

Table 41. Middle aged and old households, detailed life cycle stage by attitude to moving

Life cycle stage	Attitude to moving		Base
	In favour %	Against %	
Single, aged 35-59	54	20	41
Widowed, etc. aged 45-59 without children at home	50	20	40
Widowed, etc. aged 45-59 with children at home	39	18	28
All middle aged non-married	49	19	109
Married, aged 45-59 without children at home	40	27	99
Married, aged 45-59 with children at home	44	26	159
All middle aged married	42	26	258
Single, aged 60+	37	30	86
Widowed, etc. aged 60+	36	29	259
Married, aged 60+	39	30	197
All old	37	30	542

A radical change of housing environment may also be particularly challenging for old people. Many are set in a traditional pattern of housekeeping and feel incapable of mastering the modern technology of electric fires, lifts and central heating. Mrs C., an 85 year old widow, still cooked on an open range 'because my husband didn't believe in cookers'. She tried to work out the implications of the change:

I don't know what the new houses are like inside. I won't have to go to the dustbins every morning, that'll be good for me. But I'm worried what kind of place it shall be. I'm not very quick at taking things in now. If the gas or electricity doesn't work . . . '

At the same time it is often the lack of customary tasks which isolates old people from the life around them. Mrs B., a 75 year old widow in Leeds, did not want to move:

because at my age you're used to this sort of house. You're not so neighbourly in a flat. You don't know who you're going to get against you — you don't know whether they'll be kind and help you. People in these flats don't seem to mix somehow. You're boxed in, you don't meet people going to the toilet or the dustbins. You read about loneliness among old people in flats. I'd finish my days here if I could. The thought of moving, it's terrible, it's upsetting me very much. I don't want to leave Hunslet, I'd like to write to the papers and tell them old people don't really like it.

Almost a quarter of respondents in old households said that there was nothing they were looking forward to about the move (Table A13) and loss of the familiar was their most common fear; 31 per cent of the old cited this as their principal dislike for moving.

With some reason, therefore, older residents saw themselves as gaining less from council housing than young families. 'It's come too late for us' was a common response. Some who had invested time and money in maintenance and repair of their houses and convinced themselves that 'it's good enough for us' found it difficult to accept that their house had become 'unfit for human habitation' overnight. But their own consciousness of change in the area and the process of dereliction resulting from slum clearance itself both worked to reconcile old people to the break. When some of the oldest residents had moved in their houses represented the best of working class aspirations and they had anticipated staying 'to the end of my days'. But the deterioration of the property made the houses increasingly difficult to manage. In addition many felt that 'the young people don't keep it the way we used to' and 'the old life' had already gone.

Once a clearance area is declared the process of deterioration may be very rapid. Landlords disclaim responsibility for repairs to houses that have been 'taken over' and from which they are no longer receiving rent. The council is reluctant to repair houses it intends to demolish. As houses become vacant it is more difficult to control the children who throw stones at windows and build bonfires amongst the rubbish, occasionally mistaking occupied houses for empty ones. Whilst most local authorities attempt to board up empty houses constant vigilance is required to close up any tempting gaps as they arise. Residents, almost none of whom have a telephone, weary of trying to keep the maintenance department informed. Once the area becomes dilapidated, normal services, refuse collection, deliveries, street cleaning and lighting become more erratic, perhaps because it hardly seems worthwhile and doing a decent job is more difficult. Organised thieves begin to steal valuable lead piping, leaving residents flooded and without water supply or toilet facilities. As the area becomes more open to strangers residents retreat behind locked doors, fearing for their safety. In this situation even the sternest opposition falters. Most older residents found themselves torn between loyalty to the old place and distress at its deterioration.

The whole set of conflicting hopes and fears is perhaps best expressed by Mrs D. a competent and articulate 66 year old who had been living with her husband in a Leeds back-to-back for over 30 years. She had four rooms and an outside shared WC down the street, four doors away. They were 'good houses in their way' but she agreed with plans for clearance for the sake of a bath and toilet:

> The landlord could have put baths in years ago, but they don't break their necks even to do repairs. Sometimes I feel I don't want to move. I want to stay in Hunslet. But I want a toilet and that, we really do want something better. But they are not shoving us in no-man's land where I know no-one. On some estates you go miles for shops carrying things all that way. I'm used to bobbing round the corner. We don't live with one another, but everyone will help if you knock at the door. The old lady opposite, I keep an eye on her. That's what keeps us together. If the milk is left on the doorstep I go across to check she's all right. Neighbours are important.

> Slum people are moving in here now. This was a beautiful street when we came. Now you don't know who you'll get next to. These young people don't keep the place like we used to. Always go out to Bingo and everything. I wish it was all settled. Now we know we're going we want to go. We might have stayed in the past.

This does not mean that all older households were reluctant movers coerced by the destruction of their familiar surroundings. Some old people were well aware of the hardships they had endured for too long and welcomed the move. Many already had sons or daughters living in council housing and looked forward to joining them; 38 per cent of old households had asked to be rehoused near family and friends in a particular estate. But for the old people the affectual ties of long acquaintance with the area and dependence on a network of established relationships were particularly important factors influencing their attitude towards moving.

For middle aged households whose prospects of changing their jobs may be poor, locational factors, particularly convenience for work and shopping, were an important consideration.[1]

Fifty-eight per cent of middle aged households specified convenience to work or shops as the main reason for their choice of council house area compared with only 44 per cent of young households and 32 per cent of the old (Table A13). Lacking the pressures of a young family the convenience of a central location was often a more persuasive consideration for the middle aged than the internal amenities of a modern house.

Both old and middle aged households may achieve far less in tangible advantages by moving to council housing than the young. For many the perceived advantages were not sufficient to offset the convenience and security of their present accommodation. The loss of their present accommodation was not an expected part of an overall life plan as it was for many young people. Nevertheless, it is worthwhile recalling that, on the evidence of this survey only one quarter to one third of middle aged and old households overall were unequivocally against moving and were counterbalanced by a slightly larger proportion who were unequivocally in favour. But amongst the minority opposing clearance were households who undoubtedly had a lot to lose.

Owner Occupiers

Jennings's study of the Barton Hill area of Bristol stresses the entrenched opposition of owner occupiers to slum clearance. The 18 per cent of the families who owned their homes provided a hard core of resistance to redevelopment and the study emphasises the sense of betrayal of wage earners who felt they were being robbed of their homes and their savings by compulsory purchase.[2] On the other hand Brennan's study of Glasgow points out that, where landlords have sold off houses for a few hundred pounds to rid themselves of unprofitable properties, residents may not see the acquisition of a house as 'getting on' in the world. Purchase of such a house may be less an investment than a temporary expedient to get a roof over one's head.[3] The present study indicates that this distinction between two groups of owner occupiers is also a distinction between age groups with older households more likely to be committed owners and the younger households more likely to have become owners merely because of expediency.

The opposition to clearance expressed chiefly by owner occupiers in better property and the older age groups derived partly from their awareness of the financial and material advantages of owning a house and partly from a sense of personal pride and status. Many residents, both renters and owners, had spent time and effort on improving their houses but owners were often more thoroughgoing than renters could afford to be (Table 42). Though 'cosmetic' improvements such as installing new fireplaces and flushing doors were equally common amongst both renters and owners many more owner occupiers had undertaken substantial internal and external improvements such as installing a bath, a new sink or rewiring and some owner occupiers had virtually rebuilt their houses. But for the owner occupiers the costs of do-it-yourself improvement were closely controllable. Eighty one per cent had paid off the purchase price of the house and the expense of improving their domestic amenities could be spread over a long period. For many their housing costs were fixed while council rents were both substantial and rising. Looked at in this way, for the middle aged and old having their own house was an important defence against the poverty of old age.

Owners' efforts to improve their houses also reflected a genuine sense of pride and personal status, particularly for the old. In terms of traditional housing aspirations they represented an elite group who had achieved a widely recognised goal of security and relative comfort. For such owners the onslaught of slum clearance was sometimes regarded as both a financial disaster and a personal affront. Mr G., aged 57, lived with his wife and 19-year-old daughter in a mellowed stone house in Bingley. Although it was built back-to-back the house was quite large with five rooms and an attic;

> It needs a bathroom, you could easily put one in. It's our house so we've looked after it. Only thing the [Public Health Inspector's] report could find wrong with it was a *warped door*. Had it all in the papers, there was quite a fuss.

Despite the consciousness of personal pride bestowed by owner occupation one must not be led by conventional stereotypes of the owner occupier into supposing that owner occupiers are thereby separated

Housing Market Situation and Attitudes Towards Moving 181

from the mainstream of working class experience in their locality. In terms of their market situation most owners had more in common with tenants than with middle class owners of mortgageable houses; their perception of owner occupation as 'rent free' housing was indicative of this. Unlike the owner occupier of the 'property owning democracy' the houses of these owner occupiers did not usually represent a substantial capital asset. Sixty one per cent had been bought for £600 or less and their value had not necessarily increased with time. The handful of owners who had paid more than £1,000 for their homes had often acquired a small shop or business as well. With local prices often very low compensation, even at market value, was very low and, in any case, negotiations for compensation were unlikely to be completed in time for an owner occupier to have available the cash to help him buy another house. So many owner occupiers had no option but to accept a council house.

Table 42. Improvements to present house by tenure

Improvements	Owner occupiers %	Tenants %
Painting, decorating and plaster repairs	64	66
Fireplaces modernised, flushed doors, etc.	35	34
Constant hot water installed	12	9
WC replaced	17	3
Bath installed	27	5
Other internal	66	46
All external	25	7
Base	426	1,121

Note: percentages add to more than 100 per cent because more than one improvement was made by some households.

Nonetheless, many owners saw a council house as a definite second best. This was particularly true for the older residents who had bought their houses in the 1940s and 1950s. Buying a house in an inner city area could then be seen as having long-term advantages of security and economy and buyers could reasonably expect the house to serve them through the rest of their lives. Compulsory rehousing was therefore less attractive to this group both because, in common with other middle aged and older residents, they stood to gain little from council housing in terms of immediate calculable benefits and because rehousing inherently challenged their own prudence in making provision for their old age. Opposition for this group was in part an expression of frustration at being unable to provide for themselves.

By contrast younger couples who bought houses in the late fifties and sixties when it had become clear that all inner city areas were threatened with slum clearance, did so in a very different spirit from the older owner occupiers. In only two of the main sample areas did owner occupiers make up a significant proportion of households. Table 43 shows that in Manchester and Liverpool, roughly three quarters of all young married couples favoured moving regardless of whether they owned their houses or rented them. In 'pool' areas, however, the young married owner occupiers were much less favourable to moving than their counterparts in Manchester and Liverpool; only 44 per cent favoured a move compared with 72 per cent and 79 per cent. There was also a marked difference between young married owners and renters in the pool areas. Eighty one per cent of these renters favoured moving compared with 44 per cent of owner occupiers. The pool areas were quite small in size and usually fairly isolated patches of slum clearance compared with the broad swathes of inner Liverpool and Manchester. In such areas it seems that households may have continued to buy in expectation of a fairly long term commitment since the threat of slum clearance was typically less obvious than in the large cities.

Following this interpretation of our data, life cycle stage is an indicator not only of present household circumstances and housing needs but also of personal histories in relation to an historically changing housing situation. But while the historical context of past housing decisions and the present pattern of household needs may go a long way to explaining a household's current reaction to slum clearance and their evaluation of prospects they may give little guidance regarding the precise outcome of events. Can the apparent differences of subjective evaluation between owners and renters find expression in the adoption of different housing strategies for the future? Is there any real difference in slum clearance areas between the market situations of owner occupiers and renters?

Studies of housing administration, and most statistical series, generally distinguish only the three major sectors of owner occupiers, council tenants and private renters. While these are the important distinctions with respect to many aspects of housing legislation they lump together, particularly within the owner occupied sector, widely differing housing circumstances. The bimodal distribution of purchase prices and housing conditions of owner occupied housing has been remarked elsewhere.[4] Owner occupiers in the present sample represented the extreme lower limit of owner occupation in these respects. Having only a tenuous hold at the lower limit of this sector the owner occupier in a clearance area faced with the crisis of moving rarely has sufficient resources available to move to another bought house which will itself be free of the threat of demolition.

Table 43. Life cycle stage, tenure and area by attitude to moving (areas with 20 per cent or more owner occupiers only)

Area, life cycle and tenure		Attitude to moving		Base
		In favour %	Against %	
MANCHESTER				
Young married	Rent	79	3	33
Middle aged married	Rent	69	–	13
Old people 60+	Rent	54	12	26
Young married	Own	71	10	21
Middle aged married	Own	50	–	4
Old people 60+	Own	25	25	12
LIVERPOOL				
Young married	Rent	72	7	54
Middle aged married	Rent	60	16	24
Old people 60+	Rent	54	17	59
Young married	Own	76	8	25
Middle aged married	Own	17	83	6
Old people 60+	Own	–	100	3
POOL AREAS				
Young married	Rent	81	5	175
Middle aged married	Rent	48	26	81
Old people 60+	Rent	40	20	165
Young married	Own	44	20	75
Middle aged married	Own	15	42	78
Old people 60+	Own	18	57	132

Within the limitations of existing sociological theories of the housing market it is difficult to accommodate the diversity of circumstances and aspirations amongst owner occupiers. John Rex's theory of housing classes would categorise the entire population of the present sample as 'council tenants in slum houses awaiting demolition'.[5] This classification emphasises the possibility of access to council housing via slum clearance as the over-riding feature of residents' housing situation and ignores the distinction between tenant and owner occupier existing prior to the creation of a clearance area. Applying Rex's classification to the situation before the local authority intervened, 72 per cent of households would fall into his class of 'tenants of a whole house owned by a private landlord' but the remaining 28 per cent of owner occupiers would fall into no clear category. Few could be considered as members of the class of mortgageable owners of an appreciating asset.

The strength of Rex's model is that it identifies households in terms of the main resource available to them at the point of decision — that is, the means of access to a council house. Regardless of the difference in resources between owner occupiers and tenants in the past the intervention of the local authority places everybody in the same position, dependent on an offer of a council house.

Subsequent critics of Rex's formulation have argued that a stress on *types of housing situation* rather than *means of access to housing* obscures the real basis of differentiation.[6] Pahl has suggested an elaboration in which classes are crucially differentiated by their access to capital.[7] In Pahl's scheme previous owner occupiers fall unequivocally into the class of 'owners of capital sufficient to own their own houses and owning'. But slum clearance both forces a move regardless of the owner's immediate financial circumstances and ability to raise a further capital sum and physically eradicates another part of the low cost housing within his reach. Most owners of short life property in slum clearance areas do not have access to sufficient capital to choose to own in the 'conventional' market and are thereby forced into Pahl's final category of 'those who *must* rent'.

The weakness of both the Rex and Pahl models is the implication of a simple one-to-one relationship between households' objective market circumstances and their subjective evaluations and aspirations for the future.

For many owners house purchase was primarily a device to reduce housing costs in the long run by living 'rent free'. Many knew full well that this was only a stopgap arrangement until the council demolished their houses and rehoused them. But, while a decent council house was the ceiling of their aspirations for some, for others owner occupation represented a genuinely preferable alternative and only lack of access to additional capital was likely to force them to rent from the council.

While the great majority of residents — 85 per cent — had recognised their dependence on the council and expected to accept a council house others continued to aspire to some alternative and, at the time of inter-

Housing Market Situation and Attitudes Towards Moving 185

view, intended to rehouse themselves. There were more owner occupiers than renters intending to rehouse themselves — 18 per cent compared with only 7 per cent of tenants. Moreover, almost all owner occupiers who intended to rehouse themselves intended to buy. Table 44 shows that 17 per cent of owner occupiers overall intended to buy their next house. Over half of these were young married couples who, although more likely to be able to get some sort of loan than older households, were usually the more eager to move to council housing.

Table 44. Present tenure by expected tenure

Present tenure	Expected tenure				Base
	Council tenant %	Owner occupier %	Private tenant %	D.K. %	
Tenants	93	4	3	1	1121
Owner occupiers	82	17	1	—	426

While it is fairly easy to understand why some households should want to buy it is less clear whether they were realistically in a position to do so or whether owners were in a better position than renters in this respect. Although most owner occupiers in the sample would receive full market value compensation the settlement of a precise amount and payment of the cash was often seriously delayed and would often not, of itself, be sufficient to purchase a replacement house.

Immigrant Households

In general the population profile of the present sample confirms the widely held view that slum clearance procedure does not deal with transitional areas of multi-occupation and immigrant housing. Apart from small groups of immigrants in Wolverhampton and Doncaster only the Tower Hamlets area had a concentration of immigrant households.

In the Tower Hamlets area 41 per cent of respondents or their spouses, that is 54 households, were foreign born. Over half of these households were Indian or Pakistani, a quarter Cypriot and the remainder European Jews or Maltese. As a whole the foreign born were younger than the British born population (Table 45), amongst whom 41 per cent of housewives were aged 60 or more. The peculiar balance of age structure is obscured when the two groups are treated together. Both the two major groups, Asians and Cypriots, were considerably younger than the small European and Maltese groups reflecting in part the national pattern of immigration to this country. All the Cypriot households comprised families with children aged under 16 and half of them had been resident in the area for over ten years. By contrast, almost three quarters of Asian households had lived in the area for less than ten years and half of them for less than two years. Furthermore, 17 of the 28 households were all male households. They were usually an extended family group supporting dependents still living in Pakistan by their earnings in the local tailoring and garment industry of the East End. It was clear that the local authority regarded the area as a 'problem' area and that the position of the Asian residents was their major cause of concern.

Table 45. Tower Hamlets residents, life cycle stage by place of birth

Life cycle stage	Place of birth		
	Foreign born, Tower Hamlets sample %	British born, Tower Hamlets sample %	All households in total sample %
Young non-married	6	3	5
Middle aged non-married	15	24	7
Young married	58	21	36
Middle aged married	12	11	17
Old people 60+	10	41	36
Base	52	75	1,532

On the whole, the immigrant population of the Tower Hamlets area responded in much the same way as their British born neighbours to the prospect of moving with young families more favourable to moving than the older or unattached households. This meant that the Asian all male households were not generally in favour of moving. But their main cause of concern arose not from the move *per se* but from their often poor position in the queue for council housing. It has been pointed out many times by other authors how residence qualifications may work particularly against the chances of immigrant households. Here again was an example of the process in action.

One of the regulations of housing allocation for slum clearance cases in Tower Hamlets was that residents who were not in occupation of their house at the date of representation of the area for slum clearance (in this case December 1967) but were in residence at the date of confirmation of the CPO (in this case January 1970) received only one offer of accommodation and this an older pre-war property. This rule occasionally produced particular anomalies amongst the Asian households:

> Case ... Mr K. (40 years old) lives with his cousin (38 years) and his uncle (37 years) and a friend (30 years), all married men. The four of them between them support 59 people in East Pakistan. Mr K. is a presser at a ladies coat manufacturers locally, he has been in this country 12 years. He previously lived in a flat in the same building and moved into this flat (two rooms, a very small kitchen and inside WC) in February 1970, for which they pay £2.00 per week plus rates of approximately £21.00 per annum. Though he has lived in this *building* for some years the Council regard him as ineligible for full housing rights since he was not in this house in December 1967. He is therefore only entitled to one offer of an older property and has had official notice to that effect. Though he does not want to stay in his present house, he is worried that he will not get rehoused locally near his work and with only one offer will have no options.

While the immigrant population was likely to be poorly served by the local authority because of the residence qualification it was also vulnerable to exploitation and extortion by private interests. Several respondents reported extortion from immigrants of hundreds of pounds of key money for flats which were already 'condemned' and the press carried some details of the racket.[8] But while the cultural mixture, concentration of non-family households and overall density of a tenement area gave rise to local problems it would be wrong to overemphasise the 'social problems' aspect of the area. There were no more single parent families than elsewhere, the non-married were middle aged rather than young and there was a relatively high proportion of skilled workers. The Asians living in all male households were apparently self-effacing and desperately hard working and the housing, though grossly inadequate, was self-contained, unfurnished and, above all, cheap.

NOTES

1. For a study of the effects of slum clearance on job opportunities see H. Kasper, 'Measuring the Labour Market costs of Housing Dislocation',

Scottish Journal of Political Economy, Vol. XX, No. 2, June 1973.
2. Hilda Jennings, *op. cit.*, p. 82.
3. Tom Brennan, *op. cit.*, p. 99.
4. John English, 'Oatlands: An Area of Twilight Housing in Glasgow', *Urban Studies*, Vol. 10, No. 3, October 1973.
5. John Rex, *op. cit.*, p. 215; in this work the following housing classes are distinguished:
   1. The outright owners of large houses in desirable areas.
   2. Mortgage payers who 'own' whole houses in desirable areas.
   3. Council tenants in council built houses.
   4. Council tenants in slum houses awaiting demolition.
   5. House owners who must take lodgers to meet loan repayments.
   6. Lodgers in rooms.
6. Roy Haddon, *op. cit.*
7. R. E. Pahl, *Urban Processes and Social Structure*, paper read at a Seminar of the Research Committee on Urban and Regional Development of the International Sociological Association, Berlin, July 1972, mimeo, p. 10. Pahl suggests the following housing classes:
   1. Large property owners and capitalist speculators.
   2. Smaller landlords.
   3a. Owners of capital sufficient to own their own homes and owning.
   3b. Owners of capital sufficient to own their own homes and renting.
   4. Those who *must* rent.
8. *The People*, 3rd May 1970.

9 SUMMARY AND CONCLUSIONS

The basic objective of the present study has been an appraisal of the administration of slum clearance in England and Wales. The study was carried out at the beginning of the seventies when the post-war clearance campaign was at its height, but though the scale of clearance has since diminished the process is likely to continue and procedures have not significantly changed. The findings of the study are, therefore, of continuing relevance to policy makers and students of urban problems. The aim has been coherently to describe the clearance process, at both national and local levels, and to identify its inadequacies from the point of view of residents who are affected by it.

The relevance of slum clearance as a subject for study lies not only in its numerical importance during the past twenty years but in the power relationship between citizens and local authorities which it exemplifies. The relationship is basically one of extreme dependence on the part of residents so that councils have considerable scope to manipulate them through control of information and resources. This power relationship is manifested in a variety of contexts during the course of the clearance process. During the early stages the resident's experience is typically limited to brief and unrelated contacts with local officials who visit him to collect information or to assess the physical state of his home. Later, at the stage of compulsory purchase, public local inquiry and settlement of compensation, slum clearance is experienced as a quasi-judicial process in which procedures and the basis of negotiation with the local authority are defined by legislation. Finally, at the stage of rehousing when the neighbourhood is likely to be deteriorating around him, the resident is a supplicant for acceptable alternative accommodation; he is subject to the constraints and vicissitudes of a large-scale bureaucracy designed to match a scarce supply of council housing with the demands of many applicants. These three successive stages in the clearance process develop against a background of generally inadequate information about individual rights and what is happening. Residents have a variety of needs and aspirations which lead some to welcome clearance and rehousing whilst others vehemently oppose it. In this chapter the principal findings of the study relating to each of these stages are reviewed and some conclusions drawn.

Although local authorities have had powers to clear slum housing since the late nineteenth century these were not used on a significant scale until the clearance drive of the thirties. After a fifteen year interruption caused by the Second World War the second clearance campaign began in 1955, reached its peak around 1970, and is continuing on a reduced scale. Over the years the emphasis has shifted away from demolishing individual unfit houses towards clearance area procedure under Part III of the Housing Act 1957. In 1970 three quarters of the houses demolished were in clearance areas and within them local authorities have relied increasingly on compulsory purchase orders. Consequently the present study concentrates on this procedure which covered almost 70 per cent of houses dealt with in 1970.

The first stage in clearance procedure is for houses in a prospective clearance area to be visited by public health inspectors to determine whether they are unfit for human habitation. This usually involves a public health inspector making a detailed inspection of each house. The declaration of a clearance area by the local authority does not involve any consultation with residents or reference to them. The decision has to be approved by the relevant committee of the council but recommendations from officials are generally accepted without debate as a technical matter within a broad policy. There is no statutory requirement on local authorities to inform residents that it has been decided to demolish their homes.

Residents who might wish to canvass alternatives to clearance, for example the declaration of a housing action area to get their houses improved, are clearly in a weak position. One of their few opportunities of finding out even that clearance is being contemplated is the visit of the public health inspector. But the evidence of the survey is that the real significance of the visit is little appreciated and, even with hindsight, few residents could relate it at all coherently to subsequent stages in the process.

Although most households recalled the public health inspector's visit only 55 per cent understood its purpose and most of these only in very general terms. Residents' lack of understanding reflected the public health inspector's own emphasis on purely technical aspects of his work and the narrow interpretation of his role which the procedure itself encourages. The most important consideration for the public health inspector is that his findings will become the basis of compulsory purchase and will therefore be open to challenge by objectors and the Department of the Environment inspector. Strictly speaking the whole procedure which he is initiating may prove abortive if either the council does not declare a clearance area or the Department of the Environment

Summary and Conclusions 191

rejects the compulsory purchase order. It is hardly surprising therefore if the public health inspector is reluctant to provide definite information about the chain of events which are likely to follow his visit or if he concentrates exclusively on the technical aspects of his job.

Moving on from the declaration of a clearance area to the stage of compulsory purchase, the opportunity to object to the compulsory purchase order provides, through a public local inquiry, the only machinery for discussion of clearance proposals. But a public local inquiry is designed to deal with specific objections and is not adapted to a wide-ranging discussion of alternatives and of residents' preferences. Compulsory purchase order procedure can only be understood as a system for the protection of property rights, not as a means of public consultation. In the first place the procedure concerns only people who have legal rights in the property in an area, which excludes tenants from consideration. In the survey areas this restriction excluded almost three quarters of households from receiving statutory notification of the compulsory purchase order and related information on objections, compensation and well-maintained payments. Furthermore tenants do not even have a legal right to be heard at a public local inquiry, though this may to some extent be conceded by the government inspector.

Even for the minority of owner occupiers the statutory process appears in most cases to have provided neither clear information nor meaningful involvement. The only information statutorily required to be given to owners (Form 26 of the prescribed forms) was of little value to over half of the owner occupiers who remembered receiving it. Again, the job interpretation of the officials directly concerned, the town clerk's department, discouraged wider involvement in informing residents of their rights. The precise wording of notices is laid down in the regulations. The obligation on officials to fulfill the letter of the law is their first priority and a fear of extending the local authority's commitment is a deterrent to a more creative view of their function.

The public local inquiry concerned only a tiny minority of residents. Only 15 per cent of those who had heard of the inquiry had actually attended and the vast majority dismissed it as having no influence on the outcome of events. The subsequent visit of the government inspector was also typically misunderstood by those who recalled it. For many tenants the visit was in any case totally unrelated to any action of their own since it resulted from an objection or claim by their landlord. It is characteristic of the relationship with officialdom that almost a quarter of households remembering the inspector's visit opened their houses to him without having any idea of why he was there.

At the time of the survey the only form of compensation which tenants could claim was a well-maintained payment (WMP); although the legislation has since changed, some aspects of the situation in 1970 merit comment. Local authorities were not legally obliged to inform tenants directly of their rights to WMPs; only 54 per cent of tenants had ever heard of them and amongst these there was a good deal of misunderstanding. For example, a fifth of tenants who had heard of the payments but had not claimed were put off by the false belief that only landlords could claim.

Since both the Form 26 notes and letters issued by some local authorities stated that claims had to be made by the end of the objection period, the partial and misleading information made available to tenants about WMPs is a good example of a general failure to transform the letter of the law into constructive practice.

At the rehousing stage a local authority is little restricted by legislation and there is a wide variety of procedure and organisation between areas. The allocation systems of housing departments in the main areas have been analysed in terms of the interplay of procedural rules, the organisation of tasks and the work ideologies of staff. Using these variables the five allocation systems are evaluated against an ideal of a 'humane' system. The evaluation gives greatest prominence to the two criteria of opportunity for self-determination by residents and continuity of contact. The value judgement on which the analysis rests is broadly that allocation systems should deal with applicants as 'persons'; they should avoid the fragmentation of individual needs and personalities which can result when standardisation and specialisation reduce applicants to mere 'particulars' on a form. This ideal can only be approached if the assignment of staff to the tasks of interviewing and allocation permits continuity of contact between staff and applicants to be established. Self-determination is only likely where the stated preferences of applicants are the basis of allocation and the process of establishing household needs and preferences is meaningfully conducted.

It is not possible to arrive at a simple rank order of authorities as 'better' or 'worse' in these respects but some tentative conclusions are possible. First, the disadvantages of size can be offset by decentralisation of the lettings procedure. Both Leeds and Liverpool, which operated decentralised systems, provided opportunities for staff to sustain contact with applicants throughout the rehousing period. In Liverpool the relatively small scale of operations appeared to have encouraged a high level of commitment from interviewing staff in local offices. In Leeds the benefit of local knowledge which district managers possessed permitted an extremely careful appraisal of household requirements in relation to available dwellings. But the equally careful work of housing visitors working from the central office was a result of training and management ideology. In sharp contrast Manchester, with a large-scale centralised system, showed the most extreme fragmentation of tasks which made it unlikely that applicants were ever in contact with the same official more than once. The situation was made worse by the restricted interpretation of their roles, particularly amongst staff conducting routine home visits and by the absence of any countervailing ideology amongst senior management.

Previous writers have frequently stressed the importance of training for staff concerned with home visiting and have placed a great deal of emphasis on the importance of home visits as a channel of information and guidance in both directions between residents and housing departments. Certainly, for residents, the home visit is a highly significant event and often provides the only opportunity they may have of discussing their rehousing requirements with someone from the department. The findings of this study show that there is room for a good deal of improvement in the general performance of housing visitors; in most cases the need to check on eligibility and housekeeping standards took precedence over other aspects of the visitors' job. But the problem lies a good deal deeper than improving visitors' training. The priorities of the lower grades of staff are determined partly by departmental rules and partly by the 'tone' which senior and middle management set. At all levels of housing management inadequate training is the rule. Despite official encouragement to treat housing as a social service and to adopt a flexible and sympathetic approach to the wide range of needs of housing applicants the profession lacks the basic confidence which is needed to develop in this direction. It remains preoccupied with the protection of council property and a pursuit of formal justice which too often result in the apportionment of moral desert.

If, as some recent government statements have suggested, slum clearance is universally rejected by public opinion no amount of amelioration of an existing administrative system could make it acceptable. But the evidence of the survey is that rejection of slum clearance is far from universal; indeed, only a minority of residents in clearance areas are unequivocally opposed to the change. Though circumstances have altered to some extent since the survey was undertaken the findings indicate that a substantial proportion of the population in any area is likely to welcome the opportunity to move provided by slum clearance.

The survey results show that households' attitudes towards moving were closely related to age and household needs, to existing housing conditions and to the tenure of their accommodation. At one extreme almost 80 per cent of young married households renting houses in poor condition were in favour of moving. At the opposite pole three quarters of older households owning a good house were against moving. Owner occupiers with houses in good condition were however a small minority and only 21 per cent of the sample as a whole were unequivocally against moving. The choice of moving or remaining in one's house obviously involves a calculation of gains and losses far more complex than can be indicated by the three factors of life cycle stage, tenure and conditions; additional factors are therefore introduced in the analysis of the market position of the young, the old and owner occupiers. For many young couples slum clearance represented a chance to get a council house which had long been the objective of their housing strategy. Fifty-two per cent said that they knew before coming to live in the area that the houses would be coming down; 49 per cent had already experienced life in a council house and many saw their temporary residence in a slum clearance area as a normal way of securing a council house of their own. The perspective of older households was often coloured by the fact of very long-term residence in the area and an awareness of deterioration in recent years. For many older households slum clearance was merely the last blow in the destruction of their accustomed pattern of life and they had only limited experience of any alternative by which to judge the prospect of a council house. The attitudes of these two groups towards the performance of the local authority were therefore very different; since younger households had both specific expectations of the outcome of slum clearance and a sounder basis in experience of council housing they were far more critical.

Undoubtedly the owner occupiers in the sample were far less favourable to moving than the tenants. But the survey results point to the dangers of assuming that owner occupiers can be treated as a homogeneous group. Many owned houses which had been bought cheaply, sometimes through rental purchase arrangements, and which were acknowledged to have only a short life. In these respects they diverged sharply from the conventional image of the home owner both in their living conditions, their commitment to owning property and their position in the market for alternative housing. This important distinction between conventional home owners and ownership of cheap, short life property which is not a marketable capital asset is recognised neither in official statistics nor in existing sociological theories of housing classes. On the other hand owners of better quality houses, often improved by

Summary and Conclusions

themselves over the years, tended to see clearance as depriving them of acceptable accommodation with insufficient compensation to buy a comparable alternative.

Studies of slum clearance administration have often concluded with recommendations for specific changes in procedure or for new facilities such as better training for housing visitors, information sheets, site offices and bus trips round council estates. Similar measures have been suggested at points throughout this book. The recommendations which follow relate, first, to aspects of the clearance process which are closely controlled by legislation and DOE requirement and, second, to matters which concern only the individual local authority.

Local authorities are not required to inform residents that a clearance area has been declared so that people tend to rely on more or less inaccurate rumours about what is going to happen. But when a housing action area is declared under the Housing Act 1974, the local authority must inform all owners and residents; there is then a period during which they can make representations and the Secretary of State can rescind or modify the proposal. There is a direct analogy here with clearance areas, particularly when clearance or rehabilitation may be alternative methods of dealing with the same area of old housing. All residents and owners should certainly be informed that a clearance area has been declared and the case for giving them a definite opportunity to make representations should be considered.

Under present arrangements owner occupiers receive Form 26 when a CPO is submitted, but two improvements could be made at this stage. First, assuming that the wording of Form 26 has to remain legally watertight and cannot be substantially modified, it should be accompanied by additional information in layman's language, making clear what is happening. Second, this information should be given to all residents and the existing statutory exclusion of the majority of tenants ended.

Since the extension of full market value compensation to nearly all owner occupiers of unfit houses and the more recent introduction of home loss payments, the amount of compensation received by owner occupiers has increased substantially. Nevertheless, the compensation is unlikely to be sufficient to enable them to buy an acceptable house elsewhere. There is no hardship for those who wish to move to a council house but clearance may be deeply resented by those who are committed to owner occupation. This is particularly true of those older owner occupiers whose houses are in relatively good condition and who do not want to become council tenants but have little prospect of securing a mortgage. One way in which this group might be helped is to devise a scheme whereby additional payments are made to enable them to continue as owner occupiers. Where a household was willing to forego the right to rehousing by the council, a 'home purchase supplement' could be paid towards the cost of an owner occupied house. Safeguards would be necessary to ensure that the supplement was actually used for buying a house, perhaps with provision for repayment if it were sold within a specified period on the same lines as improvement grants. The administrative details might not be easy to devise, but the possibility should be seriously considered since the committed owner occupier of a reasonably satisfactory house is one of the few real losers from slum clearance.

Turning to aspects which are not controlled by legislation, changes could well be made in the distribution of departmental responsibilities. A number of local authority departments are involved in slum clearance and rehousing including public health, town clerks' and housing. None is usually responsible for the overall direction of the process; town clerks often have a co-ordinating role but it is usually limited to keeping the different operations in step. Housing departments are moving away from merely managing the council stock towards a more comprehensive role and it would seem sensible to give them overall responsibility for the administration of slum clearance. This would involve, for example, a much closer relationship of housing departments with PHIs. Housing departments would become directly responsible for communication and consultation with residents from initial inspection to rehousing. Since housing departments accept responsibility for welfare problems during the clearance process they should be involved in minimising their incidence from the outset. Close involvement from an early stage would establish a continuing relationship between housing staff and residents leading to a mutual increase in awareness of problems.

Once clearance is under way residents have a desperate need for information and assistance on a day to day basis. As well as questions about the timing and location of rehousing, critical problems arise as the area is gradually evacuated and services decline. Site offices or temporary caravans are obviously useful but more is needed. The kind of intensive help and support provided by community workers and information centres has proved its worth but requires the allocation of substantial resources.

These proposals for administrative change could substantially improve the experience of clearance and rehousing for residents. But modifications to the system will be of little use unless they are accompanied

Summary and Conclusions

by a change of approach on the part of officials. The problem is fundamentally one of creating a responsive bureaucracy which can both work within the constraints of limited resources and treat individuals with humanity. Whilst staffing is inadequate and much of the council housing into which people have to be moved is less than satisfactory, their task is not easy. There are, for example, severe pressures on housing departments to find tenants for unpopular property. But the scope for officials to manipulate or even coerce is enormous and the temptations are great. An official who makes 'cod-offers' for 'difficult to let' property is acting in bad faith. So is the housing visitor who covertly grades households according to their housekeeping standards.

In contrast to the other professions involved in slum clearance, housing management has developed only recently as a separate specialism. There is a need to establish a basic confidence amongst staff at all levels that would permit them to develop a more imaginative approach to their work. Better training is clearly desirable, both for senior staff and for those directly involved with the public like housing visitors. More important, however, is for housing management to establish a status in local government commensurate with the importance of its work. Only then will it attract the resources and calibre of recruits that are needed.

Many of the administrative improvements which could be made will cost money but slum clearance to date has been run on the cheap. The real cost is the uncertainty, confusion and misery suffered by clearance area residents. There has been a growing tendency in recent years to represent slum clearance as an unpopular policy and no-one now regards it as a universal panacea for the problem of bad housing. But the present study has shown that, despite shortcomings in the way it is carried out, slum clearance meets the needs of the badly housed in many areas. It clearly has a continuing role which will be more effectively fulfilled if its administration can be improved.

APPENDIX A: SUPPLEMENTARY TABLES

A1 Socioeconomic Group of household by town
A2 Households' length of residence in present house by town
A3 Households by length of residence in each town
A4 Households by stage in life cycle by town
A5 Households in each type of dwelling by town
A6 Number of usable rooms in the house (excluding bathroom and working kitchen) by town
A7 Households by possession of amenities by town
A8 Household's tenure of accommodation by town
A9 Satisfaction with present house by town
A10 Anticipation of moving by town
A11 Opinion of council's plans by town
A12 Summary attitude to moving by town
A13 Criteria for evaluating the move by household's stage in life cycle. (Young married, middle aged married and older households only.)

Table A1. Socioeconomic group of household by town

Area	Professional and Managerial %	Other Non-Manual %	Skilled Manual %	Semi-Skilled Manual %	Unskilled Manual %	Misc. %	Base
Newcastle	1	6	56	27	10	—	141
Leeds	2	7	52	23	14	3	122
Manchester	5	12	46	24	11	1	106
Liverpool	4	9	40	30	18	1	176
Tower Hamlets	4	12	32	37	14	—	110
Pool	4	11	46	26	14	—	678
All Areas	4	10	46	27	14	—	1,333
GHS 1971	18	20	33	19	6	3	11,664

Notes: For details of classification of households by SEG see Appendix B.
Comparative figures from the General Household Survey (GHS, 1971) are from Table 5.18 and refer to heads of households.

Table A2. Households length of residence in present house by town

Area	<2 years %	$2<5$ years %	$5<10$ years %	$10<20$ years %	$20<30$ years %	$30+$ years %	Born here %	Base
Newcastle	14	18	10	19	12	24	4	161
Leeds	23	25	10	8	6	25	3	145
Manchester	18	18	14	21	10	19	1	135
Liverpool	7	13	14	16	23	24	4	192
Tower Hamlets	16	28	21	16	7	10	2	131
Pool	15	15	12	19	12	22	5	783
All Areas	15	17	13	18	12	21	4	1,547
GHS 1971	15	21	23	20	8	13	—	11,981

Note: Comparative figures from the General Household Survey (GHS, 1971) are from Table 5.49 and refer to length of residence of heads of households. The base for these percentages varies slightly from figures for our own survey since the category of people born in their present house is not separately identified.

Table A3. Households by length of residence in each town

Area	<2 years %	2<5 years %	5<10 years %	10<20 years %	20<30 years %	30+ years %	Born here %	Base
Newcastle	1	1	1	2	2	3	89	161
Leeds	3	4	3	2	3	6	77	145
Manchester	1	4	3	6	2	6	78	135
Liverpool	–	–	1	–	1	3	95	192
Tower Hamlets	4	5	18	20	14	5	33	131
Pool	3	4	4	7	3	12	66	783
All Areas	3	3	4	6	4	8	71	1,547

Table A4. Households by stage in life cycle by town

Area	Young non-married %	Middle-aged non-married %	Young married %	Middle aged married %	Old 60+ married and non-married %	Base
Newcastle	4	7	36	16	38	160
Leeds	8	6	44	8	34	144
Manchester	3	16	40	13	28	134
Liverpool	2	7	42	16	33	190
Tower Hamlets	6	19	36	11	28	127
Pool	5	4	32	20	38	777
All Areas	5	7	36	17	36	1,532

Note: For definitions of life cycle stage see Appendix B.

Alternative groupings indicating presence of children at home

Non-married, childless	116	8%)	20%
Married, childless	181	12%)	
Non-married, with children	67	4%)	45%
Married, with children	625	41%)	
Non-married, over 60	345	23%)	36%
Married, over 60	198	13%)	

Table A5. Households in each type of dwelling by town

Area	Terrace house %	Back-to back house %	Tyne-side flat %	Purpose-built flat %	Other (including converted houses) %	Base
Newcastle	11	–	84	4	1	161
Leeds	4	93	–	1	2	144
Manchester	92	1	–	–	7	135
Liverpool	88	–	–	2	10	189
Tower Hamlets	–	–	–	95	5	131
Pool	69	10	9	1	12	780
All Areas	56	14	14	9	8	1,540

Note: Back-to-back houses are mostly built in terraces as are Tyneside flats. Tyneside Flats are confined to the North-east of England and are purpose-built in units of two providing a ground floor and first floor flat with separate front and back entrances.

Table A6. Number of usable rooms in the house (excluding bathroom and working kitchen) by town

| Area | Number of usable rooms | | | | | | Base |
	1 %	2 %	3 %	4 %	5 %	6 or more %	
Newcastle	1	20	49	26	3	1	160
Leeds	1	5	56	29	8	2	145
Manchester	2	4	14	58	15	8	135
Liverpool	2	4	8	45	23	19	189
Tower Hamlets	2	60	26	8	4	–	131
Pool	2	7	14	34	28	16	771
All Areas	1	12	22	34	20	12	1,531

Note: 'Usable rooms' exclude rooms in the house which were not being used by the household because of damage or excessive damp.

Table A7. Households by possession of amenities by town

A. Availability of WC

Area	Sole use inside house %	Sole use outside house %	Shared use inside house %	Shared use outside house %	None %	Base
Newcastle	4	92	1	1	1	161
Leeds	4	50	–	46	1	145
Manchester	3	97	–	–	–	135
Liverpool	17	78	3	2	–	192
Tower Hamlets	86	7	–	7	–	131
Pool	20	65	1	13	2	780
All Areas	21	66	1	12	1	1,544

B. Availability of bath and hot water supply

Area	Sole use of fixed bath %	Base	Sole use of constant hot water %	Base
Newcastle	27	161	48	160
Leeds	20	143	45	145
Manchester	19	135	46	135
Liverpool	25	192	37	190
Tower Hamlets	20	131	41	129
Pool	32	780	48	777
All Areas	27	1,542	46	1,536

Table A8. Household's tenure of accommodation by town

Area	Owners occupiers %	Tenants %	Base
Newcastle	9	91	161
Leeds	17	83	145
Manchester	33	67	135
Liverpool	20	80	192
Tower Hamlets	–	100	131
Pool	39	61	783
All Areas	28	72	1,547

Table A9. Satisfaction with present house by town

Area	Happy to stay anyway %	Happy to stay if improved %	Prefer to leave anyway %	Don't know %	Base
Newcastle	32	18	49	1	161
Leeds	39	18	41	2	145
Manchester	29	19	51	1	135
Liverpool	34	16	47	2	192
Tower Hamlets	33	16	46	7	131
Pool	50	10	36	3	783
All Areas	42	14	41	2	1,547

Table A10. Anticipation of moving by town

Area	Looking forward to living in a different place %	Not looking forward to living in a different place %	Don't know and unclassified %	Base %
Newcastle	79	19	2	161
Leeds	76	22	2	145
Manchester	82	18	1	135
Liverpool	75	24	2	192
Tower Hamlets	68	21	12	131
Pool	64	30	7	783
All Areas	70	25	5	1,547

Table A11. Opinion of council's plans by town

Area	Agree with plans %	Agree but with reservations %	Disagree with plans %	Don't know %	Base
Newcastle	78	12	9	1	161
Leeds	65	11	19	5	145
Manchester	72	13	14	2	135
Liverpool	60	14	22	4	192
Tower Hamlets	72	5	14	8	131
Pool	58	12	24	6	783
All Areas	63	12	20	5	1,547

Table A12. Summary attitude to moving by town

Area	In favour %	With reservations %	Against %	Base
Newcastle	60	28	12	160
Leeds	55	27	18	144
Manchester	63	27	10	135
Liverpool	59	23	18	192
Tower Hamlets	54	31	15	130
Pool	44	30	26	783
All Areas	51	28	21	1,544

Table A13. Criteria for evaluating the move by household's stage in life cycle (Young married, middle aged married and older households only)

Criteria for evaluating the move	Young married %	Middle aged married %	Old people 60 and over %
a) What they are looking forward to			
Bathrooms, H & C, WC	55	45	34
Modern, more suitable house	66	49	36
Nicer, socially	12	13	8
Cleaner, better outlook, etc.	13	15	14
Convenient location	1	3	10
Nothing	3	17	23
Other	7	5	5
b) What they dislike about the move			
Upheaval, uncertainty	14	16	14
Loss of the familiar	10	24	31
Rents	16	13	13
Flats	4	9	8
Inconvenient location	6	11	8
Nothing	46	33	25
Other	11	17	11
c) Main reason for choice of area			
House type	7	2	2
Near work, shops, etc.	44	58	32
Near family, friends	21	17	38
Type of people there	26	20	24
Base	546	259	542

APPENDIX B: DEFINITIONS AND CLASSIFICATIONS

1. *Socioeconomic group*

   The Registrar General's Classification of Occupations (1966) was used to classify the Socioeconomic Group of one 'worker' in each household. The household 'worker' was identified at the interview stage as the respondent, if male, or the respondent's husband regardless of whether working, retired or unemployed. Alternatively, where the respondent was female with no husband the nearest male kin living in the house was identified as 'worker', preference being given to those currently working. Where there was no such man the respondent or nearest female kin was identified as 'worker', preference being given to those currently working.

2. *Life cycle stage*

   Households were classified by life cycle stage according to the age and marital status of the 'housewife'. Additionally the presence or absence of children was taken into account. The precise full classification was as follows:

   Single young : 15 – 34 years
   ” middle aged : 35 – 59 years
   ” old : 60+ years

   Married young no children of any age (at home): 15 – 34 yrs.
   ” middle aged no ” ” ” ” ” ” : 35 – 44 yrs.
   ” older no ” ” ” ” ” ” : 45 – 59 yrs.
   ” young/middle aged with ” ” ” ” ” ” : 15 – 44 yrs.
   ” older with ” ” ” ” ” ” : 45 – 59 yrs.
   ” old with or without children : 60+ yrs.

   Widowed/separated/divorced
   young no children of any age (at home): 15 – 34 yrs.
   ” middle aged no ” ” ” ” ” ” : 35 – 44 yrs.
   ” older no ” ” ” ” ” ” : 45 – 59 yrs.
   ” young/middle aged with ” ” ” ” ” ” : 15 – 44 yrs.
   ” older with ” ” ” ” ” ” : 45 – 59 yrs.
   ” old with or without children : 60+ yrs.

3. *Housewife*

In households where there was no woman, or in circumstances where a man was responsible for running the domestic affairs of the household the 'housewife' was a man.

APPENDIX C: RESEARCH METHODS

The two main sources of data for this study are, first, interviews with staff of local authority housing departments and, second, a survey of residents living in a sample of slum clearance areas.

1. *Local authority interviews*

The local authorities were selected as a result of the sampling for slum clearance areas (see below). In each of the five authorities staff at all levels in the organisation of allocations and letting were interviewed and, where possible, a member of the research team accompanied a housing visitor on his or her rounds. In addition, details were collected of the standard forms and filing procedures on which allocation and letting was based.

Separate check lists of topics were prepared for interviews with senior and middle managers, for 'Allocators' and for 'Interviewers'. These provided the basis of focused interviews with each category of staff. As far as possible at least two members of the research team attended each interview to provide a check on both the factual details of each system recorded and on interpretations of the significance of value judgements made by staff.

In authorities operating a decentralised system of lettings staff were interviewed in at least two district offices in an attempt to identify major variations between localities.

2. *Survey of Clearance Areas*

Objectives and Constraints. The survey was designed to investigate residents' experience of slum clearance procedure in England and Wales. It was decided to concentrate exclusively on areas being compulsorily purchased under Part III of the Housing Act 1957, as this is the most important procedure.

The housing visit is a key event for residents and it was essential that the survey should be designed to inquire into residents' experience of it. But as soon as the housing visit has taken place rehousing begins so that the remaining population becomes progressively less representative of the original one. Therefore, fieldwork had to take place after the housing visit, but as far as possible before rehousing had begun.

The theoretical population under investigation was the population of households who were living in houses covered by a confirmed CPO and who had been visited by a housing visitor during some convenient period prior to the survey date. Ideally the population should be all households visited by a housing visitor during, say, one particular week. But since only about 1,000 houses are visited in England and Wales each week not only would it have been impractical to interview a sample from such a scattered population but insufficient concentration of cases within local authority areas would have been achieveable. As there is no means of drawing a national sample based on the dates of housing visits the dates of confirmation of CPOs were used as a proxy. For a part of the sample, areas were included where the CPOs had been confirmed up to one year before the survey and for the rest up to five months.

The research design required that data from the survey should permit separate presentation of sub-samples falling in a number of local authority areas to provide evidence of the effects of differences in administrative procedures between authorities. Substantial clustering of at least some of the sample cases in a limited number of areas where further study of local authority procedures could be undertaken was therefore required. But only relatively large CPOs could yield a sufficient number of cases for this purpose. It was therefore decided to split the interviews into two strata, 'main' areas and 'pool' areas, the latter being representative of smaller CPOs.

The available budget indicated an upper limit of some 1,000 interviews. Five main areas were allocated a target of 150 interviews each and the remaining 250 interviews were allocated to pool areas. Since the budget demanded strict limitation of travelling and other costs the 250 pool area interviews were divided equally between ten areas. The design therefore involved interviews in fifteen different clearance areas; five main areas with a target of 150 completed interviews in each and ten pool areas with a target of 25 completed interviews in each. Data for the ten small areas was pooled whilst the large area samples were sufficiently large to permit separate presentation. The local authority areas finally selected were:'

Main Areas
Newcastle-Upon-Tyne C.B., Leeds C.B., Manchester C.B.,
Liverpool C.B., Tower Hamlets L.B.

Pool Areas
Bingley U.D., Doncaster C.B., Gravesend M.B., Haringey L.B.,
Norwich C.B., Portsmouth C.B., South Shields C.B.,
Stoke-on-Trent C.B., Warley C.B., Wolverhampton C.B.

Appendix C: Research Methods 209

Sampling arrangements

The only centrally held records of CPOs are held by the Department of Environment. These consist of a card entry for each CPO giving details of the numbers of houses in the CPO, key dates and the name of the local authority submitting the order. This card system provided the only possible first stage sampling frame of clearance area residents having national coverage.

However, it would not have been sufficient merely to sample CPOs confirmed during, say, the six months prior to survey date. As local authorities complete their rehousing arrangements at different speeds, simply taking CPOs confirmed over a given period would have produced some areas in which the housing visits had not been undertaken but others where substantial numbers of residents had already been rehoused. An additional screening process was therefore necessary; main areas and pool areas were separately treated.

An important assumption in respect of both main and pool areas was that CPO areas which happened to reach their final stages at a time convenient for survey were a random selection of all areas being processed at that time.

Main areas. It was estimated that, to allow for some loss due to inaccuracies of local records or non-response, initial samples of about 200 cases would be required in main areas to ensure achieved samples of 150 cases. As a first step all CPOs containing at least 200 houses, confirmed or likely to be confirmed during the twelve months up to 31 May 1970, were selected. As well as CPOs confirmed up to 31 March, CPOs submitted but not confirmed up to that date were listed in the expectation that one or two might be confirmed and visited by housing staff in the two months before 31 May.

Early in April 1970 the thirty-six local authorities within which the listed CPO areas lay were asked to anticipate progress in the listed areas and to identify those areas where, in June, most of the houses would have been visited but only a small proportion of residents would have been rehoused. When these details had been established for each CPO area a final list was drawn up of twenty-five CPO areas where in June 1970 housing visits would be completed but few people rehoused. CPO areas were listed in sequence determined by the date of clearance area resolution and five areas selected by systematic sampling with probability proportionate to size of population expected to remain in the area in June 1970.

Pool areas. Ideally the 250 interviews allocated to pool areas should have been spread across CPO areas of all sizes including areas of only two or three houses. In practice the costs of interviewing in a large number of very small areas would have been too high. Interviews were concentrated in ten areas which were expected to yield achieved samples of twenty-five cases. In practice this meant confining selection to areas with at least 50 houses. It was assumed that CPO areas of fifty or more houses but less than 200 did not differ systematically from smaller areas except in size so that the exclusion of very small areas for practical reasons would not bias the results.

The sampling list contained all CPO areas with 50 but less than 200 houses which were confirmed in the three months from 1 January to 31 March 1970. The shorter period in the case of pool areas was because the smaller scale of the housing visitors' task there meant that housing visits would be completed within a relatively short time after CPO confirmation. A three month period also produced a sufficient number of CPOs, thirty-four in total. Ten of these areas were systematically selected with probability proportionate to size. Early in April the local authorities within which sample CPOs occurred were asked to anticipate progress so that areas where too many would be rehoused by June could be excluded. In two cases the areas selected were unsuitable and substitutes were taken from an alternative list selected by the same process. In one case where housing visits were delayed fieldwork was postponed until September.

The second stage of the sample depended on local authority records for a sampling frame. Preliminary visits established that many local authorities maintained log books of households living in CPO areas which were updated whenever a family was rehoused. These log books were used as a sampling frame of remaining households in each main area. As log books were constantly in use by housing department staff and constantly being updated the final sample of households was not selected until the first morning of interviewing in each area. Household names and addresses were selected systematically using a variable sampling fraction to yield the required number of interviews in each area.

In some of the pool areas where no log book was available, names and addresses were sampled from a copy of the CPO for the area making an allowance for estimated numbers rehoused.

Field work and results

Field work in fourteen of the fifteen areas was completed in five weeks

Appendix C: Research Methods

in June and July 1970. The field force consisted of twelve interviewers although not all of them worked throughout the interview period; six were university teaching or research staff including the three permanent members of the research team and the remainder were Glasgow University students, mainly graduate students on a town planning course. All except the permanent members of the team received wages or fees and expenses.

Interviewing teams spent one week in each of the five main areas working from a local church hall or office. As interviews were concentrated in relatively few streets there was no limit on the number of calls that could be made to each address to secure an interview. Interviewers worked most evenings and on Saturday mornings and sample addresses were not recorded as 'no response' until many calls had been made. Smaller teams of two or three interviewers worked in two of the pool areas most weeks, usually commuting from the same base as the main area interviewers so that constant reporting back was possible. Interviewing in pool areas was usually completed in three days.

Interviewers used a detailed questionnaire which had been extensively pre-tested and for which they were carefully briefed. All interviewers carried out practice and dummy interviews and were supervised by members of the research team in the early stages. The mean duration of completed successful interviews was 43 minutes. Copies of the questionnaire used are available on request from the Department of Social and Economic Research, Glasgow University.

The response rate in all main areas was at least 80 per cent of possible interviews and in pool areas it averaged just under 70 per cent giving an overall success rate of 81 per cent. Achieved samples in main areas ranged from 131 to 192 cases (see table). In pool areas achieved samples ranged from 20 to 32 cases.

On the assumption of relative stability of the numbers annually affected by the process (as was the case at the time of survey) the numbers of houses included in confirmed CPOs during the year is a fairly good approximation to the total numbers going through any stage in the clearance process during that year. In the twelve months preceding 31 May 1970, the number of houses included in confirmed CPOs were:

In CPOs of 200+ houses	22,033	46%
In CPOs of less than 200 houses	25,902	54%
TOTAL	47,955	100%

Interviewing success rates by area

Local authority	Original sample	Empty or demolished houses	'possible' interviews (col. 1 minus col. 2)	Total successful interviews	Success rate (successful interviews as % possibles)
	1	2	3	4	5
Newcastle	193	11	182	161	88.5
Leeds	264	83	180	145	80.5
Manchester	215	57	158	135	85.5
Liverpool	309	89	220	192	87.0
Tower Hamlets	177	27	150	131	87.5
Pool areas	494	117	377	261	69.4
TOTAL	1652	384	1267	1025	81.0

Appendix C: Research Methods

The division into large and small CPOs indicated that interviews should be allocated roughly half and half to the main area and pool area strata. But the research design required a disproportionate concentration of cases in the five main areas. The final distribution of the achieved sample of 1,025 cases was 764 cases in main areas (75 per cent) and 261 cases in pool areas. (25 per cent). To compensate for the underrepresentation of small CPO areas the results for pool areas were given a weight of three in the analysis so that the total number of cases analysed is given in the tabulations as 1,547 split into 764 main area interviews and 783 pool area interviews.

Analysis of the survey data was completed using the Statistical Package for the Social Sciences. Tabulations presented in the text were tested for significance using chi square. Tables are presented only when chi square values were large enough to indicate, at the 95 per cent level of confidence, that results were non-random.

APPENDIX D

FORM 26 / HOUSING ACT 1957

Personal notice of the making of a compulsory purchase order in respect of land comprised in a clearance area and land surrounded by or adjoining the area.

To   of
Take Notice that
(1)   the   Council
(a)   have by resolution dated   19   declared an area
      to be a clearance area; and
(b)   have on   19   , in pursuance of their
      powers under section 43 of the Housing Act 1957 made the
      Compulsory purchase Order 19   , which is about to be sub-
      mitted to the [Minister of Housing and Local Government]
      [Secretary of State] for confirmation, authorising the Council to
      purchase compulsorily the lands described in the Schedule to this
      notice;
(2)   the lands included in the order are —
      [lands in the clearance area which the Council have determined
      to purchase for securing the clearance thereof by themselves
      undertaking or otherwise securing the demolition of the buildings
      thereon;]
      [lands which the Council have determined to purchase as being
      lands surrounded by the clearance area the acquisition of which is
      reasonably necessary for the purpose of securing a cleared area of
      convenient shape and dimensions;]
      [lands which the council have determined to purchase as being
      lands adjoining the clearance area the acquisition of which is
      reasonably necessary for the satisfactory development or use of
      the cleared area;]
(3)   copies of the order and of the map referred to therein and a map
      of the clearance area have been deposited at   and
      may be seen at all reasonable hours.
(4)   the property in which you are interested as [owner] [mortgagee]
      [lessee] [occupier] is included in [that class] [those classes] of property

Appendix D

which [is] [are] not deleted from the following —
A — Houses in the clearance area which are unfit for human habitation.
B — Buildings in the clearance area which by reason only of bad arrangement in relation to other buildings or the narrowness or bad arrangement of the streets are dangerous or injurious to the health of the inhabitants of the area.
C — Properties outside the clearance area.
These classes of property are distinguished in the order and on the map referred to therein.
(5) any objection to the compulsory purchase order stating the grounds of your objection must be made in writing to [the Minister of Housing and Local Government, Whitehall, SW1] [the Secretary of State, Welsh Office, Cathays Park, Cardiff] before 19

SCHEDULE
Dated   19

                            Signed

                            Clerk of the Local Authority.

NOTES

If no objection is duly made by any of the persons upon whom notices are required to be served, or if all objections are withdrawn, the [Minister] [Secretary of State] may if he thinks fit confirm the order with or without modification, but in any other case he is required before confirming the order to cause a public local inquiry to be held or to afford the objector an opportunity of appearing before and being heard by a person appointed by him for that purpose, and to consider any objection not withdrawn and the report of the person who held the inquiry or the person appointed to hear the objector, and he may then confirm the order with or without modification.

The [Minister] [Secretary of State] is required, if he comes to the conclusion that land included in the clearance area ought not to have been included, to modify the order so as to exclude that land for all purposes from the clearance area, but if he nevertheless considers that the land may properly be purchased by the local authority as being land surrounded by the clearance area the acquisition of which is reasonably necessary for the purpose of securing a cleared area of convenient shape and dimensions, or as being land adjoining the clearance area the acquisition of which is reasonably necessary for the satisfactory development or use of the clear area, he is required further to modify the order so as to authorise to purchase the land as land outside the clearance area.

I If the order is confirmed by the [Minister] [Secretary of State] it will become operative at the expiration of six weeks from the date on which notice of its confirmation is published in accordance with the provisions of the Housing Act 1957, but if proceedings in the High Court are commenced within that period for questioning the validity of the order, the Court may, if satisifed that the order is not within the powers of the Act or that the interests of the applicant have been substantially prejudiced by any requirement of the Act not having been complied with, quash the order either generally or in so far as it affects any property of the applicant.

Compensation

If the order becomes operative, the compensation payable for land, including any buildings thereon, which is purchased under the order will be as follows:

For land within the clearance area on which there are houses unfit for human habitation (within Class A of paragraph (4) of this notice) the compensation will be its value as a site cleared of buildings and available for development in accordance with the requirements of the building byelaws or building regulations for the time being in force in the district. The compensation payable, however, will not in any event exceed the amount of compensation which would have been payable in respect of the house if it had been compulsorily purchased otherwise than at site value and if the area had not been declared to be a clearance area.

If the [Minister of Housing and Local Government] [Secretary of State] is satisfied that a house on land to which the order will apply had, notwithstanding its unfitness, been well maintained he may on confirming the order direct the local authority to make a payment in accordance with section 60 of the Housing Act 1957. The amount of any such payment, which will be calculated in accordance with Part 1 of Schedule 2 to the Act, cannot in any event be more than the amount (if any) by which the full value of the house would exceed the site value. If a person interested in the house thinks that the house has been well maintained by him or at his expense, he should make a representation in writing to the [Minister of Housing and Local Government, Whitehall, SW1] [Secretary of State, Welsh Office, Cathays Park, Cardiff,] before the end of the objection period specified in paragraph

Appendix D

(5) of this notice. A form of representation may be obtained from the Council Offices. Persons on whom this notice is served who have tenants on a monthly or lesser tenancy or statutory tenants in occupation of houses on lands in respect of which this notice is served are requested to bring this paragraph to the notice of those occupiers.

Additional compensation may be payable in respect of a house which has been occupied for business purposes, provided that certain conditions are fulfilled. Broadly these are that the house must have been wholly or partly occupied for business purposes by a person having a freehold interest or a leasehold interest for more than a year at the date of the making of the order and either on 13th December 1955, or at all times during the ten years preceding the date of the making of the order.

*There may also be additional compensation where the present owner of a freehold interest or a leasehold interest for more than a year purchased it (or is a member of the family of someone who purchased it) between 1st September 1939 and 13th December 1955, provided that the compulsory purchase order was made by the local authority before 13th December 1965 or, if on or after that date, within 15 years after the purchase. In such cases, entitlement depends upon either the original purchaser or a member of his family having occupied the house as a private dwelling on 13th December 1955 (members of the armed forces posted away, or persons changing their place of employment or occupation, being treated in certain cases as having continued in occupation).

Any person on whom this notice is served who thinks that if the order becomes operative he may have a claim to this further compensation on the compulsory purchase of the house should notify the clerk of the local authority in writing of the facts on which he relies. The question whether any compensation will be payable will not be settled at this stage, but it is important to establish the facts relating to ownership or occupation as soon as possible.

The further compensation, if it becomes payable, is the market value of the interest of the person entitled to compensation, less site value. A person who is entitled to such compensation cannot also receive a payment for good maintenance.

The total amount payable in respect of the interest of the owner occupier of a private dwelling, excluding any compensation attributable to disturbance or to severance or injurious affection, will not in any event be less than the gross value of the dwelling for rating purposes.

For other houses, buildings and land (within classes B and C of paragraph (4) of this notice) the compensation will be the market value of the interest of the person entitled to compensation, subject to the rules in Part III of Schedule 3 to the Housing Act 1957.

Any compensation paid (other than a payment for good maintenance) may in addition include an amount in respect of the cost of professional fees reasonably incurred in preparing the claim.

Mortgagors and mortgagees of unfit houses in this order, and persons either buying or selling any such house by instalments, should seek advice as to the right, which they may have in certain circumstances, of applying to the County Court for modification or discharge of outstanding liabilities under a mortgage, charge or agreement to purchase by instalments. The right applies principally to houses where additional compensation is payable under the paragraph above marked * and to owner occupied houses.

The [Minister] [Secretary of State] may disregard any objection relating solely to matters which can be dealt with by the tribunal by whom the compensation is to be assessed but the question whether the house is or is not unfit for human habitation, which decides whether site value or market value is payable, is for the Minister and not for that tribunal to consider.

INDEX

Acts of Parliament and Bills
Land Clauses Consolidation Act 1845 18
Artizans' and Labourers' Dwellings Act 1968 (Torrens Act) 16, 20
Artizans' and Labourers' Dwellings Improvement Act 1875 (Cross Act) 16-17, 18, 20
Housing, Town Planning, Etc. Act 1909 17
Acquisition of Land (Assessment of Compensation) Act 1919 18
Housing, Town Planning, Etc. Act 1919 19
Housing Act 1923 19
Housing Act 1930 20, 21
Housing (Financial Provisions) Act 1933 22
Housing Act 1935 23
Housing Act 1936 23, 25
Housing Act 1949 23, 24, 42
Housing (Repairs and Rents) Act 1954 25, 63
Housing Subsidies Act 1956 26
Slum Clearance (Compensation) Act 1956 60
Housing Act 1957, 16, 25, 38, 50, 51, 52-5, 57, 59, 63, 64, 65, 71, 190, 207
Rent Act 1957 27, 31, 63
House Purchase and Housing Act 1959 42
Land Compensation Act 1961 52, 60, 61, 63
Town and Country Planning Act 1962 51
Housing Act 1964 43
Compulsory Purchase Act 1965 60, 63
Slum Clearance (Compensation) Act 1965 61
Housing Subsidies Act 1967 32
Town and Country Planning Act 1968 51, 125
Housing Act 1969 34, 44, 61, 129, 133, 136-7
Housing Act 1971 35
Town and Country Planning Act 1971 51, 52

Housing Finance Bill (1972) 34, 35
Land Compensation Act 1973 16, 36, 52, 55, 62, 65, 139, 140
Housing and Planning Bill (1974) 37, 38
Housing Act 1974 9, 38, 62, 195
Allaun, Frank 33, 34
Allocation
criteria for evaluation of systems 78-80, 115-6, 192
not legally constrained, 55, 76
See also *Rules of Access*
Allocator role, 82-3, 84, 89-90, 94-6, 100-1, 108-9, 114-5, 116, 119
Amery, Julien 34, 35
Appeal to courts 57, 59
Attitudes to moving
consumers' preference array 164-5
expectations of council housing 176-7
house type 151-3,
housing conditions 161-8, 178, 179, 194
in other studies 156-8
in present study 158-68, 193-5
life-cycle stage 162-8, 170-9, 194
marital status 170
tenure, 162-8, 179, 185, 194
Aylesbury 28

Bad arrangement 51, 55
Bethnal Green 10
Better Housing Campaign 24, 25
Bevan, Aneurin 24, 25
Birmingham 28, 31, 38, 41
Blau, P.M. 81, 82, 121
Brennan, Tom 179
Brent 36
Bristol 10, 31, 52, 179
Brooke, Henry 26
Bull, David 11, 76, 80, 118, 124, 125
Bureaucracy
job definitions 50, 69-73, 120, 197
routinisation in 50, 55, 69, 79, 90, 108, 118, 119, 121, 123
Burnett, F.T. and Scott, Sheila F. 28

219

Central Housing Advisory Committee 25, 30, 77
  See also *Cullingworth Report* and *Denington Report*
Channon, Paul 35
Circulars (MH&LG and DOE)
  30/50 *Housing: Slum Clearance* 25
  55/54 *Housing Repairs and Rents Act, Part 1* 25
  11/65 *Slum Clearance* 30, 32
  69/67 *Housing Act 1957: Slum Clearance* 62
  68/69 *Housing Act, 1969: Slum Clearance* 62, 139
  50/72 *Slums and Older Housing: an Overall Strategy* 35
  13/75 *Housing Act 1974: Renewal Strategies* 38
Clearance Area 16-17, 21, 22, 38, 40, 51, 53, 54, 55-7, 190, 195
Clearance Order 38, 51, 54
Closing Order 19, 51
Coates, Ken and Silburn, Richard 156
Communication see *Information*
Community action and opposition to clearance 11, 36, 44, 125
Community studies 10, 124-5, 155-8, 162-4, 179-80
Compensation
  expectations and amounts of 136-40, 181, 185, 195-6
  legislation 18, 19, 23, 27, 34, 36, 52, 55, 58, 59-63, 129, 132-3
Compulsory purchase procedure
  and protection of property rights 57-8, 63-4, 73, 121, 136, 191 and bureaucratisation 69-73
  delays in 66-9, 126
  origins of 17, 21
  publicity 58
  relative importance of 50-5, 65-6
  stages of 56-9
Council housing
  as alternative accommodation 172-5, 181-2, 184
  development and scale of 16, 19, 20, 22, 24, 26-7, 30, 31-2, 34, 40, 41, 44
  residents' access to 175, 183-4, 186, 194
  residents' experience of 172-5, 194

Crossman, Richard 30, 31
Cullingworth, J.B. 27, 28, 44, 118
Cullingworth Report *(Council Housing: Purposes, Procedures and Plans)* 77, 122, 124, 125, 139

Darlington 28
Deeplish Study 33
Deferred demolition 25
Demolition order 19, 57
Denington Report (*Our Older Homes: a Call for Action*) 31, 32, 33, 42, 43
Dennis, Norman 10, 36, 149, 158, 161, 164-5
Department of the Environment (and Secretary of State) 34, 51, 56, 58, 59, 61, 62, 65, 70, 130, 190, 195
Derby 28
Dewsbury 52
District valuer 62, 142
Disturbance Payments 36, 62, 140
Doncaster 185
Donnison, D.V. 31

East Grinstead 28
Eligibility for rehousing
  of immigrant groups 79, 186-7
  restrictions on 52, 65, 78-9, 89, 90, 94, 96-7, 100-1, 105, 108, 114, 193
  understood as reason for home visit 143

'Filtering Up' 20, 21
Form No. 26
  as source of information 58, 62, 129, 135, 140, 141, 191, 192
  information in 71, 129, 132
  reproduced 214-18
  residents' recall of 129, 131
  residents' understanding of 129-30, 195
Freeson, Reginald 35
Full Market Value compensation 52, 60-1, 132-3, 136-40, 181, 185, 195-6

General Elections
  1951 24
  1955 26
  1959 27
  1964 30

1970 34
February 1974 38

General Household Survey 148-9
General Improvement Area 34, 37, 38, 44
Glasgow 124, 179
Government Inspector 51, 58, 59, 62, 70, 131, 133-4, 142, 190, 191
Government Social Survey 31
Grading of applicants
  as covert process 83, 88, 105, 122, 143, 197
  criteria of 79, 85, 96, 97, 110, 121-2
  in survey areas 85-8, 89, 96, 97, 105, 110
'Gradual renewal' 36, 37, 38
Gravesend 65
Gray, P.G. and Russell, R. 29, 31
Greater London Council 97
Greenwood, Anthony 33
Greenwood, Arthur 21

Hill, Dr Charles 28, 30
Home Loss Payments 36, 62, 140, 195
Home Purchase Supplement 196
Housing Action Area 9, 37, 38, 44, 190, 195
Housing classes, theory of 12, 183-4, 194
Housing conditions 16, 21, 28, 31, 32-3, 151-5, 161-8, 178, 194
Housing Corporation 36
Housing departments
  comparison between 115-21
  organisational structure 86-7, 92-3, 98-9, 106-7, 112-3, 117
Housing managers
  as professional group 76-7, 79, 80-1, 84, 197
  ideology of, 12, 80-1, 84, 109, 111, 115, 116-23, 192-3
  training of 79, 119, 121, 193, 197
Housing surveys 31, 32-3
Housing visitors
  and ideology 80, 81, 118, 192-3, 197
  importance 77, 142-3, 193
  purpose of visit 83, 85-8, 90-1, 96-7, 104-5, 110, 120, 143-6
  residents' perception of 126, 143, 145-6
  training 77, 121-2, 193, 197

Ideology, occupational
  commitment to clients 81-2, 94-5, 118-20, 121-3
  definition of 80-1
  organisational structure 12, 81, 84, 118-20, 193
  view of clients 116-8, 192
Immigrants
  access to housing 170, 185-7
  eligibility for rehousing 79
Improvement 9, 28, 30, 33-4, 35-8, 42-4, 148
Improvement Area 43
Improvement Grants 9, 24, 35, 42-4, 196
Improvement Scheme 17, 18-19
Information
  about compensation 129, 139-40
  adequacy of 124-6, 134-6, 189-91
  and choice of housing 125, 143-7
  from housing visitors 85-8, 90-1, 104-5, 110
  from PHI 127-8
  'information points' 91-4
  prerequisite for participation 11, 79, 125
  statutory requirements 57-9, 62, 191, 195
Institute of Housing Managers 76
Interviewer role 82, 83, 85-9, 90-4 96-100, 104-8, 110-11, 116-18, 121

Jennings, Hilda 10, 125, 179
Job definition 50, 69-73, 91, 97, 109, 110-11, 120, 147, 191, 193
  see also *Housing departments, Public Health Inspectors* and *Town Clerk's departments*
Joseph, Sir Keith 30, 31

Landlords 24, 32, 43, 60, 61-2, 64, 135, 140, 141, 155, 177, 179, 192
Lands Tribunal 58
Leeds 13, 31, 37-8, 41, 65, 96, 104-9, 119, 120-1, 124 *passim*, 149 *passim*, 163, 177, 178, 192
Life-cycle stage 150-1, 164, 166-8, 170-9, 182, 194, 205
Liverpool 13, 26, 28, 36, 41, 63, 65, 68, 70, 72, 96, 109-15, 120-1, 127 *passim*, 149 *passim*, 172, 175, 176, 182, 192

Local Government Board 17-18
London 16, 17, 18, 119, 138
    see also *Tower Hamlets*
London County Council 18

McKie, Robert 36
Macmillan, Harold 24, 26
Macey, J.P. and Baker C.V. 76
Manchester 13, 20, 26, 28, 30, 38, 41, 65-6, 76, 90-6, 97, 100, 119, 120-1, 124 *passim*, 182, 193
Medical Officer of Health 16, 18, 55
Mellish, Robert 32
Metropolitan Board of Works 18
Middle manager role 82, 118, 120, 193
Milner Holland Committee 30, 31
Ministry of Health (and Minister) 18, 20, 21, 22, 24
Ministry of Housing and Local Government (and Minister) 24, 25, 26, 28, 29, 30, 31, 32, 33, 34, 62, 72
Muchnick, D.N. 79

National Building Agency 32, 36, 41
National House Condition Survey 33-4, 35, 154-5
National Housing and Town Planning Council 20, 24
Needleman L. 28
Newcastle-upon-Tyne 13, 38, 65, 68, 85-90, 95, 97, 101, 118, 120, 127 *passim*, 149 *passim*
Norris, June 11, 79, 125
Norwich 68
Nottingham 31, 70, 156

Objection 57-9, 63-4, 129-33, 135
Official Representation 56
Oldham 26, 41, 163
Overcrowding 23, 24, 32
Owner occupiers
    and compensation 60-1, 132-3, 136-40
    and objection 63-4, 129-32
    attitudes to moving 164-8, 170, 179-85, 194
    proportion in sample 155
    types 179-81, 183-4, 194-5

Pahl, R.E. 12, 184
Participation 10, 11, 77, 79
Pembroke 28

Pepper, Simon 36
Portsmouth 68
Power relations
    as theme in previous studies 9-12
    scope for manipulation by officials 83, 88, 89, 189, 197
Principal Grounds Notice 58, 70
Professionalism
    development in housing management 76-7, 79, 81, 84, 120, 193, 197
    of PHI 70, 72
    of town clerk 71-2
Public Health Inspector
    as source of information 70-1, 127-8, 140, 191
    job definition of 70-1, 190-1
    residents' understanding of 126-8, 190
    visit of 57-8, 68, 69, 127-8, 133, 180
    'worst first' principle 55
Public Local Inquiry 58-9, 66, 68, 126, 130-1, 142, 191
Purchase by agreement 52, 54

Rehousing
    limitations on offers 79, 95, 100, 104, 108, 125, 143-5, 187
    obligations of local authorities 16-18, 21, 24, 52, 55, 64-5, 76
Relets 41, 97, 105, 175, 187
Rent 21, 24, 27, 34, 43, 85, 88, 89, 104, 114, 155, 177
Rental purchase 194
Re-organisation of local government 76, 77
Research methods 12-13, 65, 115, 126, 152-5, 207-13
Rex, John 12, 183-4
    and Moore, Robert 50
Rippon, Geoffrey 35
Royal Commission on the Housing of the Working Classes 18
Rules of Access
    13, 50, 57, 60-1, 63-5, 89-90, 94-6, 100-1, 108-9, 114-15, 122, 170, 189
    see also *Eligibility and Grading*

Salford 33
Sandys, Duncan 26
Second World War 60, 61, 163
Section 170 Notice 71

Seebohm Report 77
Senior Manager role 82, 97, 118, 193
Sheffield 41
Shelter 9, 36, 124
Simon, E.D. 20
Site Value compensation 52, 60-1, 133, 136-40
Skeffington Report (*People and Planning*) 11
Slum Clearance procedure
　development of 16-38
　opposition to 36, 179-80
　progress, local 28, 37, 41
　progress, national 18, 19, 22-3, 27, 38-44
　residents' opinion of 10, 159, 174-5
　residents' understanding of 14, 126-34, 190-1
　social arguments against 25, 37, 44, 148
　use of various procedures 50, 53-5, 65, 190-2
Socio-economic groups 149, 205
Solicitors 133, 135-6
South Shields 65
Southwark 36
Stereotypes, operational 81, 84
Stoke-on-Trent 65, 66
Stone, Alan 36
Subsidies 18, 19, 21-2, 23, 26, 27, 32, 34, 35
Sunderland 10, 36, 158
Survey areas, 'Main' and 'Pool' areas defined 13, 208

Tenants
　access to information 63-4, 130-1, 135, 140, 191
　and WMPs 61-2, 131, 140-2, 191-2
　attitudes to moving 162-8, 182, 194
　rights of objection 57-8, 63-4
Tower Hamlets 13, 68, 96-101, 119, 120-1, 127 *passim*, 149 *passim*, 185-7
Town Clerk's departments 69, 71-2, 191
Twelve-point standard 42, 48-9 n.

Unfit Housing
　and compensation 60-2, 132-3, 136, 142, 195-6
　definitions of 16, 21, 25, 26, 45-6 n., 51
　estimated numbers local, 22, 26, 28-9, 30-1, 32
　estimated numbers national, 9, 24, 26, 27, 28-9, 30-1, 32, 33, 35, 38, 42
Unfitness Order 52, 53, 54
Ungerson, Clare 36, 77, 80, 81

Vereker, Charles and Mays, J.B. 156

Waiting List 41, 55, 89, 94, 95, 100, 172, 173-4, 175
Walker, Peter 34, 35
Well Maintained Payments 23, 58, 61-5, 71-2, 131, 133-5, 140-2, 192
White Papers
　Cmd. 8996, *Houses – The Next Step*, 1953 24
　Cmnd. 1290, *Housing in England and Wales*, 1961, 28, 30
　Cmnd. 2050, *Housing*, 1963 30
　Cmnd. 2838, *The Housing Programme 1965 to 1970*, 1965 31
　Cmnd. 3602, *Old Houses into New Homes*, 1968 33
　Cmnd. 4728, *Fair Deal for Housing*, 1971 34
　Cmnd. 5280, *Widening the Choice: the Next Steps in Housing*, 1973 36
　Cmnd. 5339, *Better Homes, the Next Priorities*, 1973 37
Wilkinson, R. and Sigsworth, E. 124, 149, 156, 163
Wolverhampton 185

York 149
Young, Michael and Willmott, Peter 10, 77, 163

For Product Safety Concerns and Information please contact our EU
representative GPSR@taylorandfrancis.com
Taylor & Francis Verlag GmbH, Kaufingerstraße 24, 80331 München, Germany